High Yield BONDS

Identifying Value and Assessing Risk of Speculative Grade Securities

Martin S. Fridson

Probus Publishing Company
Chicago, Illinois

This publication is designed to provide accurate and authoritative information in regard to the subject matter covered. It is sold with the understanding that the publisher is not engaged in rendering legal, accounting or other professional service.

Library of Congress Cataloging-in-Publication Data

Fridson, Martin S.
High yield bonds : identifying value and assessing risk of speculative grade securities / Martin S. Fridson.
p. cm.
ISBN 1-55738-052-X : $55.00
1. Junk bonds. I. Title.
HG4651.F75 1989
332.63'234—dc20 89-37594
CIP

Printed in the United States of America

2 3 4 5 6 7 8 9 0

DEDICATION

To Elaine Sisman

Contents

Foreword

High yield bonds have taken their place among the investment alternatives considered by mainstream institutional investors. Buyers of these securities (which are generally defined as obligations rated below Baa3 by Moody's Investors Service or below BBB- by Standard & Poor's), now include insurance companies, investment advisors, public and private pension funds, commercial banks, thrifts and corporations, as well as the high income mutual funds that fueled the initial boom in issuance.

To attain its present level of acceptance among mainstream investors, the high yield market has had to build an infrastructure comparable to that which is available in other sectors.

Growth in market-making, for example, has been a necessary development. In the early 1980s, only a handful of issues traded on a regular basis with several firms making two-sided markets. Today, that list has expanded to around 100. A dramatic rise in average new issue size (from $58 million in 1982 to $196 million in 1988) has facilitated this trend, since a large float encourages dealer activity in a bond. Favorably, too, primary market share has become more dispersed in recent years, with six firms individually underwriting $1 billion or more of high yield debt in 1988. Investment banks have had to expand their secondary trading to achieve those volumes of new issue business, since buyers shy away from underwriters who fail to support their deals in the aftermarket.

Credit research is another element of infrastructure that is essential to a full-fledged institutional market. Here, too, the high yield sector has made major strides over a short period.

Only a few years ago, Wall Street high yield research was

for the most part conducted on an ad hoc basis that reflected the scarcity at that time of regularly quoted issues. A typical setup consisted of a single high yield specialist within a research group that focused primarily on investment-grade securities. Instead of following a defined group of companies on a consistent basis, the high yield analyst mainly did on-the-spot analysis of whichever names happened to turn up in the secondary market on a given day. After the transaction, the investor could not count on availability of ongoing research. Lack of continuity was the unfortunate situation in new issues, as well; the underwriter typically provided a barrage of information to support the initial distribution, but did not commit sufficient resources to keep buyers informed of subsequent credit developments.

From these early, hand-to-mouth efforts, Wall Street research on lower-rated credits has rapidly advanced in professionalism and sophistication. Major high yield underwriters now support research staffs of eight to 12 analysts, who typically specialize by industry and cover the more actively traded issues on a continuous basis. In bonds for which there are multiple market-makers, investors can generally assume that there are also several firms conducting research, since trading desks find it essential to have in-house credit information when taking positions in speculative-grade names.

Missing Pieces

Notwithstanding the marked improvement in the volume and quality of high yield credit research, some significant gaps remain. In contrast to the equity and high-grade fixed income markets, the high yield sector has not yet been studied intensively from perspectives other than the analysis of individual issuers. It is understandable that company-by-company research has taken precedence so far. Investors rightly view the minimization of defaults as essential to their success in high yield. From the brokerage firm's standpoint, credit analysis of individual issuers is the type of research that can most easily be exploited to generate transactions.

Because of these incentives to concentrate research resources in company-specific activities, broader topics that have by now been explored in detail in other sectors have been examined only superficially, if at all, in high yield. Much important work remains to be done to gain an understanding of the behavior of various high yield subsectors (defined by industry groups, quality tiers, maturity or duration ranges and other classification criteria). In addition, while there are now many individuals engaged in credit analysis of high yield bonds, there has been too little rigorous study of the validity of the methods they are employing. (There is voluminous research on correlations between financial ratios and defaults, but where are the tests of analysts' methods for identifying undervalued and overvalued bonds?)

Perhaps the sharpest contrast between the state of research on high yield debt and on other securities is the comparatively undeveloped linkup of scholarship with the marketplace, that is, of theory and practice. Academics have no doubt been hampered by the limited availability of reliable pricing data—a problem endemic to all fixed income research. (Unlike listed equities, which trade on centralized exchanges that record transaction prices, the bulk of corporate bond volume occurs in over-the-counter trades for which no price record is generally available. Dealer quotations are the best substitute for exchange prices.) Much of the scholarship to date, moreover, has been directed toward a narrow range of topics, particularly the documentation of historical returns and the construction of quantitative default risk models utilizing financial statement data. Perhaps because researchers have received few alternative suggestions from market participants, they have too often chosen to refine existing work in these admittedly worthwhile areas instead of breaking new ground. (The very recent literature offers some encouraging signs of innovation, however.)

In the absence of credible research on many topics that must be addressed in the course of buying and selling high yield securities, investors have had to rely for the most part on three sources of information:

- Marketing material prepared by brokerage firms
- The media
- Folk wisdom (widely accepted—but unproven—beliefs about the behavior of securities).

Each of these sources, while occasionally providing some useful data or provocative ideas, has serious shortcomings as a guide for investors.

Promotion versus Research

Marketing material describing high yield bonds has appeared all too often in the guise of research. While there is nothing wrong with a dealer or investment advisor producing promotional material, buyers must take care not to mistake such publications for serious analysis. A marketing campaign, after all, begins with the assumption that the product has merit, then constructs arguments and collects facts that support the premise. In the course of gathering the facts, the marketing specialists may consult periodical indexes, conduct surveys or reproduce excerpts from books and articles, but these activities do not by themselves constitute research. Genuine research consists of following the scientific method, which—in contrast to persuasive technique—places the findings at the end, rather than the beginning of the process. A true researcher poses a problem, collects the data necessary to test a hypothesis and presents a conclusion. Bona fide research points out to the reader alternative explanations that cannot be rejected based on the available evidence, as well as imperfections in the data and techniques employed that may make the findings less than wholly conclusive.

To consider the difference between promotion and research in more concrete terms, let us suppose that one desires to study whether the boom in issuance of high yield bonds has had a beneficial or detrimental effect on the U.S. economy. If conducted according to rigorous analytical standards, such a study could be a valuable addition to the economics literature.

The same question, however, if approached as a public relations exercise, would probably generate nothing of serious intellectual interest.

For example, given a mandate of persuading people that high yield bonds strengthen the economy, a capable marketing consultant might travel to a rural hamlet where the construction of a factory financed with speculative-grade debt was followed by an improvement in economic conditions. "Before-and-after" statistics on unemployment levels and per capita income could very well appear to support the argument that high yield bonds create prosperity. To make their case to the public, the sponsors of this undertaking might publicize the findings by producing a television commercial featuring the beneficiaries of the economic stimulus (or actors hired to portray them).

However effective such an exercise might be from a public relations standpoint, it cannot by any reasonable definition be classified as research. The process employed in producing the television commercial fails to satisfy the accepted standards of scientific inquiry. Instead of examining a randomly selected sample of communities affected by high yield financing, the hypothetical study described here focuses exclusively on what may have been a highly unrepresentative case. The statistics have not been normalized for factors such as the economic trend throughout the region; the reported employment surge may have largely reflected a statewide, cyclical recovery. Furthermore, "research" of this type neglects externalities—side-effects of the high yield financing that may have appeared outside of the small town where incomes rose after a factory opened its doors. Perhaps there is no truth whatsoever to critics' charges that "junk bonds" pose extreme risk to the U.S. financial system. Without even addressing that contention, however, it is not valid to offer the experience of a single community as evidence that high yield debt's economic impact represents a net benefit to society-at-large.

Perhaps an enterprise of this sort could qualify as documentary journalism (although journalists might protest that it lacks the objectivity demanded by their professional code). It is also possible that an advertisement based on limited data will achieve its intended—and entirely legitimate—purpose of swaying public opinion. One thing that is certain, though, is that the "findings" of such marketing exercises cannot be regarded as the basis of informed investment decisions.

A Report on the Media

Notwithstanding the emphasis that its ethical code places on accuracy, the press has not proven to be a source of consistently reliable information on high yield bonds. Structural flaws of the news-gathering industry, attributable both to historical circumstances and to systematic tendencies in editorial policy, have produced a great deal of misleading coverage.

One basic problem is the shortage of qualified financial reporters that has resulted from the boom in business coverage. A 1987 survey by James T. Hamilton and Joseph P. Kalt of Harvard University reported that 80% of responding news organizations had increased their economics and business coverage over the preceding five years. Some 62% of the surveyed editors, however, said they would increase coverage even more but for the constraint of the quality of reporting. According to the study, conducted by the Foundation for American Communications for the Ford Foundation, "Journalists who primarily cover business/economics news have much less experience than other reporters: business/economics reporters average 10.2 years in journalism, versus 15 years for other reporters . . ." Hamilton and Kalt add, "The educational backgrounds of business/economics reporters confirm that they are not specialists chosen because of their training, but rather are young and less experienced journalists with backgrounds similar to other reporters." Given this profile, it should come as no surprise if the average business reporter finds it difficult to master a subject requiring the technical expertise that high yield debt does. The market's growth has simply outpaced the media's ability to cover it effectively.

Competence and experience are not the only issues, moreover. The observation that the press prefers bad news to good news, while trite, is nevertheless true when it comes to high yield debt. Lurid tales of securities manipulation and prophecies of financial doom make juicer reading than cogent analysis of speculative-grade debt's role in the capital markets. Reporters speaking off the record tell of editors who try to enliven sound, objective reporting with sensational headlines and illustrations. Exacerbating this institutional bias toward negative coverage, it appears, is a distrust of businessmen among young reporters. In a 1986 study conducted by Ted Kidds of Western Kentucky University and reported in *Editor & Publisher* (October 24, 1987), 58% of the more than 500 college journalism students surveyed disagreed with the statement, "American businessmen are basically honest."

Despite its frequent lack of balance, media coverage of high yield bonds is something that knowledgeable fund managers would shrug off, but for its influence on readers who are not close to the market. Potential high yield clients, legislators and regulators seem inclined to regard superficial newspaper accounts of "junk bonds" as authoritative and reliable. Readers who readily recognize biased political reporting often fail to detect similar one-sidedness in articles dealing with business matters with which they are not intimately familiar. Any rebuttal that high yield managers offer is likely to be regarded as self-interested and therefore treated with skepticism.

Folk Wisdom Debunked

Although high yield professionals are generally unfazed when they read press articles written by reporters less informed than themselves, they are not immune to the appeal of folk wisdom. This is not surprising, for there is an understandable attraction in investment precepts imbibed across the table from grizzled traders who entered the business prior to the invention of the electronic yield calculator. Shorn of its romantic trappings, however, much of this bond lore is a throwback to pre-scientific societies, where truth is equated with anything that people have believed for a long, long time. If it is the received wisdom in such cultures that tomatoes are poisonous or that handling frogs causes warts, no one thinks of conducting a simple experiment to verify that it is so. People rely on authority and custom rather than their own senses to try to understand how the world around them operates.

Although thoroughly modern in other aspects of their lives, fixed income investors cannot fully claim to have abandoned pre-scientific behavior in their professional capacities. Many rules-of-thumb and seat-of-the-pants methods persist where sound analytics ought by now to have become standard.

One piece of folk wisdom, for example, holds that the winning strategy in high yield is to buy the "rising stars"—growth companies currently rated below investment-grade solely (it is alleged) because of their comparatively small size. These dynamic young corporations, say their advocates, represent the IBMs and Xeroxes of tomorrow. When they inevitably attain investment-grade ratings, bondholders will realize a whopping capital gain on top of the generous yield received along the way.

The notion is exciting and, if true, potentially a quite profitable concept. Before adopting the strategy, however, a serious investor must seek empirical confirmation that the "rising stars" are indeed rising. Surprisingly, many portfolio managers seem content with anecdotal evidence in the form of citations of individual companies that have been upgraded to Baa3/BBB- or higher. A more scientific mind would demand to know what percentage of the rising stars are represented by these showcase success stories and whether the examples of credit have been more frequent or less frequent than instances of credit deterioration.

The presentation of non-randomly selected data, by the way, is not a technique employed solely in connection with the rising stars concept. Soft, anecdotal evidence is in fact a chief buttress of the folk wisdom that permeates much of the high yield market.

Consider, for example, the abuse heaped on Moody's and Standard & Poor's over the years by earnest advocates of high yield bonds who have gotten carried away in their enthusiasm. These zealots have cited instances where yields in the secondary market correlate imperfectly (sometimes very imperfectly) with bond ratings as proof that the ratings understate the true value of high yield securities. They have neglected to mention, however, that by design, ratings address only a few of the factors that determine trading levels and, moreover, are not intended to be investment recommendations. Excessive zeal for the high yield cause has led to other—presumably unintentional—misstatements that have further undermined the agencies' credility. For example, critics of Standard & Poor's have delighted in pointing out that it is possible for a company's subordinated debt to carry a rating of (for example) B- while its preferred stock (which is junior to subordinated debt) is rated B+. The ratings, conclude the critics, imply that the debt is riskier than the stock—an obviously absurd result. In their eagerness to discredit the ratings, the zealots have apparently not taken the trouble to find out that S&P's preferred stock rating scale is not directly comparable to its bond rating scale, even though both use similar notation. That is, a company with AA senior debt will ordinarily carry a rating of AA on its preferred stock, but S&P does not by any means suggest that the preferred dividend (which can be omitted at the board's discretion) is as safe as a bond coupon (for which failure to pay can precipitate a bankruptcy).

The energetic if sometimes errant efforts to publicize the rating agencies' shortcomings may reflect nothing more than a desire to help investors make more precise credit decisions. To be sure, assistance of this sort, if offered in good faith by competent individuals, is welcome. No one (not even the agencies themselves) would deny that ratings have sometimes proven far too high or too low in hindsight. In this sense, the folk wisdom regarding the unreliability of high yield ratings is not entirely unfounded. If the fault-finders sincerely want to aid investors' performance, though, they should also investigate ways in which ratings can play a constructive role. For example, there is evidence that even though the absolute level of a company's bond rating may not always represent its credit risk accurately, the *trend* of ratings provides useful information. Defaults have usually been preceded by downgrading and for many investors a signal that the risk of a failure is increasing is the primary benefit sought from any source of credit information.

In conclusion, folk wisdom, like a folk tale, has an author, even though the author may be unknown to those hearing the story. The genres further resemble each other in that they gain popularity through frequent retelling. With folk wisdom, this repetition has the effect of transforming untested propositions into presumed truths.

Investors who wish to break out of the pack must take the trouble to explore whether widely accepted beliefs stand up to rigorous empirical testing. Otherwise, they are no better off than the multitudes who, over many centuries, believed in the proposition that a 20-pound weight falls to earth at twice the speed of a 10-pound weight. Until Galileo disproved it by experiment, it seems that no one bothered to test the hypothesis, since Aristotle had attested to its truth. This sounds laughable now, but high yield investors may find the joke is on them if they buy and sell on the basis of propositions that have never been subjected to systematic analysis.

Plan of the Book

In essence, this book is an attempt to advance the understanding of high yield debt beyond the prejudices of its impassioned supporters and vehement opponents, beyond the superstition engendered by pre-scientific methods. The book's point of view is not that of the proselytizer or the pundit, but of the student.

It is impossible to pursue this ambitious goal without treading on a number of sacred illusions. The author hopes that where this has been necessary he has managed to trample without malice. Throughout the book he has sought to leaven his iconoclasm with gentle humor. In the end, though, the objective must be a true, not a prettified picture. High yield bonds' continued integration into the securities mainstream will depend on investors' confidence that they can base their strategies on carefully documented facts, rather than mere assertions of what interested parties fervently hope is the truth.

The 20 chapters in this volume fall, in a reasonably natural manner, under the following four broad topics.

Managing Credit Risk

No one should invest in speculative-grade bonds without first having established sound principles and a systematic method of managing credit risk. Note that the task is to manage risk, not necessarily to minimize it, which is only one of several options. Given that returns are generally correlated positively with risk, the optimal way to manage risk for many investors is to tolerate more than the minimum that can be achieved within the universe of lower-rated bonds. The manager must carefully define the portfolio's risk level, which should be consistent both with standards of suitability for the investor and with the internal and external resources available for analyzing credit risk. Then, before buying the first security, the manager should make sure that criteria for credit approval and procedures for monitoring quality are firmly in place.

Unfortunately, the tasks of defining and analyzing credit risk are not as straightforward as they might appear. Chapters in this section point out that the most common criteria—bond ratings and standard financial ratios—provide less than perfect guidance in the dynamic environment of high yield bonds. Shibboleths uttered by some speculative-grade buyers, such as "asset protection" and "stock prices," also prove under close scrutiny to fall short of qualifying as credit-monitoring panaceas. Even legal recourse, as represented by covenants designed to protect bondholders, can at times turn out to be a thin reed. The purpose of these chapters, however, is not to persuade the reader that managing credit risk is a futile exercise. Rather, the author hopes to convey that it is a complex task requiring far more than a pro forma effort.

Segmenting the Market to Find Value

Analysis of differential performance among various market subsectors is far less developed in speculative-grade debt than in other sectors of the securities market. In equities, academics and sophisticated money managers have exploited advances in data management technology to slice up the universe in countless ways—small-versus large-capitalization, high-versus low-price-earnings-ratio, accelerating-versus decelerating-earnings-trend, and so on. These exercises have uncovered documentable opportunities for superior risk-adjusted returns. Similarly, certain investment-grade managers have built their strategies on exploiting temporary abnormalities in the relationships between full coupons and discounts, long bonds and intermediates, corporates and Treasuries, and so forth. In the high yield market, such techniques are less widely practiced for a variety of reasons. These include comparatively short trading histories from which to determine "normal" spreads; the difficulty, until fairly recently, of implementing active management strategies because of relatively low liquidity; and the dedication of most research capacity to the critical task of controlling credit risk.

The chapters on segmenting the high yield market seek to adapt for high yield investors the relative value methods that have proven successful in other markets. While the supporting data may be less extensive than in equities or high-grade bonds, the exploitable opportunities may be greater, since fewer investors have focused on them. Among the high yield market's many identifiable subsectors, this section of the book focuses on just a few: "rising stars," divisional buyouts and legal risk bonds, plus one that is largely hypothetical at this point—securitized debt of less-developed countries. Using these studies as models, creative portfolio managers should be able to identify and analyze various other classes of bonds that afford exceptional opportunities.

Maximizing Performance

The first three sections of this volume form a progression from specific to more general issues. "Managing Credit Risk" addresses tactical issues of individual security selection. Strategic issues of sector selection are the primary focus of the second section, "Segmenting the Market to Find Value." The third section, "Maximizing Performance," deals with still broader themes of portfolio management.

The chapters in this section discuss high yield bonds in the context of portfolios that also include other classes of securities. Here readers will find ideas on adapting their particular skills to the unique characteristics of the speculative-grade market, as well as enhancing returns by varying the amount of exposure to high yield. One chapter examines the applicability of a top-down, industry-oriented approach to a market that some regard as analyzable only in a company-specific manner; the findings have important implications for the deployment of research resources. Finally, two chapters explore the way in which the high yield market assimilates and adapts to information. Low-rated bonds do not always respond in the manner that financial theory or popular wisdom suggests, a fact that portfolio managers should recognize in determining the strategies they will adopt in pursuit of superior performance.

Value of the High Yield Sector

While this book's primary purpose is analysis, rather than advocacy, the author would be remiss if he failed to address the question of whether there is intrinsic investment value in high yield bonds. Indeed, to many thoughtful investors and other interested parties, this is the most important question of all. Such readers should begin by studying the final section, which consists of a single chapter. Stepping back from the various factors influencing short- and intermediate-term performance, the author attempts in this chapter to quantify the long-term risks and rewards of investing in high yield debt. the standard analysis-cum-sales pitch ("The yield premium over high-grade bonds exceeds the historical default rate differential, so investors are getting a free lunch.") is flawed in several ways. Besides implicitly assuming that future default rates will not exceed historical levels, it ignores the risk of principal deterioration as the result of a widening in quality spreads. "The Time Factor in High Yield Market Risk," this volume's final chapter, enables investors to use their own assumptions regarding expected default rates and expected future quality differentials to asses the long-term merits of high yield debt.

The author hopes that these remarks have helped to explain the sense of mission that has been his support through the long gestation of this book. High yield debt is a dynamic market, rich in opportunity but punishing to those who approach it without proper respect for its hazards. May the reader derive as much pleasure from the reading as its creator did from the writing of *High Yield Bonds: Assessing Risk and Identifying Value in Speculative-Grade Securities.*

Acknowledgements

The author could not possibly have produced this book without the help of his colleagues at, and support of the management of, Morgan Stanley & Co., Incorporated. He is no less indebted to his wife, an outstanding scholar as well as a great provider of encouragement, to whom this volume is dedicated.

Even the lengthy list that follows represents no more than a fraction of the total to whom the author owes gratitude. He apologizes to those he has not mentioned by name but attests to the essentiality of their contributions.

Debra Alu
Megan Beecher
Richard Bookstaber
Lawrence J. Brainard
Barbara C. Brizzi
Thomas Dzwil
Thomas J. Flynn III
Robert Gay
David Germany
David Goesling
Harold Goldberg
Magarita Gonzalez
Samuel Gordon
Brian T. Grady
Gail Hessol
Glori Holzman
Aida Der Hovanessian
Michael B. Kushma
Michael Long
Philip Maffei
Michael Marocco
Lorraine McCorry
Krishna Memani
Robert M. Miller
Mariann Moore
Elizabeth Mulhare
David Nixon
Robert B. Platt
Elsie Rodd
Kerry Rucidlo
Norman Schindler
William S. Schreier
Barbara Shaw
Mark Shenkman
Ramona Soltero
Stephen Waite
Edna A. Walker
Mark Walsh
Patricia Wells
Robert C. Whitehand
Benjamin Wolkowitz

The author thanks the following individuals for their contributions to the chapters indicated:

Barbara Dughi	4
Lawrence Dyer	19
Igor S. Fuksman	8
Michael C. Heaney	2, 6, 9, 10
Steven B. Jones	2, 13, 17
Peter Kaufman	12
Carlos P. Lima	6, 17
Fritz Wahl	1, 4, 7, 14, 15, 16, 19, 20

PART I

Managing Credit Risk

CHAPTER 1

Establishing Investment Guidelines for a High Yield Portfolio

Many financial institutions that have not previously invested actively in high yield bonds are now seriously studying the sector's potential benefits. Besides desiring to increase their spreads over the cost of funds, these institutions wish to diversify their assets. High yield bonds consequently appeal to savings and loans with heavy concentration in their local real estate markets, as well as established buyers of high-grade bonds, who recognize that high yield securities' comparatively low covariance with the Treasury market can help them reduce their overall portfolio volatility.[1] Furthermore, the high yield market's rapid expansion has made it increasingly difficult to ignore. Speculative-grade bonds now represent over 20% of the corporate sector (nonconvertible) and 5% of the total taxable bond market, so a 0% weighting represents a substantial bet against average or better performance for these issues.

Strong though these incentives may be, few institutions initiate high yield programs without careful deliberation by senior policy-makers. For many investment committees, the purchase of speculative-grade bonds represents a radical cultural change and some cannot quite bring themselves to authorize it. Even the most innovative senior managers, who can make a rational, economic decision on the merits of high yield debt, will generally not approve the concept without strong assurances that effective controls are in place.

Unfortunately for the portfolio managers and analysts who shepherd high yield business plans through the institutional approval process, relatively little research is available on the subject of appropriate portfolio guidelines. Investment banks have understandably focused their efforts on helping institutions with the decision of whether to enter the high yield market. Once the institutions have decided to get into the game, they have been left to their own devices with respect to establishing ground rules.

To redress this past neglect, we offer below some facts we have collected in the course of responding to institutions as they have set up high yield portfolio guidelines. We have attempted to put this knowledge into a semblance of order by addressing, in sequence, the investment objective, formal guidelines and credit review procedures. In discussing these topics, we draw heavily on data compiled from a sample of high yield mutual fund prospectuses. While the specific quantitative rules observed by the mutual funds may not be suitable for other institutions, they cover pretty thoroughly the range of issues that investment guidelines must address. Mutual fund investment rules can therefore serve, if not as a model, at least as a checklist for investment committees that hope to avoid overlooking any essential safeguards.

The Investment Objective

Before telling portfolio managers the rules, it makes sense to tell them what they are being asked to accomplish. High yield mutual funds list a high level of current income, without undue risk, as their primary objective. Capital appreciation, provided it is consistent with the primary objective, is a secondary objective of these funds. This simple statement of purpose leads, in logical fashion, to all of the funds' rules on quality, permitted and prohibited transactions, portfolio concentration and turnover.[2] Other types of institutions will likewise find their task of setting guidelines greatly eased if they begin by clearly stating their objectives. A portfolio that is intended to match a specific set of liabilities requires guidelines that enable the manager to go after a high enough yield to cover default and call risk as well as management costs, and still net the desired spread. On the other hand, if total return is the primary objective, the manager should have the flexibility to upgrade a substantial portion of the portfolio when there is better short-term value in high-grades.

Formal Guidelines

We generally advise institutions to go lightly on formal portfolio restrictions. Unlike mutual fund shareholders, who cannot be informed weekly or monthly of the managers' actions, a thrift or insurance company investment committee can keep close tabs on transactions. A pension fund sponsor with outside managers may have somewhat less frequent communication, but even in this case we favor general guidelines over extensive, detailed rules. The best situation is to have a manager who clearly understands the (internal or external) client's tolerance for risk and has freedom to capitalize on opportunities, not all of which may be anticipated during the guideline-writing stage. Nor should financial institutions write elaborate diversification and turnover rules to appease the regulators; we have found agencies such as the Federal Home Loan Bank Board to be more concerned about the credit review process, discussed below under "Procedures."

With the caveat that it is counterproductive to hamstring a high yield manager with too many rules, we list below the portfolio issues that might warrant establishment of formal policies. We include under each point a discussion of how the high yield mutual funds have approached the issue. The mutual funds' guidelines are included, not because they are appropriate for all investors, but because many of the funds have been in existence for several years and have presumably benefited from their experience. One indication that they have learned from the experience of dealing with the high yield market's realities is that their prospectuses for the most part contain flexible, rather than rigid, guidelines.

Minimum Quality

An example of the flexibility afforded most high yield mutual fund managers is the fact that the prospectuses do not set absolute rating cutoffs. They typically have general policies against buying issues rated less than Caa by Moody's or CCC by Standard & Poor's, or in some instances less than Single-B.[3] In almost all cases, though, they permit the purchase of issues rated below these levels but which the managers consider underrated. Similarly, the guidelines permit managers to buy unrated issues that they believe would, if correctly rated, be at or above the required level, provided the yield is satisfactory. The prospectuses sometimes list the general analytical considerations by which the managers make these judgments (cash flow, asset value, management experience, etc.) but never set quantitative requirements (such as a minimum fixed charge coverage ratio) for approving a credit. Incidentally, the mutual fund prospectuses include in the high yield segment all securities rated Baa/BBB or lower, even though Moody's and Standard & Poor's define the speculative-grade category as beginning at Ba/BB.

Percentage Invested in High Yield

High yield mutual funds give their managers the latitude to seek superior value by shifting assets to the investment-grade sector when quality spreads narrow. It is also typical for portfolio managers to have the authority to put funds into money market instruments pending delivery of high yield securities. A common guideline is that under normal conditions 80% of assets[4] (but ranging between 65% and 100% in different prospectuses) will be invested in securities that are consistent with the primary objective of high current income and the secondary objective of capital appreciation. This generally includes convertible and non-convertible debt, and usually preferred stock, although preferred is sometimes classified as equity. The prospectuses provide, however, for circumstances (presumably severe economic distress) in which the manager might think it prudent to go into a defensive mode, which may be defined as up to 100% in top-quality money market instruments (government and agency paper, certificates of deposit, prime commercial paper, etc.). Clearly, this sort of authority has the potential for abuse. A manager who feels competent to anticipate swings in the Treasury market could cross over the line between upgrading in response to market conditions and recklessly speculating on interest rates. That should be a small worry, however, in an organization where there is close communication between portfolio managers and senior investment officers. On the presumption that portfolio managers will act in good faith, it makes sense to authorize an emergency flight to quality well before it becomes necessary to execute it.

Maturity

Prospectuses that even bother to address this topic establish no limitations and state that the proportions of long, intermediate and short paper will vary, based on market conditions. Admittedly, the mutual funds' emphasis on current income encourages them simply to concentrate on the highest point along the yield curve, which is most often the long end. Such freedom does not exist for institutions that must match relatively short-lived liabilities. Nevertheless, it would be a mistake to restrict a high yield manager to too narrow a range of maturities, which might at times make it impossible to find reasonably priced merchandise. At such times, a superior yield may be achievable through buying longer-term high yield paper, combined with shorter-term high-grade corporates, to obtain the required duration.[5]

Concentration

Unlike other guidelines, high yield mutual funds' concentration requirements tend to be specific rules, rather than mere statements of what will prevail under normal conditions. (Even so, these rules are in many cases subject to change without shareholder approval.) Because of the importance we place on diversification, we consider it prudent to institute safeguards against infatuation with industries that appear destined to "grow to the sky," e.g, the oils circa 1979. Adopting a disciplined approach to concentration, while still allowing for strategic under- and overweighting within reasonable bounds, is the best policy, in our view.

Simply establishing quantitative diversification standards does not fulfill the investment committee's fiduciary responsibility in this area. When confronted with numerical constraints, the human mind has a propensity to finagle. Therefore, investment committees must scrutinize the industry definitions being applied. It is common, and we think reasonable, to define electric, telephone, gas and water utilities as separate industries. Less legitimately, though, a portfolio manager could—in an extreme case—comply with a 25%-per-industry rule, yet make a 100% bet on the energy sector, by defining oil refiners, oil producers, contract drillers and oil tool manufacturers as separate industries.

Keeping in mind that mutual funds' specific standards may not be appropriate for all investors, here are the typical concentration rules they have established. (Note that no category below is restricted by all funds, while some categories are ignored in most prospectuses.)

- *Industry:* 25% maximum concentration.
- *Issuer:* 5% maximum concentration. (U. S. government and government-guaranteed issues are exempt.) 10% maximum on any class of securities[6] of a single issuer. (In some cases the 10% limit applies to all securities or all voting securities of a single issuer.)
- *Issues of Companies in Business Less Than Three Years:* 5% maximum concentration. One prospectus further limits the 5% to regulated utilities and oil, gas and electric transmission companies. Another imposes a 5% limit on the sum of illiquid issues and issues of companies in business less than three years.

- *Private Placements*: 5% to 10% maximum concentration. (Some prospectuses prohibit privates or permit them only if the issuer intends to register the issue subsequently). Another variant imposes a 10% limit on the sum of private placements and illiquid issues.
- *Issues for Which Market Quotations Are Not Readily Available*: 5% maximum concentration.
- *Issues in Default or of Bankrupt Companies*: 10% to 15% maximum concentration for prospectuses that authorize purchase.
- *Issues Known to Have Significant Ownership by Officer, Director or Investment Advisor of the Fund*: 5% aggregate ownership by individuals holding ½ of 1% or more precludes retention, as may the fact of individuals being directors or officers of both the fund and the issuer in question.

Alternative Investments

The primary vehicles for high yield mutual fund managers, as indicated in preceding paragraphs, are fixed income securities of Triple-B and lower quality, including convertibles. Higher-grade bonds and money market instruments are used for liquidity needs and when unusual market conditions prevail. Aside from these main categories, mutual fund prospectuses generally permit some selection of the investment alternatives listed below, subject to the indicated limitations.

1. *Equity*. Mutual fund prospectuses commonly permit investment in common stocks, rights and warrants. Formulas vary, with maximum concentration ranging from 10% to 20%, a limitation from which equity securities acquired as parts of units that include fixed income securities may or may not be exempted. (In some cases, *only* the latter type of equity securities may be held.) To comply with certain state regula-

tions, some prospectuses limit warrants to 5% of assets and non-listed warrants to 2% of assets. Non-dividend-paying common stocks may be limited to 4% of assets. Some prospectuses permit buying puts, calls and futures contracts on common stocks and stock indexes and writing covered calls on common stocks. Arbitrage activities may be forbidden.

2. *Repurchase Agreements.* Repos are permitted by many high yield mutual fund prospectuses, subject to varying constraints. Most commonly, the other party to the transaction must be either a Federal Reserve System member or a primary dealer in U.S. government securities. There may be a further requirement that the underlying security be a permissible purchase under the fund's other guidelines. The prospectuses either put no ceiling on the volume of repos or limit them to 25% or 30% of assets. Some forbid transactions extending beyond seven business days or limit them to 5% to 10% of total assets or, in a variation, limit the sum of repos longer than 10 days and illiquid securities to 10%.
3. *When-Issued Securities.* These are specifically authorized by many prospectuses (sometimes with a 5% to 25% maximum concentration), with a requirement that an equivalent amount of cash or marketable securities be set aside in a segregated account.
4. *Interest Rate Futures and Options.* Most prospectuses that mention these instruments limit their use to hedging. Put and call options (sometimes only if listed) on futures contracts may be permitted, either in addition to or in lieu of futures contracts themselves, and a ceiling of 5% of total assets may be specified. Other variants include a 5% to 10% limit on purchase of options (listed only) on debt securities themselves, plus a 20% to 50% limit on writing of such options and a requirement that options be covered by deliverable

securities or segregated, liquid assets. Still another variant permits the purchase of calls only to close out calls previously written.

5. *Foreign Securities.* A limit of 5% to 20% of total assets is common in prospectuses that specifically authorize foreign securities. These are defined as obligations both of foreign issuers and of foreign branches of U. S. banks, possibly limited to securities purchased with and payable in U.S. dollars. Other variants include a 25% limit on securities of foreign governments, a 5% limit on securities of any single foreign government, and a 5% limit on foreign securities that are not publicly traded in the United States. Eurodollar certificates of deposit or Canadian issues payable in U S. dollars may be excluded from the percentage-of-assets limit and forward purchases and sales of foreign currencies may be permitted in connection with investment in foreign securities.
6. *Securities Lending.* Some high yield mutual fund prospectuses permit securities lending if 100% collateralized by cash or government (or government agency) securities. Maximum concentrations range between 10% and 30% of assets. Alternatively, the prospectus may impose no limit, provided the loans are callable at any time.
7. *Short Sales.* Some prospectuses authorize short sales up to a maximum of 10% of total assets, if offset by an equivalent long position, call, or conversion or exchange privilege.
8. *Mutual Fund Shares.* May be permitted for closed end fund shares only, or solely in connection with a merger, consolidation, reorganization or acquisition of assets.
9. *Municipal Bonds.* One prospectus authorizes investment of up to 10% of assets in municipals.

10. *Real Estate.* Some funds, while prohibiting direct investment in real estate, permit purchase of marketable securities of real estate firms and securities that are secured by real estate.

11. *Oil and Mineral Exploration and Development Programs.* Some funds authorize purchase of these securities or permit only the purchase of securities of companies that offer such programs.

Turnover

Portfolio turnover in high yield mutual funds tends to be subject to a general guideline, rather than a strict rule. The usual provision is that turnover is not ordinarily expected to exceed 100% (200% in one case) per year, but will vary depending on market conditions. In practice, it is not a rare occurrence for turnover to exceed 100%. Some prospectuses state that turnover will not be a consideration in investment decisions.

We endorse the general guideline approach in this area. Certainly, excessive turnover should be avoided, for although taxable fixed income markets operate largely on a net price basis, transaction costs are real, even if hard to measure. Indeed, the costs can be considerable in high yield, given the sector's relatively wide bid-to-asked spreads. Too large a volume of transactions might even suggest unethical activity by managers seeking to inflate the compensation of certain salesmen who call on them. The remedy in such cases, however, is to replace the managers, rather than attempt to reform them through quantitative limits on turnover. If fundamental trust characterizes the investment committee's relationship with the managers, the policy on turnover should provide sufficient latitude to capitalize on the arbitrage opportunities that frequently arise in the secondary market.

Another legitimate activity that contributes to a high yield portfolio's turnover is the purchase of new issues during periods when there is no net new cash flowing into the portfolio. This activity can be quite profitable, since the present balance of power between issuers and investors obliges underwriters to price high yield offerings to go to a premium shortly after issue.[7] Investment committees should be aware, however, that managers who overdo this and acquire reputations as short-term "flippers" will find themselves receiving minimal allocations in heavily oversubscribed offerings.

Credit Review Procedures

More important than precise, quantitative investment rules, both in our own opinion and as indicated by the regulators' approach to the high yield sector, are the procedures an institution puts in place for analyzing the credit quality of each holding. An investment organization could have its assets perfectly distributed by industry and type of security but still underperform by failing to cut its losses on deteriorating credits.

Avoiding the big problems requires a selling discipline, a willingness to book a small loss before the situation worsens, notwithstanding internal embarrassment and the inability to replace the income on a bond sold at a depressed price. Overcoming the inherent organizational resistance to biting the bullet will become easier if the case for selling the position is built on a thorough documentation of credit deterioration over many months.

It is impossible to prescribe a single set of credit review procedures that will perfectly meet the needs of all investment organizations, given variations in size and sophistication of professional staff, number and average quality of holdings, and demands on available man-hours for client contact, attendance of new-offering roadshows, and administrative chores. Credit review is too important a function in high yield investment to be treated as the residual of these other activities, however. Instead, an organization should take as axiomatic the necessity of a plan along the lines outlined below, then assess whether its remaining available resources are adequate for the other assigned tasks. If not, tradeoffs must be made, such as adding specialists to handle new business development or reducing the number of names in the portfolio to cut down the time required for credit review. Using third-party research—especially contact with fixed income analysts at brokerage firms and rating agencies—can be an effective means of stretching available in-house research resources. (Institutions have the responsibility, however, of "consumer-testing" these outside experts to make sure they are both competent and free of any bias related to underwriting relationships or trading desk positions.)

Acknowledging that special circumstances will dictate some modifications, the following elements should produce a satisfactory credit review process for most institutions.

Personnel

The high yield sector's dramatic growth has put a premium on experienced credit analysts, so not every institution can expect to recruit a staff with the resumes one would ideally hope for. Without minimizing the difficulty of analyzing lower-quality issuers, however, we believe institutions can achieve satisfactory results by hiring individuals with some relevant educational background (financial statement analysis, in particular) and, if possible, related work experience (commercial lending, private placements, etc.).

These analysts' training will primarily be on-the job, but can be supplemented by learning from buy-side peers (who can be met through professional organizations and at roadshows) and by periodically making the rounds of investment banks' credit research staffs. The key to getting credit risk under control (and not incidentally, to satisfying the regulators) is to make analysis a bona fide, independent function, rather than a department called into being solely to foster the illusion that research plays a role in security selection. What the regulators will come down hardest on is staffing a credit research department with amiable but unqualified individuals who get their jobs through "connections."

Periodic Credit Reviews

Analysts dream of obtaining the occasional unique insight that enables them to recognize an exceptional value before the rest of the crowd sees it. Investment organizations hope to recruit the gifted individuals who get these insights, and the high yield market affords many opportunities to profit from such flashes of inspiration. When it comes to dodging bankruptcies, however, the essential analytical trait is conscientiousness, rather than brilliance. As Edward Altman's work demonstrates,[8] most defaults are anticipated far in advance by techniques that do nothing more than process (admittedly in a sophisticated manner) reported financial data. Gifted analysts may spot decay before it becomes apparent in the issuers' financial reports, and thereby get their institutions out early and at advantageous prices, but it takes no genius to identify companies that are close to collapse before they actually fold. Although some of the price damage will already have occurred by that point, the analyst who systematically monitors holdings for credit deterioration can contribute significantly to an institution's performance over time.

To derive the greatest possible benefit from periodic credit reviews, an institution should establish internal rules concerning the frequency with which reviews must occur. In general, frequency should increase as credit quality declines. For most institutions, we believe the following four-level review process is appropriate and necessary, and should be fully provided for in the high yield unit's budget.

1. *Initial Purchase Review.* For internal control and regulatory reasons, institutions should create files on first-time purchases. On primary issues, analysts should file prospectuses and notes from roadshows. Documentation on issues purchased in the secondary

market should include current financial statements, plus any relevant news items and outside research reports. Whether for a primary or secondary item, the file should above all include some sort of investment rationale, a demonstration that an analyst has thoroughly studied the issue and concluded, in conjunction with the portfolio manager, that it is fairly priced with respect to its credit risk.

2. *Quarterly Review.* Every company in the portfolio should be subject to a routine review of its Form 10-Q quarterly report to the Securities and Exchange Commission.[9] In most periods and for most issuers, this process will be quick and uneventful, for analysts are concerned mainly with the surprises. Nevertheless, a 10-Q review must be thorough. The analyst must be on guard for nonrecurring items and accounting changes that may make a three-month period appear more in line with expectations than was the economic reality. Footnotes must be read closely for mounting risk in the area of contingent liabilities. Management's discussion of financial condition may reveal important changes in the availability of credit or future funds needs. As a final observation, the 10-Q analysis cannot be performed in a vacuum. A flat, or even a modestly improved quarter may signal trouble if the issuer's competitors are concurrently enjoying large percentage earnings increases.
3. *Unscheduled Review.* Academic studies have demonstrated that the bulk of the information contained in financial statements is disclosed prior to release of the statements. Therefore, important as the quarterly review is, it cannot be relied on exclusively. Rather, the analyst must stand ready to investigate signs of potential credit trouble that occur at random times during the reporting cycle. It is a good policy to monitor the stock prices of publicly held issuers for

market signals of changes in their fundamentals.[10] A price decline of 25% within a few days or a succession of new lows should trigger an investigation and assessment of the causes. Bond pricing services and dealer quotations are additional sources of clues that a particular credit may require an unscheduled review, with significant deviation from the market trend being the chief criterion. News items may likewise signal the need for review, but it is difficult to establish rules for what sorts of items merit such attention. Newspapers often publish retrospective articles that are aimed at the general reader and contain nothing that is truly new to the analyst. By the same token, a seemingly innocuous news item sometimes leads, upon investigation, to the discovery of a significant credit development that the publication lacked the space to print in its entirety. Finally, rating changes can serve as a check for ensuring that unscheduled reviews occur when needed. Downgrades are typically preceded by news developments that ought in their own right to generate reviews, but even the most conscientious analyst may miss a news story occasionally.

4. *"Intensive Care Unit."* On the theory that avoiding the catastrophes is at least as important to performance as spotting the bargains, high yield analysts should reserve a significant portion of their time for particularly close monitoring of the weakest names in the portfolio. Institutions should be conservative enough in their purchases, and disciplined enough in their selling, to avoid having more troubled holdings at any one time than their available analysts can review thoroughly on at least a monthly basis.

For a high yield buyer with average risk aversion, companies can be assigned to the "Intensive Care Unit" according to several objective criteria. A company rated Caa or lower by

Moody's or CC or lower by Standard & Poor's will generally qualify.[11] Likewise, users of Altman's Zeta scores should initiate monthly or more frequent reviews of companies with scores of less than zero. Market risk premiums are another basis for identifying candidates; at most times a yield of 1.25 times the yield on core issues, e.g., 15% versus 12%, is a reasonable threshold. Note that these three criteria will not independently select exactly the same companies for the "Intensive Care Unit." Nor should these objective criteria be used to the exclusion of an analyst's judgment that a particular company bears close watching, even though ratings, ratios and market prices (which may not be readily available, in any case, for certain issues) may not yet raise a caution.

Conclusion

We believe that by addressing the issues covered in this article, an institution can satisfy itself and its regulators that it has duly dealt with the issue of investment guidelines. Policy-makers need not agree with each of our specific prescriptions, but to fulfill their fiduciary responsibility they should reach some conclusion on each matter we have discussed.

In closing, we reiterate that mutually understood, general guidelines, implemented in an environment of open communication and trust, are preferable to inflexible, detailed formulas. The former bring the best out of entrepreneurially minded, opportunistic managers, while the latter will not restrain ingenious loophole-finders. Finally, even general guidelines should be subject to revision upon due consideration, for the high yield market is evolving too rapidly at this point to ensure that a charter devised today will still be workable five years hence.

Endnotes

1 Richard Bookstaber and David P. Jacob found correlation coefficients of 0.51 between Treasuries and bonds rated B to Caa, 0.77 between

Treasuries and bonds rated Baa to Ba, and 0.86 between Treasuries and bonds rated Aaa to A. See "The Composite Hedge: Controlling the Credit Risk of High Yield Bonds," Morgan Stanley (March 1985): p. 2.

2 In practice, mutual fund managers' lives are not quite as simple as their prospectuses suggest. Although the income objective is clearly paramount in the prospectuses, potential share purchasers do not look solely at current yield when comparing the funds. Instead, in the process of selecting a high yield mutual fund individuals often consult published total return figures, which are by definition heavily influenced by capital appreciation (or deterioration). The income and capital appreciation objectives may consequently come into conflict through pressure for performance from the salesforce that distributes a mutual fund's shares. Such conflicts do not mean, however, that the prospectuses' formal guidelines have no effect on managers' actions. On the contrary, the tug of opposing demands underscores the importance of written principles of action, without which a portfolio manager might lose direction entirely.

3 A minimum standard of Single-B at both leading agencies is no longer a logical policy, since Moody's Caa rating implies lower quality than Standard & Poor's CCC. In brief, a Caa rating still implies that a company has "one foot in the grave," whereas S&P now uses its CCC to make finer distinctions among the speculative but viable companies all formerly lumped in the B category. For a fuller explanation, see Chapter 2, "Bond Ratings: Should High Yield Buyers Care?".

4 For many of the quantitative rules discussed in this chapter, definitions vary among the different mutual fund prospectuses. Percentages of assets may be calculated on the basis of either cost or current market value. "Assets" may refer to total assets or to assets net of certain payables or net of cash.

5 To the extent that this strategy is implemented through a "barbell" (for example, 50% one-year maturities and 50% 15-year maturities for an eight-year average maturity), the portfolio will incur some risk of failing to meet its objective as a result of a change in the yield curve's shape. The portfolio manager can lessen this risk by constructing a "ladder"—a portfolio composed of issues equally spaced over a range of maturities, resulting in the desired average term.

6 "Class of securities" of an issuer raises another definitional issue. The rulemaker must decide, for example, whether debt and preferred stock constitute a single "fixed income" category.

7 That, at least, is the intent. Portfolio managers are acutely aware that underwriters do not always have the market savvy or the distribution

capability to ensure that their deals will trade up in the aftermarket. Investment banks that consistently fail to do so will tend to underwrite less volume as time progresses.

[8] See, for example, Edward I. Altman and Scott A. Nammacher, Investing in Junk Bonds: Inside the High Yield Debt Market (New York: John Wiley & Sons, 1987): pp. 145-163.

[9] Private companies that are not legally required to file with the SEC typically provide bondholders a quarterly statement in the same format as the 10-Q, so analysts can conduct the same quarterly review that they would for public companies. Surveillance is far more difficult when private companies elect not to provide financials, a fact that should be carefully weighed when contemplating purchase of an issue for which there will be no regular reporting.

[10] Analysts should be careful to regard changes in stock prices as possible red flags, not as embodiments of a mystical, collective wisdom that should be heeded, rather than investigated. See "How Useful Are Stock Prices in Monitoring Credit Quality?" in this volume.

[11] As explained in Footnote 3 above, Standard & Poor's equivalent of Moody's Caa rating is not CCC, but CC or lower. A rating of CCC does not imply financial distress and should not automatically place a company under extra-heavy surveillance.

CHAPTER 2

Bond Ratings: Should High Yield Buyers Care?

"Rating agencies? What good are they? They lag behind, rather than lead the market, which proves that they're out of touch."

"If we were to liquidate our company tomorrow, we would have enough cash to pay bondholders in full twice over. How can the rating agencies conclude that we're speculative-grade?"

"The problem isn't that the ratings are too conservative—they're too liberal. Did you realize that W. T. Grant carried an investment grade-rating right up until two years before it went bankrupt in 1976? The agencies are so understaffed that they cannot respond promptly to credit deterioration."

"We underwrote a company that received a B3 rating even though its fixed charge coverage was fully two-tenths of a percent higher than another company that received a B2 rating. That's ridiculous! The real problem with rating agencies is that they are inconsistent and arbitrary. Why don't they just publish standard cutoffs for the various rating categories? That would enhance their credibility by making the process more scientific."

"Their analysis is backward-looking, rather than forward-looking."

"They give no credit to the most valuable assets of all—the ingenuity and drive of an entrepreneurial management."

"They look at historical cost instead of real economic value, as established by the stock market."

"We pay zero attention to ratings in our shop. The agencies do fine

with high-grade companies but they just don't understand the high yield market. Judging by the way these bonds trade, I'd say the ratings are irrelevant once you get below Triple-B."

"Those @#!?%! number-pushers gave us a CCC! Would I have invested my life savings in this company if it was on the verge of bankruptcy?"*

* * *

An individual who cannot tolerate complaints would be ill-advised to go to work for a rating agency. A certain amount of customer dissatisfaction is inevitable when one's actions have the power to raise borrowers' cost of money and reduce the value of investors' holdings. In the end, however, rating agency personnel find the flack bearable because it proves that someone cares. Enough people care, in fact, to cough up fees sufficient to support five recognized rating agencies in the United States.

If the agencies have provoked a response other than apathy, however, they have not made an equally deep impression everywhere they have ventured. In Europe, their influence is growing but many investors in that market still focus more than their American cousins do on the issuer's name recognition, the underwriter's record for supporting its deals in the secondary market and the original placement of the bonds. The high yield sector, too, appears to be less under the sway of the agencies than is the investment-grade market. Granted, it is the agencies' ratings that define the sector (below Baa3 at Moody's, BBB- at Standard & Poor's or 10 at Duff & Phelps). It is also true that investors sometimes use low ratings when arguing for higher yields on primary and secondary offerings, whatever their own views of the credit. (Nor is it unknown for dealers to cite ratings to their advantage, even as they bemoan the agencies' misperceptions of the high yield market.)

Exhibit 2–1 shows, however, that ratings do not predict yields in the low-grade sector as well as they do in the investment-grade arena. For the period studied, ratings explained only 57% of the observed yield on bonds rated Ba1/BB + or lower, versus 89% for those rated Baa3/BBB- or higher. (See

Test of Correlation Between Ratings and Bond Yields, at the end of this chapter, for details.)

A popular interpretation of such data is that the ratings are "wrong," a corollary of which is that the "market rating," or credit quality implied by trading levels, is invariably right. By this reasoning, the ratings are more wrong on high yield bonds than on investment-grade issues. It is a short step from there to the conclusion that the rating agencies, although competent when looking at Double-A credits, do not know how to rate Single-Bs. A closer examination of the facts, however, suggests the plausibility of a far different, if somewhat paradoxical conclusion, namely, that the lack of correspondence between ratings and yields may indicate that the agencies are doing their job well, rather than poorly. Those who conclude differently may simply misunderstand what the rating agencies' job—as defined by the agencies themselves—really is.

Exhibit 2–2 depicts eight factors that determine the value of a corporate bond. Only two of these are factors explicitly considered in the determination of bond ratings. The agencies consider one factor only partially and the majority—five of eight—are deliberately ignored in the rating process. This being so, it would be surprising ever to find the market perfectly in line with the agencies. To the extent that high yield bonds are more sensitive than investment-grade bonds to the five factors not considered in assigning ratings, one would expect a lower correlation between ratings and yields on bonds rated below the Triple-B category. Moreover, the rating agencies have valid reasons for sticking to the areas they know best, even though they realize that bond prices reflect a number of other factors.

Default Risk

A rating by Moody's, Standard & Poor's, Duff & Phelps or Fitch is primarily an assessment of the likelihood of timely payment of principal and interest. Anything other than payment on

Exhibit 2–1
Do Bond Yields Reflect Ratings?

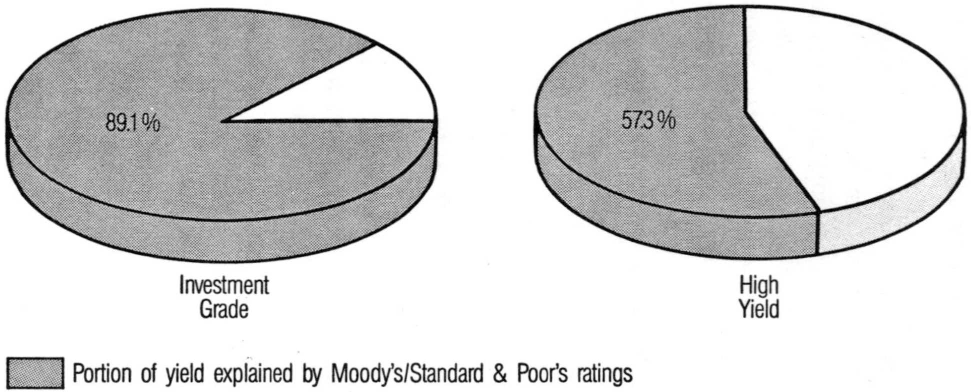

The correlation between yields and bond ratings is higher in the investment grade sector than in the speculative grade sector. One possible explanation is the greater price sensitivity of low-rated issues to short-term credit changes that may not affect ratings.

Exhibit 2–2
Determinants of Bond Value

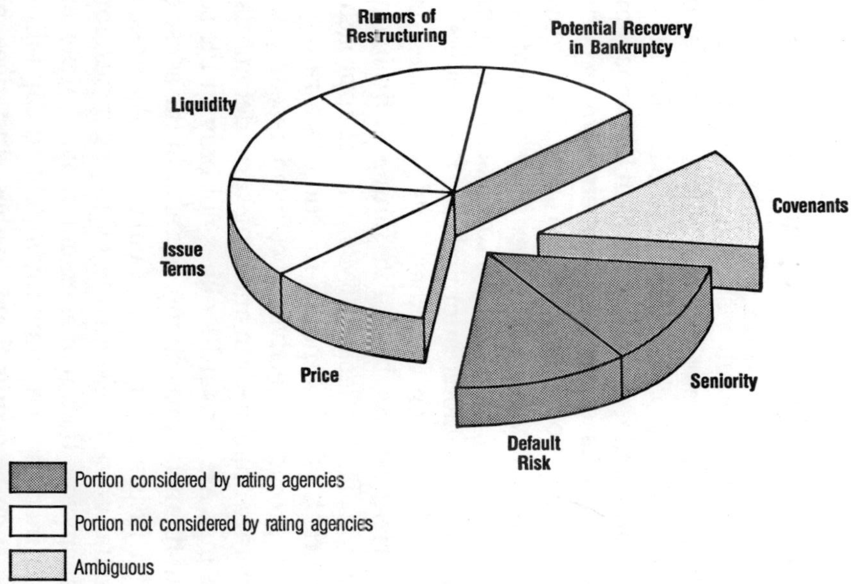

Ratings are not meant to be investment recommendations. The agencies intend them to deal with only a few of the determinants of value. It should therefore come as no surprise that bond prices do not correspond perfectly with ratings, even if the agencies have correctly assessed default risk.

schedule constitutes a default and for the purposes of assigning ratings, it makes no difference whether the issuer quickly cures the default and pays investors all the money owed them or remains in Chapter 11 proceedings for five years and then pays its creditors 10 cents on the dollar. As discussed below, under "Potential Recovery in Bankruptcy," failure to understand the agencies' limited objective may give rise to mistaken notions about the accuracy of ratings.

In assessing default risk, the rating agencies do not, as many bond market participants believe, consider only historical data. Both Moody's and S&P examine the confidential financial projections provided to them by management and adjust the forecasts according to their own expectations. One reason this may not be apparent to subscribers to *Moody's Bond Survey* and *Standard & Poor's CreditWeek* is that both agencies have qualms about publishing forecasts that are informed by non-public projections supplied by the issuers. (McCarthy, Crisanti & Maffei, on the other hand, publishes projections in its high yield reports, basing its figures entirely on non-inside information. This reflects MCM's general approach to the high yield market, which is not to function as a rating agency, but rather to provide objective investment research that includes commentary on near-term and long-term default risk.)

Ratings are forward-looking not only in the sense of considering financial projections, but also in the sense of reflecting potential future balance sheet changes. "Aggressiveness" is a term usually used pejoratively by the agencies, for it signifies their suspicion that management may sharply and without warning increase the company's debt to capitalize on opportunities such as acquisitions. In these instances, management usually argues that the rating agencies *should* look only at historical ratios. Lest issuers fear that only negative perceptions of management influence ratings, the agencies affirm that they give weight to managers' ability to fix problems, particularly when their track record is good.

Seniority

Aside from default risk, seniority is the only factor in Exhibit 2–2 that clearly plays a major role in ratings. Typically, subordinated debt is rated two notches lower (e. g., B3 versus B1, B+ versus BB) than senior debt if the senior debt is rated less than investment-grade, although there are numerous exceptions to this rule.

By differentiating on the basis of seniority (including secured versus unsecured debt), the ratings reflect the verifiable fact[1] that in bankruptcy subordinated debt holders generally recover less of their investment than senior lenders do. Recognizing this fact, interestingly, contrasts with the agencies' policy of not considering the potentially higher recovery in bankruptcy that certain very liquid assets offer vis-a-vis illiquid assets such as specialized or outdated machinery.

Covenants

As suggested by Exhibit 2–2, the role of restrictive covenants in ratings is neither black nor white, but in a grey area. The rating agencies clearly pay some heed to covenants, since they refuse to rate issues that lack them entirely. This insistence has helped to preserve such rudimentary provisions as the negative pledge clause (which prohibits securing other creditors without also securing debenture holders) as other covenants have gradually been dropped from indentures. On the other hand, the agencies do not ordinarily assign different ratings to two issues of the same obligor, with equivalent seniority, solely because one has a less restrictive debt limitation than the other, or because one lacks a dividend restriction that the other has. (Moody's, in one notable exception to the rule, has recently begun to recognize in its ratings the presence of certain protections against financial restructuring.) In short, covenants are considered only to a limited extent by the rating agencies.

Potential Recovery in Bankruptcy

Consistent with their policy of basing ratings primarily on default risk, the agencies do not consider liquidation value in bankruptcy, a factor that can be quite significant in the market's valuation of a bond.

To illustrate, captive finance subsidiaries (i.e., companies engaged primarily in financing parent receivables) generally receive the same ratings as their respective manufacturing or retailing parents. This policy reflects the agencies' expectation that a bankruptcy at the parent will probably draw the finance subsidiary into Chapter 11 as well, notwithstanding a legal structure (i.e., two separate corporations) that might suggest otherwise. Wickes Companies's unsuccessful effort to keep its captive finance subsidiaries out of its 1982 Chapter 11 filing supports this view. Conceding that the parent and the finance subsidiary have equivalent chances of default, however, is not an admission that equivalent-coupon-and-maturity bonds of the two entities have identical value. Particularly when default risk is perceived to be high, the market reflects the likelihood that a lender to the finance subsidiary, assets of which consist primarily of high-quality, liquid receivables, will emerge from reorganization or liquidation with a higher percentage of principal than the creditor of a failed manufacturing firm, which has assets that will probably be greatly devalued on the auction block. The phenomenon of a captive finance subsidiary's debt trading at a substantially lower yield than its equivalently rated parent's obligations will cause yields to correlate poorly with ratings. It does not, however, prove that the agencies are poorly executing their task (as they define it).

Readers should note our use in the preceding paragraph of the phrase "liquidation value *in bankruptcy*" to describe the aspect of asset values that lies outside the rating process. Contrary to what is sometimes alleged against them, the rating agencies do take into account the liquidation value of assets as a source of financial flexibility, i.e., as a means of raising cash through divestments. Moreover, the agencies are fully aware that potential sale prices may diverge significantly from book value, even though the canard persists that they consider only historical cost.

Rumors of Restructuring

In recent years, takeovers and restructurings have been a major cause of downgrading, particularly in the industrial sector. The high yield universe is not immune to this risk, even though many low-rated companies already have such heavy debt burdens that further leveraging to effect a takeover might seem inconceivable. Republic Health, Caesars World and Allegheny International are examples of speculative-grade companies that have been affected by the merge-and-borrow frenzy.

In restructuring situations, ratings will not typically change until full financial details are available, although Standard & Poor's often indicates the direction and potential magnitude of change as the situation unfolds. The agencies will ordinarily watchlist a company for potential downgrading once a proposed transaction is made public, but they draw the line at taking action solely on the basis of takeover rumors, even if the alleged target company's stock is soaring. A mere whisper of a tender offer, however, can be sufficient to drop the price of a potential victim's bonds. This is another reason why at times ratings may be out of line with market prices, but as in other instances, the implication is not that the ratings are wrong. While it is often true that where there is smoke there is fire, changing ratings in response to rumors would raise thorny ethical questions, not to mention vociferous protests from issuers.

Liquidity

Liquidity is an important determinant of a bond's value but plays no direct role in ratings. The only aspect of liquidity that affects both value and ratings is issue size. If a small company (equity of $50 million, for example) floats a small (say $25 million) bond, the agencies will probably rate it lower than a $250 million bond of a company with $500 million of equity, even though the two companies stack up similarly on other financial measures. This would, as it happens, be consistent with the market's assigning of a larger risk premium to the smaller, less liquid issue. The rating differential would not, however, be premised on liquidity, but rather on the agencies' perception (which has considerable empirical support)[2] that small companies are more prone to default than large companies. If the larger company subsequently repurchases 90% of its issue, so that with just $25 million outstanding it becomes as illiquid as the smaller company's issue, it will nonetheless retain its higher rating. In short, it is only by coincidence, not by design, that the agencies sometimes rate less liquid (and therefore less valued) bonds lower than more liquid issues.

Issue Terms

Coupon and maturity are as inconsequential to ratings as they are critical to bond pricing. Plainly, a 30-year obligation has a greater chance than a one-year note of defaulting before maturity, and some have suggested that ratings ought to reflect this difference. Perhaps so, but implementing such a policy could be an administrative nightmare. Each long-term issue would have to be automatically upgraded as it approached maturity. Moreover, to be thorough the agencies would have to judge whether a callable bond was likely to remain outstanding only until its call date or until its final maturity, in order to classify it as a higher-rated short issue or a lower-rated long issue.

Price

At a 12% yield, a certain bond may represent fair value. At 14% it may be an outstanding value. At 20% it may be the investment opportunity of a lifetime, but it will still have the rating it had at

12% if its default risk has not changed. Similarly, a bond trading at 60 will fall further if interest rates rise than a bond trading at 102. That fact affects perceptions of value, but it does not affect ratings, for ratings are not investment recommendations.

In response to demand from investors, one organization, McCarthy, Crisanti & Maffei, has elected to address the price component of the *quality ÷ price = value* equation. MCM, as noted earlier, does not rate high yield bonds, but instead provides buy, hold and sell recommendations premised on its perceptions of relative value.

Moody's and Standard & Poor's have stuck to the traditional rating agency role, but have increasingly integrated market information into their activities. At Moody's, a computerized information system enables senior managers to identify unusual stock price movements and dividend actions that might point to a credit quality shift not yet recognized by an analyst. In the future, bond yields may also be introduced into the system as signals that the market has perceived a change in credit risk. Similarly, Standard & Poor's officials say they would not ignore a sudden, drastic change in an issuer's stock price, since it might suggest that the analyst has missed some significant development. S&P does not, however, passively accept the view that a rise in equity market capitalization ipso facto implies an improvement in credit quality. In the agency's view, the stock market is too volatile and too sensitive to quarterly earnings fluctuations to serve as a basis for ratings, which are meant to reflect long-term creditworthiness.

A Different Interpretation

The preceding paragraphs should make it clear that investors cannot value bonds solely on the basis of ratings, and that the agencies do not intend that they do so. Furthermore, the discussion of factors that influence value but not ratings may help to explain the lower correspondence of ratings to yields in the speculative-grade sector, vis-a-vis the investment-grade sector. In particular, the agencies' focus on long-term credit quality causes ratings to change less frequently than market perceptions, which reflect short-term fluctuations in companies' earnings prospects. (It is logical for low-rated bonds, more so than high-rated bonds, to behave like equities, since the holder of a Single-B bond is more likely than the holder of a Double-A bond to end up owning the firm as a result of bankruptcy.) Combined with the high yield market's generally lesser liquidity, the greater sensitivity to short-term changes in perceived credit quality seems likely to produce a lower correlation of ratings and yields than in the investment-grade sector, even if there is no dispute about the accuracy of ratings.

Danger—Default Ahead!

Clearly, though, there is considerable difference of opinion about the accuracy of the ratings. Many vested interests are involved in this controversy, so it is difficult to eliminate subjectivity from tests of ratings' usefulness.

One objective way to evaluate the rating agencies' performance that is especially suited to high yield investors' needs is to assess how well they warn investors of impending defaults. Our discussions with rating agency personnel in connection with this chapter indicated that they themselves view this as an important indicator of their effectiveness. Perhaps sensitized to the matter by past complaints that they were slow in downgrading failing credits, they appear to have become increasingly determined to raise red flags. A Standard & Poor's official, for instance, told us that analysts nowadays try to avoid having their issuers rated as high as B- when they default, whereas in the past merely getting the company down to speculative-grade in advance of default might have been considered satisfactory.

Exhibit 2–3 presents one measure of ratings' effectiveness as harbingers of default. The summary statistics show that the average company that defaulted in 1986 was rated B1/B one year before default, B2/B- six months before default, and B3/CCC one month before default. Clearly, the rating trend on companies that ultimately failed generally signaled deterioration. (Moody's did, however, upgrade Petro-Lewis and Savin debt within a year of default.) Both agencies rated the majority of defaulting companies below Single-B (in most cases Caa/CCC) one month before default. Investors might have wished for still earlier and more dramatic warnings, but the agencies' record does not betray any gross lack of vigilance.

You Can't Please Everyone

No matter how well the rating agencies perform on this sort of test, however, it is still their lot to hear complaints. Occasionally the din of deprecating comments is relieved by a constructive criticism. As the agencies readily admit, they are not perfect, but neither have they ignored the rhubarbs.

One indication of the agencies' responsiveness is that they have expanded their staffs over the years. A Standard & Poor's official estimated in discussions with us that the firm's Corporate Finance Department had grown more than sixfold in the past decade. One S&P analyst noted that his workload had been cut from 55 to between 30 and 35 companies during the past six years. Moody's pointed to its increased employment of research associates to relieve analysts of routine number-crunching, and to improved computer capabilities to facilitate sensitivity analysis.

While increasing their personnel, the agencies have also sought to hire more experienced analysts. Moody's has emphasized recruitment of trained credit specialists from commercial banks and Standard & Poor's likewise looks for backgrounds in lending and financial analysis. McCarthy, Crisanti & Maffei has hired from a variety of sources, including insurance company private placement departments.

Many investors believe that high yield bonds are so dissimilar to high-grade issues that they require separate analytical teams using techniques unlike those employed in the investment-grade sector. McCarthy, Crisanti & Maffei has gone furthest in adopting the first part of this advice, currently

Exhibit 2–3
Rating Experience of Companies That Defaulted in 1986

The columns indicate the number of companies in each rating category at selected intervals prior to default. For example; seven companies had B3 ratings at Moody's six months prior to defaulting; thirteen companies were in Standard & Poor's CCC category one month prior to default.

	Moody's				**Standard & Poor's**		
	Months Prior to Default				Months Prior to Default		
Rating	12	6	1	Rating	12	6	1
A3	1	0	0	BBB	0	1	1
Baa1	0	0	0	BBB-	0	0	0
Baa2	0	0	0	BB+	1	0	0
Baa3	0	1	1	BB	2	0	0
Ba1	1	0	0	BB-	2	0	0
Ba2	1	0	0	B+	2	3	1
Ba3	2	1	1	B	2	2	1
B1	5	4	1	B-	7	8	4
B2	2	3	2	CCC	7	9	13
B3	6	7	4	CC	1	2	3
Caa	4	5	13	C	0	0	2
Ca	0	1	1				
Average Rating	B1	B2	B3	Average Rating	B	B-	CCC

Ratings are for actual issues that defaulted, whether senior or subordinated. To avoid double-counting, certain defaulting issues have been eliminated where a related credit defaulted simultaneously. Not all companies were rated in all periods by both agencies.

dedicating eight analysts to its high yield effort. In contrast, at Moody's and Standard & Poor's industry specialists continue to follow all grades of companies within their areas of expertise. Moody's does not approach high yield analysis in a way radically different from its high-grade analysis, but puts special emphasis on such factors as:

- Potential impact of the unexpected, in light of relatively narrow margins of protection,
- Ability to sell assets to raise cash, and

- Maintenance of access to credit.

Standard & Poor's pays less attention to conventional leverage ratios when rating high yield issues and focuses more on cash flow coverage and on management's demonstrated financial philosophy and operating record.

In addition to the quality of high yield research, effectiveness in communicating it has also received considerable attention at the agencies. Moody's *Corporate Credit Reports* on speculative-grade issues are designed to reach investors before pricing on new issues. Standard & Poor's has created a special section devoted to the high yield sector in *CreditWeek,* with emphasis on analyses of new deals and large-capitalization issues. McCarthy, Crisanti & Maffei publishes new-issue reports and updates. Electronic publishing is an increasingly important medium for the agencies' opinions on high yield companies.

One final area of controversy involves the use of a limited number of speculative ratings to cover a wide range of credit quality. On a selected date in 1987, actively quoted, long-term issues rated in the six Standard & Poor's categories from BB + to B- traded across a 729-basis-point range. The three categories of CCC to C added another 1,618 basis points of spread. In contrast, the 10 investment-grade ratings covered a range of only 133 basis points (based on long-term, new-issue levels). Under these circumstances, the label "Single-B" conveys about as precise a picture as the term "mammal" does to someone who has never seen a giraffe.

Standard & Poor's has attempted to rectify this problem by making greater use of its CCC category, formerly reserved for companies "on death's doorstep," in an official's phrase. Risky yet viable companies now regularly receive ratings in the CCC category at S&P, differentiating the rating from Moody's Caa, which still connotes "one foot in the grave," according to a spokesman. Because of this difference in rating definitions, the common institutional guideline of minimum B3/B- quality no longer makes sense. Anyone willing to own a B3 credit should also be willing to own a CCC. As evidence that the two ratings are applied to similar companies, there were 38 companies rated some combination of B1, B2 and B3 by Moody's and CCC+, CCC or CCC- by Standard & Poor's in July 1987, versus just 12 rated Caa by Moody's and CCC+, CCC or CCC- by Standard & Poor's. One implication of this rating quirk is that issues rated in the B category by Moody's and in the CCC category by S&P may become more valuable as institutions switch from a B3/B- to a B3/CCC- minimum quality standard to reflect S&P's change in policy.

Conclusion

Although we have emphasized the criticisms endured by the rating agencies, we do not perceive that they are looking for sympathy. In recent years, the demand for their services has been bolstered by increased volume of debt financing, accompanied by greater instability in credit quality. The high yield market's rapid expansion has provided them another major opportunity, but it has also necessitated innovation on their part. At this point, many high yield buyers claim to pay almost no attention to bond ratings and it is by no means certain that their attitude will change in the future. The agencies' success in expanding their influence in the high yield world will depend at least in part on their ability to adapt to the customer's special needs. In addition, it will be important that they get the customer to understand what they do and what they expressly decline to do. Equipped with this understanding, investors will be able to judge accurately the agencies' effectiveness in their chosen task.

Technical Note

Test of Correlation Between Ratings and Bond Yields

Description of Experiment

To quantify the relationship between bond ratings and secondary market yields, we selected five investment-grade and five speculative-grade issues. Within each category, we limited our selection to issues trading at dollar prices between 90 and 100 and with maturities of six to nine years. By keeping these factors uniform, we minimized possible distortions related to call vulnerability and the yield curve. In addition, we used only issues specifically priced on a regular basis by the Morgan Stanley high yield trading desk. This avoided the circularity of matrix pricing, which is itself largely determined by ratings. As a result of these selection criteria, observed yield relationships within our samples should have been as nearly pure reflections as possible of the market's perceived credit quality. By regressing the ratings against the yields, we were able to evaluate the extent to which market perceptions corresponded to ratings. (To plot the ratings, we averaged the Moody's and Standard & Poor's rating for each issue by converting each rating to a numerical score, e.g., Aaa = 1, Aa1 = 2, etc.)

We observed the yields on the two samples on 10 dates, at intervals of two weeks, between April 1 and August 14, 1987. During this period, the yield on 10-year Treasuries ranged between 7.58% and 8.81%.

Results

The correlation between ratings and yields proved to be higher in the investment-grade sector than in the high yield sector. For investment-grade issues the R^2 factor was .891, versus .573 for the high yield bonds. These results were significant at the 98.1% and 85.4% levels, respectively.

A possible explanation for the lower correlation in the high yield sector might be simply that the subinvestment-grade ratings cover a wider range of secondary market yields. By this logic, the investment-grade bonds are bound to show a close fit with ratings, since their yields are squeezed into comparatively few basis points. We can reject this hypothesis, however. For our investment-grade sample, residuals (the portion of yield not explained by ratings) approximated 2.3% of observed yield, versus approximately 3.9% for the high yield sample. In other words, the correlation for high yield bonds was looser, even normalized for the wider range of yields.

Composition of Samples

Investment-Grade		
Bausch & Lomb	8%	04/15/96
C.I.T. Financial	7 3/4%	04/15/93
Du Pont	7 1/2%	08/15/93
General Motors Acceptance Corp.	8%	07/01/93
Occidental Petroleum	8 95/100%	04/15/94
High Yield		
Fruit of the Loom	10 3/4%	02/15/95
Holiday Corp.	10 1/2%	04/01/94
MCI Communications	9 1/2%	08/01/93
Price Communications	11 3/4%	02/15/95
Union Carbide	9 3/4%	04/15/94

Endnotes

[1] See Martin Fridson and Fritz Wahl, "Overvaluation of Subordinated Debt," *High Performance* (June 1985): pp. 2-7.

[2] See for example Maggie Queen and Richard Roll, "Firm Mortality: Using Market Indicators to Predict Survival," *Financial Analysts Journal* (May/June 1987): pp. 9-16.

[3] For a fuller discussion of this opportunity, see Martin S. Fridson, "B/CCC Paper Undervalued Because of Rating Anomaly," (Morgan Stanley, August 12, 1987).

CHAPTER 3

Covenants in Context

Few topics in the bond market generate as much controversy, or as much confusion, as covenants. When a high yield issue is coming to market, the underwriter has the dual task of explicating for investors the dense legalese in which the covenants are written and mediating the sometimes heated debate between the issuer and potential buyers regarding the adequacy of the provisions. Frequently, competing investment banks' salespeople are on the sidelines, providing helpful consumer advice (as they see it) or trashing the underwriter's deal (as those who are trying to sell it perceive). The decibel level rises even higher when a financial problem at the issuer triggers a covenant. At that point, the parties find that even when the language of the covenant is reduced to Basic English, the meaning can still be unclear (from a legal standpoint). In the end, the bondholder's overriding emotion may be anger, derived from a perception that the issuer has evaded the clear intent of the indenture through trickery and been upheld by a court supposedly ordained to preserve the sanctity of contracts.

Beginning in 1987, a new dimension was added to the already controversial subject of covenants as releveraging became a more clearly recognized hazard for high yield bondholders. Previously, balance sheet restructuring was a concern primarily in the investment-grade market, where many Single-A and Double-A companies were instantly transformed into Single-B credits through recapitalizations or leveraged buyouts. Bonds that lacked strong safeguards fell sharply in value as credit quality declined. More recently, high yield buyers have found that they, too, are vulnerable to debt-financed actions designed to enhance shareholder value. The loss of market value as a result of releveraging represents a significant hazard for bondholders.

To many investors, the obvious solution to the releveraging problem is to tighten covenants. In our view, a more accurate statement is that covenant reform is part of the answer for bondholders seeking better insulation against price shocks. For one thing, investors cannot hope to dictate terms to borrowers who have alternatives to raising public debt containing strict covenants. Second, even if lenders succeed in imposing tighter covenants, they may find that the protection they obtain thereby is illusory. Over the life of a bond, market conditions often change in ways that nobody contemplates when drafting the covenants. Furthermore, issuers and their attorneys sometimes devise ingenious means of circumventing covenants that might appear airtight to the layman. In some cases, protective covenants ultimately backfire, making bondholders worse off than they would have been without the provisions. Accordingly, high yield buyers should not pin their hopes for economic justice entirely on covenants. Instead, they should view covenants in the context of all actions they can take to maximize their returns and limit their risks.

A Give-and-Take Process

Perhaps there was a golden age in which investors, issuers and underwriters universally regarded covenants as a sacred right, although we doubt it. In any event, that is certainly not the case today. Whatever one's private conscience may say about the ethical correctness of bonds issued with weak covenants, the marketplace treats indentures primarily as a process of give-and-take. (One notable exception is that some underwriters have held the line on requiring that issuers regularly report their financial results to bondholders, even when not compelled to by Securities and Exchange Commission regulations.[1])

In this environment, bondholders find that there are limits to their bargaining power. A strong Single-B company seeking to raise $150 million in today's market can attract more than enough willing buyers for its paper. Elementary game theory suggests that these conditions are not ideal for collective action by buyers hoping to hold out for unusually strong covenants. Just as sellers' cartels typically arise in oligopolistic industries and disintegrate in industries characterized by atomistic competition, buyers' cartels work best when a few major institutions have the power to make or break the deal. This is more likely to be the case when the issuer is a comparatively weak credit trying to borrow $500 million. In point of fact, the most carefully crafted covenants occur in leveraged buyouts and recapitalizations, where uncertainties about the feasibility of planned asset sales can create substantial risks.

Further strengthening the issuer's hand is the alternative of borrowing privately. Particularly as commercial banks have indicated a willingness to venture beyond bridge loans into providing permanent financing, borrowers have enjoyed an increasing variety of options. A chief executive officer can now reasonably ask, "Why should I traipse around the country on a three-week roadshow in order to be handcuffed by covenants? I might as well borrow privately in that case." Again, it is the big, ugly borrowers who are most likely to submit to demands for tight covenants, due to their need for public market access in order to float the sheer volume of paper they require. By virtue of their prominence, these megadeals may establish stricter standards for bondholder protection.

Even if bond buyers succeed in extracting detailed covenants through this Hobbesian struggle, however, they cannot let down their guard. Instead, investors must take it as an axiom that some covenants being written today will fail to protect bondholders in the desired fashion when push comes to shove. The only uncertainty is whether that failure will result from an unforeseen change in economic conditions, a deliberately contrived loophole or a sly reading of the covenant by the issuer and its counsel.

Status Quo Not Maintained

An excellent illustration of how changing economic conditions can alter the effect of covenants is the history of electric utilities' maintenance and replacement (M&R) funds. These provisions were originally understood to protect investors by preserving a minimum of secured property to outstanding mortgage debt. As the value of plant and equipment declined through wear-and-tear, the utility could keep the ratio constant either by reducing the amount of debt outstanding (i.e., retiring bonds) or by replacing the asset value that had been lost through use. Because utilities tended to add capacity over time, their invariable practice was to satisfy the M&R requirements by obtaining credits for their capital expenditures, which were more than sufficient for the purpose.

When interest rates rose sharply during the early 1970s, utilities issued bonds at painfully high rates and (as was the custom) with five-year refunding prohibitions. Well before those refunding restrictions expired, interest rates fell precipitously and utilities yearned to rid themselves of debt that had become extremely costly. Suddenly, companies realized that the M&R funds provided an out. Instead of crediting property additions to the M&R funds, some companies began to retire bonds—concentrating, naturally, on their highest outstanding coupons. The redemption prices were well below the prevailing secondary market values of the issues, which were being priced to the refunding dates, with no contemplation of earlier calls. Bondholders suffered sizable losses as a result of the surprise redemptions.

Through these unexpected redemptions the maintenance and replacement covenant, originally conceived as a protection for bondholders, ultimately backfired on lenders. Unforeseen economic conditions—an unprecedented increase in interest rate volatility—radically changed the issuers' use of the covenant.

Limitations of the Debt Limitation

Readers should not infer from the M&R example that unpleasant surprises for bondholders are invariably surprises to the issuers as well. Rather, companies often succeed in crafting covenants that satisfy investors' appetite for restrictions while subtly preserving management's future flexibility. Buyers who merely adopt a checkoff approach, instead of examining the actual contents of the covenants they have managed to obtain, can leave themselves vulnerable to significant financial deterioration.

A "debt limitation," for example, may not restrict total debt incurrence but may restrict only senior debt, or only senior funded (i.e., maturity exceeding one year) debt. Such a provision protects the subordinated lender's position in bankruptcy (by limiting the amount of debt that will rank higher) but does nothing to prevent the issuer from borrowing its way into Chapter 11 on a subordinated basis.

Bondholders are better protected by a limitation on incurrence of all classes of debt, but the flaw in even this tighter test is revealed by the key word, "incurrence." Generally, the issuer is not obligated to *maintain* debt at a level below (for example) 50% of consolidated net tangible assets, but merely to refrain from incurring new debt that would push its leverage over the specified limit. An amusing parlor game consists of devising ingenious new ways to do violence to the spirit, while observing the letter of the debt-incurrence test. For instance, a company could sell an asset and apply the proceeds to stock repurchase. In this scenario, equity would decline, so the ratio of debt to equity would rise (possibly above the "limit") without new debt being incurred. Alternatively, a company might issue redeemable, cumulative preferred stock (thereby increasing financial risk, but not debt, technically speaking) and buy in common stock with the proceeds. This scheme would particularly appeal to a company in a non-taxpaying mode, a condition the equity holders could preserve (by keeping interest payments high) until they had an opportunity to cash out their investment. Still another possible circumvention would be to issue new debt, right up to the maximum level permitted, then dividend out the proceeds. Technically, the resultant crossing of the debt ratio threshold would be caused not by the debt incurrence but by the later dividend payment.

Loopholes Aplenty

Corporate treasurers who do not care for these mental exercises can get around a debt restriction with the far simpler device of a leveraged acquirer. The history of ANR Pipeline (formerly known as Michigan-Wisconsin Pipeline) illustrates this technique. As of early 1989, ANR's first mortgage debt is rated Baa2/BB+, yet the company's ratio of total debt to total capital (32%) seems more in line with its Duff & Phelps rating of "5" (high Single-A). The explanation is that ANR is a wholly owned subsidiary of Coastal Corporation, a much more highly leveraged company with senior debt ratings of Ba1/BB. Moody's and Standard & Poor's, as well as the market, take into account the contingent risk that if its parent were to falter, ANR could be compelled to borrow heavily and upstream the proceeds. This risk was created in 1985 when ANR was acquired by Coastal for $2.5 billion. At that time, a covenant limited ANR's total outstanding bonds to $750 million and also subjected new issuance to a fixed charge coverage test. Fortunately for Coastal, however, ANR's indenture said nothing about how much debt its parent could incur. By putting all of the acquisition debt onto its own balance sheet, Coastal steered clear of ANR's covenants and compelled bondholders to absorb a portion of the cost of the transactions through downgrading of their securities from A2/A+ to (initially) Baa2/BB. (Coastal would have been obliged to comply with the ANR covenants if it had merged ANR into itself. By not taking that step, Coastal kept outstanding debt that carried coupons as low as 5 3/4%.)

Poison Puts and Principal Property

Long-established covenants like the debt limitation are vulnerable partly because issuers have had lots of time to figure out how to evade them, but newfangled covenants have their pitfalls, as well. For example, the "poison put" provisions that gained popularity in 1988 were supposed to protect the investor against releveraging by allowing the holder to put the bonds back to the issuer in the event of a change of control. In some cases, though, friendly transactions (i.e., those approved by the company's outside directors) were excluded from the provisions. The weakness in this structure is that if management itself decides to leverage the company—possibly to avoid being taken over by a hostile raider—or approves a sweetened tender from a raider who initially bid on an unsolicited basis (as typically occurs these days), bondholders suffer maximum damage from the releveraging. Other poison put issues have closed the friendly transaction loophole but have permitted defensive acquisitions, transactions designed to reduce the target company's vulnerability by using up all excess debt capacity and thereby reducing credit quality.

Even the seemingly straightforward negative pledge clause, the most basic covenant in an unsecured obligation, can have hidden traps.

The concept of a negative pledge clause is to protect the unsecured lender from becoming effectively subordinated through the granting of liens to other lenders. If such liens are created, the unsecured lenders must be equally and ratably secured.

This covenant does not purport to limit debt incurrence, but merely to preserve the lender's standing in bankruptcy. Even the latter objective may not be achieved, however, due to numerous exceptions and definitions that typically accompany the basic provision. For instance, there may be an exception allowing incurrence of purchase money mortgages, i.e., secured debt issued in connection with the acquisition of new assets. The rationale is that as long as the borrower keeps intact the asset base that existed when the unsecured lender purchased the bonds, no impairment should occur. Meanwhile, the borrower retains flexibility in purchasing new assets. Over time, however, a rapidly growing company could acquire so much property with purchase money mortgages that its unsecured debt could end up ranking below a much larger class of secured debt.

A still subtler flaw in some negative pledge clauses involves a key definition. The covenant may restrict the creation of a security interest in "principal property" of the issuer. In some instances the definition of principal property excludes any property that the board of directors reasonably determines not to be a principal property. That is, the issuer could create secured debt, notwithstanding the negative pledge clause, on any asset its directors decided not to define as principal property. One source that we consulted in preparing this essay recalled an instance in which a manufacturer had so many different plants and properties that none individually represented as much as one percent of its total assets. The company's directors determined that nothing the firm owned in and of itself qualified as a principal property, effectively rendering the negative pledge in its debentures meaningless. Another loophole sometimes observed in negative pledges is the exclusion of stock of subsidiaries from the definition of principal property. The issuer may thus be free to transfer assets to a subsidiary and offer the stock (rather than the assets) as collateral for a loan, thereby creating a security interest without having to equally and ratably secure the debenture holders.

Issuer's Choice

Hazards for bondholders are not limited to technicalities of this sort that are explicitly written into indentures. Investors can also fall victim to what attorneys politely term "sailing close to wind." Emboldened by a literal-minded tendency among judges who are called upon to rule on such matters, many issuers aggressively interpret covenants to their own benefit. In such cases, the outcome for bondholders may depend primarily on whether the issuer is inclined to emphasize the spirit of the covenant, rather than on how the covenant is worded.

A case in point involves the Jim Walter 9 ½% debentures due 2019 and the Allied Stores 6% notes due 1992. Exhibit 3–1 reproduces the dividend restrictions of the two issues. To a reader with just a passing knowledge of covenants, both appear to present formidable obstacles to leveraged buyouts and recapitalizations. The issuer in each case is barred from paying dividends or buying in stock in an amount exceeding a "basket" ($100 million for Jim Walter, $90 million for Allied Stores) plus cumulative earnings, proceeds of new equity sales and proceeds of convertible debt conversions subsequent to the issue date.

When Kohlberg Kravis Roberts & Co. led a leveraged buyout of Jim Walter, the covenant apparently had its desired effect.[2] Issues containing the dividend test (including the 9 ½s of 2016) were retired, so holders were not harmed by the October 1987 downgrading of Jim Walter from Baa1/A- to B1/B. Three other Jim Walter issues that lacked the dividend test remained outstanding after the LBO and the attendant reduction in credit quality.[3]

In contrast, the Allied Stores 6s remained outstanding throughout the company's leveraged buyout and its February 1987 downgrading from A2/A+ to B1/B. Real estate magnate Robert Campeau structured the deal in such a way that no dividend payment or stock repurchase occurred at the issuer level. Instead, a shell corporation borrowed the necessary funds and purchased the Allied Stores shares. The shell then merged into Allied. Although the effect of absorbing the highly leveraged acquisition vehicle sharply raised Allied's debt ratio —just as a direct share repurchase by Allied would have—no covenant was found to have been violated. Campeau kept low-cost debt on the books and Allied's bondholders suffered a loss in market value. Although some have argued that a merger of this sort economically violates the dividend test, the courts

Exhibit 3–1
Selected Dividend Restrictions

Jim Walter 9 ½% Debentures due 2016

"The company will not declare any dividend or make any distribution (except dividends and distributions payable in shares of its capital stock) in respect of, or purchase, redeem or acquire for a consideration (except shares acquired upon the conversion thereof into, or in exchange for, other shares of stock of the Company), or permit any of its Restricted Subsidiaries to purchase or acquire, any shares of the Company's capital stock (except for shares of the Company's capital stock) if immediately thereafter the aggregate payments for such purposes since August 31, 1985 exceed the sum of (i) the Consolidated Net Income of the Company and its Restricted Subsidiaries since August 31, 1985, (ii) $100,000,000, (iii) the aggregate net proceeds received (whether in cash, stock or other property) after August 31, 1985 from the issue of capital stock of the Company or of warrants or rights to purchase such capital stock and (iv) the aggregate net proceeds received by the Company in respect of any Indebtedness which is converted into shares of its capital stock after August 31, 1985. (Section 5.06)"

Allied Stores 6% Notes due 1992

"No dividend may be paid or declared or other distribution made (except in stock of the Company) on any stock of the Company, and neither the Company nor any Subsidiary may acquire any such stock, if, after giving effect thereto, the aggregate payments for all such purposes subsequent to January 31, 1981 would exceed the sum of (i) Consolidated Net Income subsequent to January 31, 1981, (ii) the aggregate of the net proceeds received by the Company and its Wholly-owned Restricted Subsidiaries from the issuance or sale (other than to a Subsidiary) of the Company's stock subsequent to January 31, 1981, (iii) the aggregate of the net proceeds received by the Company from the issuance or sale (other than to a Subsidiary) for cash or other property of any Indebtedness of the Company which is converted into shares of its stock subsequent to January 31, 1981, and (iv) $90,000,000. The foregoing restriction, however shall not prevent the acquisition of stock of the Company solely in exchange for other shares of stock of the Company, or the acquisition of stock of the Company through the application of the net proceeds of a substantially concurrent sale for cash (other than to a Subsidiary) of other shares of stock of the Company, or the payment of any dividend within 90 days after the date declaration thereof, it at such date such declaration complied with the provision of the Indenture. (Section 1009)" have to date adhered to a narrow, literal interpretation of the covenant.

Based on the dissimilar responses of Kohlberg Kravis Roberts and Robert Campeau to similar provisions, investors seeking to evaluate covenants may find it more worthwhile to study the principal players' past behavior than to match wits with lawyers who are adept at subtle and innovative readings of indentures. Certainly, economic motivations play a part in the willingness of those in control to "sail close to the wind." An issuer contemplating no additional financing in the foreseeable future may not worry about leaving a bad taste in bondholders' mouths. On the other hand, an investment bank hoping to organize and invest in a series of restructurings could impair its ability to raise capital if it acquired a reputation for overly clever interpretation of indentures.

Investors should not neglect this angle in their analysis, but attorneys caution that litigation involving covenants tends to be quite "fact-specific." In other words, the precise language of the provision in question, which varies from indenture to indenture, will be critical in deciding the case. Therefore, a firm that decided not to attempt to circumvent a covenant in the past might try an aggressive interpretation in the future on the strength of slightly more favorable language.

What's It Worth to You?

The many pitfalls we have described, ranging from changing economic conditions to loopholes to aggressive interpretation by borrowers, may lead some readers to the conclusion that all protective covenants are worthless. We would certainly not go that far, but we consider it essential for portfolio managers to recognize that the value of covenants is finite. While this statement sounds obvious, some investors overlook it, judging by their actions. A portfolio manager who says, "I absolutely refuse to buy this issue unless the underwriters put in a dividend restriction" is in effect placing an infinite value on the covenant. The statement implies that no yield incentive—not 50, 150, or even 1,500 points—would be sufficient to induce the portfolio manager to buy the bond without the covenant, in lieu of a comparable-credit issue that has it. Expressed another way, a categorical rejection means that the investor would in theory *give up* any amount of yield to sell the covenantless issue and replace it with the covenant-protected one.[4] Perhaps this is carrying the argument to the point of absurdity, but it underscores the necessity of putting some ceiling on the value that one will attribute to a covenant—particularly since, as we have shown, the protection it affords is unlikely to be airtight.

Establishing a ceiling, unfortunately, is easier said than done. Precise valuation of an anti-releveraging covenant is impossible, given the numerous uncertainties about whether it will come into play and, if it does, whether it will work as bondholders expect it to.

One might try to infer a value from the market, i.e., by comparing yields. That approach, however, requires a pure case—which is unlikely to be found—of two bonds identical in every respect except the presence of the covenant. Moreover, there is no assurance that the market is efficiently pricing the existence of covenants. Following Wickes's initial leveraged buyout proposal in 1988, the market apparently began to reflect a minimum net worth provision only after a one-day delay, at which point the bonds started to recover from their initial post-announcement lows.

As an alternative to trying to isolate a market spread attributable to a covenant, one can attempt to calculate its intrinsic value. While highly dependent on assumptions, this exercise at least gets the investor into the ballpark regarding the maximum one ought to pay for a perfect covenant. In the real world, the value will be something less than the figure derived by calculation.

One approach to estimating the intrinsic value of a covenant uses the following variables:

1. *Expected impact of a releveraging.* The purest measure of the impact of a releveraging announcements is the

widening of the yield spread versus a high yield index. Past experience offers some indication of the basis point response one might expect to see in such circumstances.

2. *Probability of a releveraging.* Releveraging is a diversifiable risk. Unless one assumes that every bond in the portfolio will be devalued through releveraging during one's measurement period, it does not pay to insure against 100% of the downside in each bond. This reasoning is analogous to the rationale for reserving against default losses only up to a reasonable expectation of future default experience, rather than to the approximately 60% of total portfolio value that might be lost if every issuer went into Chapter 11.
3. *Measurement period.* The total return impact of a five-point drop in a single holding can be substantial over a one-day period, but portfolio mangers are not generally evaluated on their daily performance. A truer sense of the value of a covenant can be obtained by looking at the impact of a releveraging over the evaluation period, which may be three months, a year, or longer.

As conceptually simple as these three variables are, implementing a model based on them is surprisingly difficult. The impact of releveraging, for example, is not only highly variable but difficult to measure, as well. Does the impact include the market's anticipation of the releveraging, which has become more pronounced as high yield investors have become more conscious of the threat? Because of this anticipation, will future responses to the announcements be less dramatic than in the past? If the spread widens only gradually or fluctuates for an extended period after the announcement, how does one determine the appropriate base date and post-announcement measurement date? Further complicating the measurement is the fact that each releveraging is unique; the incremental risk created varies according to (among other factors) the amount

Exhibit 3–2
Impact of Selected Releveragings of 1988

Issue	Observation Period	Basis Point Widening Versus Core Holdings
Colt Industries 12 ½% due 2001	March 2 to March 31	42
Foodmaker 13% due 1998	August 22 to August 23	28
Imo Delaval 12 ¼% due 1997	August 18 to August 25	33
Macy 14 ½% due 1998	March 2 to March 31	116
Macy 14 ½% due 2001	March 2 to March 31	152

The disparity in the releveraging impact observed for the two Macy issues may be a function of seniority. One would expect the senior subordinated 14 ½s of 1998 to show less response to an increase in financial risk than the subordinated (i.e., riskier) 14 ½s of 2001. The observed increases in spread, 116 and 152 basis points, respectively, are consistent with this expectation.

of debt capacity eliminated by the transaction and the stability of the company's operations. Finally, if issues in the observation sample contain anti-releveraging covenants, then the findings will not purely represent the desired information, i.e., the effect of releveraging a non-covenant-protected issuer. In light of the extreme variability observed in selected releveragings of 1988 (Exhibit 3–2), any assumption about future releveragings is necessarily arbitrary. We have posited an impact of 100 basis points for the purpose of illustrating our model, but readers may be wise to test alternative assumptions.

As for the probability of releveraging (or the expected percentage of issues in the portfolio that will suffer releveraging), the sharp increase in such activity during 1987-1988 limits the relevance of historical experience. Accordingly, it may be advisable to make the probability of releveraging the unknown variable for which one solves the equation. Plugging in a one-year measurement period for sake of illustration, we can then ask: *Given a stated giveup in yield as payment for covenant protection, what probability of releveraging is implied?*

The Technical Note shows how we derive the solution. (Observe that the model requires additional assumptions regarding average coupon and maturity of the portfolio.) In the example shown, a 50-basis-point giveup to obtain an anti-releveraging covenant implies a 10% risk of releveraging. Working the equation "in reverse," an assumed 25% releveraging probability in theory justifies a 124-basis point giveup. As a practical consideration, though, it is questionable whether an investor would be likely to accept the implied yield of 11.26% (i.e., 12.50% minus 1.24%). The sheer credit risk might argue against so rich a yield, bearing in mind that the anti-releveraging provision in no way eliminates default risk, but merely reduces the company's freedom to borrow its way to bankruptcy.

Readers should also remember that the model in the Technical Note shows the value of a perfectly airtight covenant, something one is unlikely to find in the real world. Given the many flaws and escape hatches described above, an investor must knock a fair amount off any theoretically derived value of a covenant.

The key point is that the value of any covenant is finite. It is therefore not rational to reject a bond on the basis of a lack of covenant protection without considering how much yield one forgoes by doing so. Suppose, for example, Company A is a better credit than Company B, to the tune of 100 basis points at prevailing risk premiums. If the value of an anti-releveraging covenant is shown to have a maximum value of 60 basis points, it is not rational to buy Company B's covenant-protected bond when Company A's non-covenant-protected bond is available at an identical yield.

Conclusion

Covenants must be assessed in the context of other factors that affect investment performance. It pays to be knowledgeable about covenants, for they can add value to a security. Losing sight of their intrinsic value can be costly, however. Certainly, buying an inferior credit to obtain superior covenant protection is a dubious strategy. Neither should a portfolio manger place an excessive value on a covenant that is likely to be circumvented; a contract with a scoundrel is worth little. Most important, performance-driven investors should not put their primary emphasis on the desirability of covenants in the abstract. Instead, they should focus on each covenant's monetary value and resolve to pay not one penny more than the protection is objectively worth.

Technical Note

Calculating the Value of an Airtight Anti-Releveraging Covenant Model

$$V = Y_n - Y_c$$
$$Y_c = [R_{lt} \times P] + [R_{nt} \times (1 - P)]$$

Where:

V	=	Value of anti-releveraging covenant
Y_n	=	Yield available on a non-covenant-protected bond
Y_c	=	Yield available on a covenant-protected bond
R_{lt}	=	Expected return on a non-covenant-protected bond that is releveraged, measured over period t, corresponding to investor's performance measurement period
R_{nt}	=	Expected return on a non-covenant-protected bond that is not releveraged, measured over period t, corresponding to investor's performance measurement period
P	=	Probability of releveraging

(Note that $Y_n = R_{nt}$ for any value of t if the general level of interest rates remains constant)

Example:

Assumptions:

Impact of Releveraging	100 basis points
Measurement Period	One year
Average Coupon of Portfolio	12½%
Average Maturity of Portfolio	10 years

Solve for: Probability of Releveraging, based on a given value assigned to the covenant

Solution:

		Total Return Over One Year*
Bonds Not Affected by Releveraging (no price change)	=	12.50%
Bonds Affected by Releveraging	=	7.52%

*The value assigned to the covenant is the maximum number of basis points an investor will give up to own a covenant-protected bond rather than a non-covenant-protected bond of equivalent credit, term and liquidity risk.

Suppose the investor is willing to give up 50 basis points. The implied probability of releveraging can be calculated by determining the percentages of releveraging and non-releveraging bonds that produce a weighted average return of:

12.50 (Yield on non-covenant-protected issue)
- .50 (Giveup)
12.00

Solving for P, the percentage of releveraging issues, we get:

$$[7.52 \times P] + [12.50 \times (1 - P)] = 12.00$$
$$7.52(P) + 12.50 - 12.50(P) = 12.00$$
$$-4.98(P) = -0.50$$
$$P = 9.96$$

A 50-basis point giveup to obtain the covenant thus assumes a 10% probability that a given issue in the portfolio will be subjected to releveraging over the next year. Note that the model can also be used to determine a value of the covenant given an assumed probability of releveraging. For example, if we expect 25% of the companies in the portfolio to releverage, then we solve for Y_c, the yield we would be willing to accept to own a bond with an airtight covenant.

$$[7.52 \times .25] + [12.50 \times (1-.25)] = Y_c$$
$$11.26 = Y_c$$

The value of the covenant is the resulting giveup versus the prevailing non-covenant-protected rate.

$$\begin{array}{r} 12.50 \\ \underline{-11.26} \\ 1.24 \end{array}$$

* Assumes no change in the general level of interest rates.

LITERARY NOTE

Circumventing Covenants: A Celebrated Tradition

Literature and folklore abound with tales of sly rascals who wriggle out of contracts by ingenious means. By and large, the character who evades the covenant is the hero of the piece, more esteemed for his wits than despised for his lack of honor. Perhaps this glorification of artful dodgers reflects deeply rooted cultural attitudes that also explain society's tolerance for the undoing of covenants through technicalities.

The most celebrated example of covenant evasion occurs in "The Merchant of Venice." In Shakespeare's play, the borrower (Antonio), serenely confident of his ability to repay a 3,000-ducat shipping loan well before maturity, readily agrees to secure the obligation with a pound of his own flesh. After the fleet he has financed is reported lost at sea, however, Antonio defaults. A friend offers to repay the principal on his behalf, but the lender (Shylock) elects instead to foreclose on the collateral, which is indubitably his right. The matter goes to litigation, where nobody disputes the validity of Shylock's claim. Unfortunately for the lender, however, the "judge" (actually an impostor who is clearly partial toward Antonio) decides the case on the basis of an extraordinarily literal reading of the contract. The lien is on a pound of Antonio's flesh and does not expressly permit the creditor to draw blood during the process of foreclosing. If Shylock does shed a drop of blood, the bogus judge rules, all of his assets will be seized by the state. Not satisfied with this travesty of justice, Antonio's ally refuses to allow Shylock to revert to recovering his principal in lieu of foreclosing, then introduces an extraneous criminal charge against Shylock into the civil proceeding.

So lightly does the public regard such legal chicanery, evidently, that even Abraham Lincoln's reputation for rectitude has survived his confession of preposterously self-interested literalness in interpreting a contract. According to a tale Lincoln himself told, once as a young lawyer he and a certain judge got to bantering about their respective skills as horse traders. They contracted to meet the following morning and swap horses, sight unseen, with a penalty of $25 to either party who attempted to renege. The judge appeared on schedule, leading the most emaciated oatburner the onlookers had ever set eyes upon. Lincoln arrived shortly thereafter with a wooden sawhorse on his shoulders. Amidst profuse laughter from the crowd, Lincoln perused the judge's creature and exclaimed, "Well, judge, this is the first time I ever got the worst of it in a horse trade."

Evading the clear intent of the contract is such a common theme in popular stories that the occasional character who scrupulously fulfills the terms of a deal is regarded as somehow more than human. The Irish hero Cuchulain, for example, was rumored to be the son of a god (Lugh of the Long Hand), no doubt because he acted so unlike the mortals in most other legends and dramas. On one occasion, a fearsome giant appeared at the great hall in Armagh and challenged anyone present to cut off his head with a huge axe that he carried. The sole condition was that the giant could return the next night and reciprocate by cutting off the head of the one who accepted the challenge. Cuchulain's rival Laegire, believing he had found a genuine rube, immediately agreed to the terms. Imagine his surprise when, after cleaving the giant's neck, he saw the brute arise, collect his head and walk out of the hall. When the giant returned intact the next night, Laegire was nowhere to be seen, notwithstanding the unambiguous clause that commanded his presence. Cuchulain's cousin and rival Connall Cearnach, who had not witnessed the previous night's events, accepted with delight when the giant again made his proposition. Connall, too, lopped off the oversized noggin then failed to appear 24 hours later despite his promise. At that point the scene was once again reenacted as Cuchulain, who was present for the first time, became the third in as many nights to chop off the giant's ugly head.

Cuchulain alone of the three heroes reappeared to fulfill his pledge, telling his uncle, King Conor of Ulster, that he would sooner die than violate a covenant, either by absconding or through knavery. With the youth's neck stretched before him the giant raised his axe to the rafters and crashed it to the earth . . . blunt side downward and several inches away from Cuchulain's body. Cuchulain opened his eyes to behold not a giant but the wizard Curoi of Kerry, who declared the brave and honest lad Champion of the Heroes of Ireland, thereby settling a longstanding dispute over that title. Who can deny that Cuchulain deserved this singular honor, when the vast majority of protagonists in world literature—most of whom had far lesser incentives than Cuchulain to seek a loophole—declined to honor the terms of their agreements?

Endnotes

1 Unlisted companies with fewer than 300 security holders are not obliged to file SEC financial statements even though they may have public debt outstanding. Many privately owned bonds issuers qualify for this exemption.

2 The issue is complicated by the fact that there was also a senior debt limitation in the Jim Walter indenture. Although as we have already pointed out, that provision is no more foolproof than a dividend restriction, the facts do not establish whether the dividend test alone would have prompted redemption of the bonds. Nevertheless, the contrast with the Allied Stores experience is informative. The casual reader of covenants would have judged in both the Jim Walter and the Allied Stores cases that the dividend restriction alone precluded a drastic financial restructuring. As it turned out, the issuer had flexibility to escape the strictures and Allied Stores chose to exploit that flexibility.

3 Jim Walter also retired certain issues that did not contain either the dividend restriction or the senior debt limitation.

4 The rejectionist stance may be viewed as rational if it is adopted as part of a collective action by investors to hold out for certain covenants. If successful, a boycott could produce a tangible benefit. Unless an investor has sufficient buying power to make or break a deal, however, unilateral rejection of an issue can have a negative impact on perfor-

mance by prompting the selection of a riskier credit in exchange for less-than-offsetting covenant protection.

CHAPTER 4

How Much Value in Asset Values?

Judging by asset coverage, as shown in Exhibit 4–1, which of the six bonds listed would you guess proved to be the best investment from the date 12 months prior to bankruptcy through its emergence from Chapter 11?

Exhibit 4–1
Selected Post-1978 Bankruptcies Ranked by Asset Coverage

Issue (All Senior Debentures)			Total Assets/Total Liabilities One Year Before Bankruptcy
White Motor	7 ¼%	12/01/93	127.6%
Braniff	9 ⅛%	1/01/97	106.4
Wickes	7 ⅞%	5/01/98	105.1
AM International	9 ⅜%	6/30/95	104.2
Wilson Foods	7 ⅞%	3/01/97	101.0
Itel	10 ½%	3/01/98	84.6

Surprisingly, Wilson Foods, which ranked near the bottom of the group by the asset protection measure used here, had the highest rate of return, both in absolute terms and adjusted for overall market performance. (See Exhibit 4–2, Columns 5 and 7.) The White Motor issue, with by far the best asset protection (measured by book value), returned -1.69% over a period in which a risk-free (i.e., Treasury) bond of similar coupon and maturity produced a 7.76% total return. Clearly, the simple-minded asset protection sales pitch ("These bonds are money-good because the assets are greater than the liabilities.") has not proven an infallible guide to investment value in troubled companies that have gone bankrupt. In general, two things went wrong—(1) assets were worth less than their stated values and (2) the passage of time eroded rates of return, even when bondholders recovered a high percentage of their claims. Asset protection can be a useful concept, especially in the larger context of financial flexibility analysis, as described later in this article. Investors can, however, come to woe in several different ways when they seek protection in assets of corporations that subsequently seek protection from their creditors.

Note that we are not discussing speculation in companies already in bankruptcy. Rather, our focus is on the purchase of high-risk bonds in the belief that the issuer will probably remain solvent, while looking to asset values for downside protection. Less risk-averse investors who are willing to buy bonds already in default may achieve higher returns than those cited in this chapter.

Less Than Meets the Eye

By definition, any company with positive net worth has stated assets greater than stated liabilities. Unfortunately, assets' economic worth may be less than their carrying values at a given point; in a failing company such discrepancies are likely. Column 2 in Exhibit 4–2 shows that no bondholder in any of the Chapter 11 proceedings surveyed (all from the period following the 1978 Bankruptcy Code reform) received as much as $900 in market value of new securities for his claim of $1,000 (par) plus pre-petition accrued interest.

A reorganization plan cannot be confirmed unless it awards creditors least as much as they would receive in liquidation. It follows that the liquidation value of the assets was less than $900 per bond in all cases cited, even though the stated values were as high as $1,276 a year prior to the bankruptcy (Exhibit 4–1). Ironically, Itel creditors, who had

Exhibit 4–2
Rates of Return in Selected Bankruptcies

Pre-Petition Issue			(1) Market Value 12 Months Before Chapter 11 Filing: Price	(1) YTM	(2) Market Value of Reorganization Securities at Issue Date		(3) Percentage Recovery of Investment	(4) Months in Reorganization	(5) Annual Effective Internal Rate of Return	(6) Total Return on Comparable Treasury	(7) Return Minus Risk-Free Return
AM International	9 3/8%	06/30/95	613.80	16.49%	682.27	(10/30/84)	111%	30	3.11%	16.25%	-13.14%
Braniff	9 1/8%	01/01/97	540.00	18.00%	741.90	(12/15/83)	137%	20.5	12.44%	14.26%	1.81%
Itel	10 1/2%	12/01/98	520.00	20.65%	883.70	(9/19/83)	169%	33	13.60%	13.83%	0.23%
White Motor	7 1/4%	12/01/93	602.50	13.66%	551.84	(12/01/83)	92%	38	1.69%	7.76%	-9.45%
Wickes Cos.	7 7/8%	05/01/98	593.75	14.28%	867.71	(1/26/85 WI)	146%	29	15.28%	17.43%	-2.14%
Wilson Foods	7 7/8%	03/01/97	471.25	18.43%	790.30	(4/30/84)	168%	12	32.35%	13.97%	18.38%

Notes: The issues listed represent all issuers of straight, taxable, public debt that filed Chapter 11 after the 1978 Bankruptcy Code revision and emerged from reorganization proceedings through the date of this study.

"Value of Reorganization Securities" includes coupons paid on original securities in the year between purchase and default. Reorganization Securities includes all distributions (including cash) awarded by the plan of reorganization to holders of the pre-petition issue.

"Months in Reorganization" is calculated from Chapter 11 petition to issuance of reorganization securities.

For each company listed, the figure in Column 7 is the difference between the figures in Columns 5 and 6.

asset coverage of just $846 per bond, recovered the highest proportion of their par value: $884.

The lesson here is that type of asset is critical; Itel's railcar lease fleet provided more value than White Motor's outmoded manufacturing facilities. Technology companies such as AM International are prone to slippage in asset values because of obsolescence and the limited number of potential buyers of their highly specialized facilities. Erosion can also result from industrial companies' tendency to die slowly. Asset protection may look splendid a year before bankruptcy, but management still has plenty of time before throwing in the towel to dissipate those assets through further operating losses. Also, subject to indenture constraints, a company can, in effect, begin the liquidation process before filing bankruptcy, in some cases selling off strong operations to try to save the weak ones, which alone are finally left for the creditors. For all these reasons, investors must resist the unelaborated argument that the balance sheet asset values "assure" payment at par if the company defaults.

The Clock is Running

The alert reader will by now have pointed out that the buyer of a problem credit need not recover 100% of par to be whole, but merely 100% of his purchase price (Column 1 of Exhibit 4–2). By this standard, the majority of issues ultimately paid 100% or more to holders who bought one year before default (Column 2). These high recovery rates underscore an important point about high yield bonds, namely, that a default does not typically cost the investor his entire principal. Within a diversified portfolio, possible principal losses of the magnitude suffered by White Motor holders (Column 3) may be acceptable risks, considering the high yields available in troubled situations (Column 1). The analysis must, however, take into account the time value of money. At AM International, for example, those who bought the 9 ⅜s a year prior to bankruptcy recovered 111% of their investment, but had to go through a two-and-a-half-year Chapter 11 reorganization (Column 4). Their 3% return (Column 5) on a high-risk investment represented an opportunity loss of over 13% versus the 16% total return they would have obtained by owning a Treasury security with no credit risk for the same holding period. Further underscoring the sensitivity of returns to time, the best performer, the Wilson Foods issue, had the shortest Chapter 11 proceeding—12 months, some 40% shorter than the next quickest to emerge. Wilson 7 ⅞s holders earned over 1,200 basis points above the comparable-coupon Treasury total return, while the issue with the longest reorganization proceeding, White Motor (38 months), provided almost 950 basis points less than Treasuries (Column 7). Here the lesson appears to be that in high-risk investments, one should prefer simple situations to complex ones that may require lengthy reorganizations in the event of bankruptcy. Wilson Foods was an uncomplicated company (a meatpacker) with a straightforward objective in filing Chapter 11—relief from a high-cost labor contract. Thanks to that clear focus, Wilson managed to achieve its aim and emerge from the reorganization proceeding in just 12 months. Furthermore, with its single purpose of reducing wages, Wilson was able to protect bondholders' interests by accruing interest during the reorganization proceeding (not mandatory on unsecured debt under bankruptcy law) and even interest on the accrued interest. In contrast, Wickes Companies's myriad subsidiaries complicated its reorganization. Workout specialist Sanford Sigoloff's team won praise for restructuring Wickes's operations, but the company's sheer complexity and many conflicting creditors' claims stretched the reorganization out to 29 months, contributing to a return on the Wickes 7 ⅞s of 200 basis points below the available Treasury return.

Conclusion

Our survey of post-1978 bankruptcies has demonstrated that asset coverage (as determined by balance sheet figures) is only one of several factors that influence the return on an investment in a company that subsequently defaults. When a bond salesman says, "They're money-good—assets are 120% of liabilities!," the shrewd investor should respond, "What are the assets really worth, notwithstanding what the financial statement says?" Harder to judge, yet critical in the equation, is the probable length of time necessary to bring the company out of Chapter 11.

Admittedly, there is more to the story of asset protection. We have not, for example, discussed the flip side of the overvalued asset story. In the Penn Central bankruptcy, certain assets were worth substantially more than book value and creditors benefited thereby. Furthermore, many financially distressed companies have managed to avoid bankruptcy because they had valuable and readily salable assets. Particularly in this latter case, seen in the context of the larger issue of financial flexibility asset protection can provide valuable insights for credit evaluation. Even with this more helpful view of asset protection, though, the investor must avoid certain pitfalls:

- Is the company cutting off a limb to save the trunk or simply liquidating the best assets first and leaving the worst for the creditors?
- To whom can the "salable" assets be sold? (Competitors might be precluded by antitrust considerations. Perhaps the underlying cause of the bankruptcy is excess capacity in the industry.)
- If the plan is to sell a division to management in a leveraged buyout, could such a deal actually be financed in a period of increased caution by lenders?

In short, book value can be just as deceptive when viewed as a source of financial flexibility as it can when regarded as the source of recoupment if default does occur. By asking the tough questions in both instances, however, investors can distinguish between authentic asset protection and the mere illusion.

CHAPTER 5

Asset Protection: What You See Is Not Necessarily What You Get

A contrarian acquaintance of ours is a fiend for high returns, but never invests his money without being well protected. In 1982, he decided to profit from the asbestos panic by buying Manville bonds, confident that the company's *insurance protection* made bankruptcy an impossibility. Scoffing at the timid souls who feared that megamergers would cause credit quality to deteriorate, he purchased Houston Natural Gas bonds in 1984, relying on *covenant protection* to stay clear of any runup in financial leverage. Later, he sneered at the nervous Nellies who dumped their high coupon issues when rates plunged in early 1986 and bought Minstar 14 ⅞s, since *refunding protection* promised to lock in his yield for three years.

Insistence on various sorts of protection ultimately did the contrarian little good. He lost heavily when Manville announced that its asbestos liabilities far exceeded previously disclosed amounts (and Manville's insurance coverage) and filed Chapter 11. His performance suffered again when Houston Natural financed some large, defensive acquisitions with short-term debt, resulting in a downgrading of its bonds. Only then did our friend realize that a funded debt test placed no limitation on the amount of *unfunded* debt that a company could take down. Minstar dealt him yet another blow by exercising a little-known minimum net worth provision that permitted the company to call 10% of its 14 ⅞s, even though the issue was nonrefundable.

Despite his disappointments with insurance protection, covenant protection and refunding protection, our contrarian friend continues to pursue excess returns. Where is he focusing his efforts currently? In distressed companies that afford good *asset protection.* We fear that if he continues on this course, he may one day be forced to seek another type of protection—from his creditors.

The allure of asset protection is understandable, for although perceived by many high-grade portfolio managers as bold (even reckless) risk-takers, most high yield investors are in fact a conservative lot, at least in one respect. While they stretch for yields of 300 to 1,000 basis points above Treasuries, they also invariably think carefully about their downside. Pressure to maintain dividends forces this mindset on high yield mutual fund managers. Total return investors find that consistency depends on avoiding the catastrophes. Even the most aggressive fund managers, who buy bankrupt companies in the hopes that spectacular gains on the ones that make it will offset losses on the rest, try to improve their odds by paying no more than the rock bottom value they perceive. (If possible, they will take advantage of a company's distress, and limited options, to pay even less than this minimum value, thereby obtaining a still better risk-reward ratio.) Nothing gives all of these investors the confidence that they have reached the bedrock the way hard assets do. "Peel off the goodwill, the corporate culture and the synergy," they say, "and give us a knockdown quote on the machines and the furniture. At that price we will buy the debt of any company in the Free World." So powerful are the images of solidity conveyed by the very phrase "asset protection" that some bond salesmen employ it as an incantation for inducing portfolio managers to buy securities that, aside from promising to pay off in full after they default, have no discernible investment merit.

High Yield's Maginot Line

Like many seductive concepts, asset protection is a valid notion but in our opinion much oversold. Investors who regard it as a justification for holding the debt of a company with no viable business plan, rather than as an insurance policy on one that will probably remain solvent, are doing their credit analysis backwards. This wrong emphasis reminds us of France's military strategy prior to 1940. Many then believed that a strong army was redundant, since the Maginot Line, an imposing system of fortifications, was an impregnable barrier to a German invasion. Despite this impressive defense, France fell in 18 days. Asset protection may prove to be the Maginot Line of high yield bond buyers who rely on it to the neglect of analysis of ongoing operations.

There are three major reasons why asset values, while affording bondholders some protection, fall short of invincibility. We will discuss each in sequence.

1. Accurate asset values are not easy to come by, even though Wall Street publishes reams of purported breakup analysis.
2. Even if the true economic value of a company's assets is determinable, the legal process of bankruptcy does not ensure that each class of creditors will receive the amount to which it is entitled.
3. Even if a claim's future value, after litigation, is known, the present value is subject to massive erosion through a protracted reorganization.

Breaking Up Is Hard to Do

The takeover craze that began in the mid-1980s created a huge appetite for breakup analyses of companies that might become targets. Wall Street analysts were happy to fill this often undiscriminating demand with studies prepared in Manhattan office buildings on the basis of 10-K reports. These Securities and Exchange Commission filings provided the operating earnings of each business segment and analysts could assign to each of these an appropriate multiple (assuming there was a comparable public company). By publishing this type of superficial research, which gained additional stature through being picked up by the press, Wall Street created the impression that public companies' hard asset values were easily determined and widely known.

In reality, valuations based on public filings may have little relation to the potential proceeds of a liquidation. Capitalizing an income stream is valid only if the income is sustainable. It may not be, due to labor problems, impending foreign competition or contingent liabilities—matters about which companies, in their public financial statements, often seem to follow the rule of disclosing the minimum that the lawyers will permit. Getting bankable answers to these questions requires extensive discussions with management, on an insider basis. Investment bankers might charge $150,000 or $200,000 for this sort of valuation. Even allowing for a fair markup in that fee, it is clear that the cost of obtaining a reliable estimate of asset protection is high. So high is the information cost, in fact, that a study of this type is not worth undertaking unless one is taking a large position in a defaulted security trading at such a deep discount to par as to promise a staggering return. Accordingly, it seems to us implausible that information of this quality is available gratis from some friendly salesman (whose firm just happens to be long) on each of the dozens of issues that cannot be sold without strong assurances of limited downside.

The firm's value as an ongoing concern is irrelevant in any case to the true rag-picker, who is concerned only with what the assets will fetch at auction. Surely, one would think, debt priced on this basis cannot fall further. Unfortunately, not all types of assets have active auction markets. According to David Goesling, Manager of Machinery and Equipment Appraisal for Valtec Associates, Inc. of Chicago, weekly quotes are available on oil rigs and standard metalworking equipment trades daily, but for more specialized machinery an appraiser must obtain price estimates from dealers—a classic one-sided market.

When no recent "comparables" are available, an appraiser may have to fall back on the cost approach, which theoretically deducts wear-and-tear from the purchase price to obtain fair market value. According to Goesling, the accuracy of this approach frequently suffers from the necessarily arbitrary adjustments for functional and economic obsolescence that are also required. Another problem with the cost method is that large items, such as three-million-pound mining machines and electric arc furnaces, decline precipitously in value if not usable at their existing sites, since moving costs are exorbitant. High-technology equipment, on the other hand, may be worth substantially less on the open market than cost minus depreciation, for although it is essential to a specific process, it has little value elsewhere. Given the difficulty of making accurate estimates in the field, the investor who relies on financial statements faces insuperable barriers.

Actively traded markets would seem to eliminate many of these problems in the case of natural resources, but in this area price fluctuations can seriously undermine the value of asset protection. Oil company lenders take a double whack when energy prices fall. Not only does the present value of all reserves decline, but some reserves become valueless altogether as they cease to be economically producible. Public financial statements provide too little detail to enable an investor to determine how many barrels become uneconomical at a given price, and companies rarely volunteer such data. To compound the problem, these unpredictable declines in value do not typically permit the public bondholder to accelerate principal payment. As a result, "solid" asset protection may crumble before the powerless investor's eyes.

Nor are price fluctuations the only hazard for lenders who derive comfort from the tangibility and liquidity of natural resources. Oil companies' financial statements do not report reserves, but rather reserve estimates, a critical distinction. Estimating the amount of producible hydrocarbons a mile underground is not a precise science; geologists rely on indirect evidence and a lot of assumptions. Until a reservoir has been producing for some time, there is no assurance that pressure will be maintained, and consequently no way of knowing what percentage of the oil will be recovered. Different geologists react with varying degrees of conservatism to this uncertainty, so investors cannot obtain a reliable asset valuation by simply multiplying estimated barrels by recent per-barrel transaction prices. Moreover, not all barrels are equal in the market for reserves. For one thing, hydrocarbon pools generally produce at their highest rates during the early years of production. In present value terms, therefore, a million barrels in a young field are worth more than a million barrels in a mature field that may take 20 years to produce. Reserve life estimates in financial reports do not solve this puzzle, since they are merely averages of various properties, generally broken down no more specifically than by country. The Securities and Exchange Commission's mandatory reserve valuation disclosures consider present value, but because companies are required to report these figures just once a year, the investor may lack useful information in a period of rapidly falling prices.

Value Judgments

We have shown that neither capitalized earnings nor liquidation analysis can quantify asset protection in a wholly satisfactory way, but even supposing they could, bondholders might never realize the correctly predicted value of their claim. Our legal system, regrettably, does not dispense that excellent a brand of justice. The imprecision of asset valuation often permits other parties in a bankruptcy to persuade the court to accept a value that works to the bondholder's disadvantage. For instance, under the Bankruptcy Code, a secured lender is entitled to "adequate protection," which may imply cash payments during the reorganization unless the secured holder is found to be substantially oversecured (i.e., collateral value greatly exceeds the secured claim). It is therefore in the secured bank lenders' interest to minimize the court's valuation of their collateral, in order to get hold of cash that might otherwise be employed to rehabilitate the company, which would in turn increase the value of the subordinated holders' claim.

Secured holders not only have an interest in shifting the court's valuation away from the analyst's objectively determined number, but they frequently succeed, and it is all within the rules. According to Robert M. Miller, a partner in the law firm of Berlack, Israels & Liberman, "Bankruptcy is a game of leverage and it's a contractual process, the end result being a plan of reorganization. Like any other contractual process, those parties that participate in the process tend to be rewarded over those parties that don't participate." Miller argues that subordinated holders should take a more active role in bankruptcy proceedings to protect their interests, i.e., to emerge with a larger portion of the value to which they are entitled according to a disinterested asset valuation.

Institutional investors have the economic power, he believes, to obtain considerable leverage. By gaining permission to form a separate committee for bondholders (or for subordinated bondholders), institutions can exercise more clout, since courts tend to take committees' views more seriously than minor players' opinions, according to Miller. While bondholders may be able to get a fairer shake than they have in the past, the fact remains that the asset valuation one does when deciding whether to purchase a bond may ultimately prove less important than the courtroom jockeying. As Miller puts it, "Maximizing that clout and maximizing that leverage is what bankruptcy is all about."[1]

"Every Hour Wounds . . . "[2]

A final reason why assets often provide less protection than meets the eye involves the time value of money. We are obliged here to make clear one of our fundamental assumptions, namely, that our readers' objective is to maximize returns. If, on the other hand, an investor is striving mainly to avoid accounting recognition of economic losses, what follows may have little relevance. The latter motive, we realize, can be a powerful one—witness money center banks' resistance to forced writedowns of Latin American loans that have for a long time provided no economic return. To a portfolio manager concerned more about returns than about bookkeeping, however, half a loaf today is better than a whole loaf five years hence, discounted at 15%. In the present context, the key point is that even if a claim will assuredly be worth a bond's $1,000 face value as of the issuer's emergence from reorganization proceedings, its present value is only $800 (discounted at 25%, the rate we have generally used in bankruptcy studies) if the reorganization takes one year. Moreover, the investor would be getting off easy in that case. Edward Altman found an average reorganization period of 27 months in his study of public bond defaults.[3] A three-year reorganization reduces the present value of a $1,000 claim to $512, again assuming a 25% discount rate, and at four years, present value declines to $410. (The last figure, incidentally, equals the average trading price for defaulted issues, one month after default, observed by Altman and Nammacher.[4]) To the writedown-averse lender who is under no performance pressure, none of this matters, as long as the bond eventually gets back to par. If rate of return is paramount, however, then it may behoove the investor to sell a deteriorating credit at a 30-point loss, rather than risk an even steeper decline, followed by a default and period of interest suspension, even though asset protection is such that the bond will eventually pay in full.

Time value would present less of a problem if there were less uncertainty about the interval required to reorganize a given company. At least one would then know how deep a discount to take on a company's asset-protected value. Unfortunately, we have discovered no infallible formula for predicting the duration of a reorganization proceeding. The variables commonly noted—complexity of the company, motivation for seeking protection (e. g., genuine insolvency or massive legal claims)—-are difficult to quantify. Moreover, measurable economic factors are not the sole influences. According to Mark Shenkman, president of Shenkman Capital Management Inc., management's response to default may be critical. "In my experience," says Shenkman, "while there's an initial shock on the part of management from going into bankruptcy, after they recognize that they're still accepted in the community, even though their company is bankrupt, they get comfortable in bankruptcy. All of a sudden, they don't have contentious litigation, they don't have to pay interest on their debt; management can accumulate cash. They generally run the company on the normal course of business, as if they weren't bankrupt." Aside from such attitudinal variables, the legal wrangling discussed above can similarly affect the timing of a company's emergence from reorganization proceedings. Ironically, as bondholders attempt to influence the court's valuation in their favor by forming a separate creditors' committee, they may give back some of their gains (through time value) by prolonging the bankruptcy.

Given so many unpredictable factors, portfolio managers who are conscientious about protecting their investments with substantial asset values are likely to learn to their sorrow that payment delayed is payment at least partially denied. Shenkman concludes, "I've found these bankruptcies tend to take longer than they should, and this has a big impact on what the ultimate returns are."

Conclusion

We would never advise a high yield investor to be blase about asset protection. Chances are that if a company controls valuable productive resources, its management—or another one—can exploit them in a manner that will assure debt service, or at least recovery of principal. Furthermore, it is easier to obtain property rights in hard assets than in management skill and insight, even though the latter may be more important to an enterprise's success. This essay's purpose is merely to counsel portfolio managers against putting more weight on assets than they will bear. Assets are not obliged to sell for their apparent worth, nor does the legal system promise to make up the shortfall. Time is the most intransigent arbiter of all. Recognizing the multiple sources of slippage in asset protection, the prudent investor will not resort to it as a justification for buying (or holding on to) the debt of a company that lacks a credible plan for staying out of receivership.

Endnotes

[1] Adding to the uncertainty that remains even when asset values are well known is the fact the amount of secured debt may increase sharply between an investor's purchase of subordinated debt and bankruptcy. Unlike many senior debentures, subordinated issues typically lack negative pledge clauses, which restrict the amount of debt that may be secured without the debenture holder being secured as well. As a result, asset values that appeared sufficient to preclude adequate protection payments to the secured holders may become insufficient as the amount of secured debt increases.

[2] "Every hour wounds, the last one kills."

[3] Edward I. Altman, *Corporate Financial Distress* (New York: John Wiley & Sons, 1983): p. 254.

[4] Edward I. Altman and Scott A. Nammacher, "The Default Rate Experience on High Yield Corporate Debt" (Morgan Stanley & Co. Incorporated, March 31, 1985): p. 14.

CHAPTER 6

How Useful Are Stock Prices in Monitoring Credit Quality?

If you walk into a high yield portfolio manager's office you are likely to see a computer terminal monitoring the stock prices of companies in which he has a major bond position. Elsewhere in the office you may find spread sheets that track the equity market capitalizations of those companies, possibly comparing the figures with the corresponding debt balances. You will be mistaken if you infer from your observations that the high yield manager is spending too much company time trading his personal stock portfolio. These equity-related paraphernalia reflect widely practiced techniques for monitoring the credit risk of speculative-grade bond holdings.

The popularity of stock-watching among high yield bond investors is understandable. For one thing, the manager of a large high yield mutual fund may hold more than 100 different names.[1] Any low-rated sample of that size inevitably contains some companies that are susceptible to sudden, dramatic swings in credit quality by virtue of being comparatively undiversified, highly leveraged or prone to large-scale merger activity. Monitoring this sort of portfolio is a daunting task, especially when the fund manager is simultaneously preoccupied with responding to arbitrage swap proposals, attending underwriters' road shows, preparing for performance reviews and participating in new-business presentations. With so many chances of missing news that could affect his returns, the portfolio manager is naturally inclined to watch for distress signals, including falling stock prices. Because they purportedly represent the value of future earnings, moreover, equity prices have the additional appeal of promising to act as early warnings of problems that investors do not yet foresee. The ready availability of stock quotations further explains their popularity. Finally, the notion that the complex process of analyzing credit quality can be reduced to a single, easily calculated measure (for example, a ratio of debt to market capitalization) is seductive in its simplicity.

Watching stock prices is not only an eminently practical credit-monitoring technique, but also has a solid theoretical basis. As the work of Bookstaber and Jacob shows,[2] a speculative-grade bond's price has, to a much greater extent than is true for a high-grade bond, a strong element of an option on the firm's equity, in addition to the pure interest rate risk component. The bondholder is effectively short a put on the company's equity in the event of bankruptcy, which is considerably more likely for a Single-B than for a Double-A company. There is also theoretical support for using market capitalization (i.e., number of shares outstanding multiplied by share price) in lieu of book value as a measure of net worth, to calculate financial leverage. Book value, after all, merely represents the historical cost of a firm's assets, depreciated according to accounting rules at rates that may bear little relationship to the actual decline (or possibly increase) in their economic value. The economics literature generally follows this reasoning, defining net worth as market capitalization, rather than book value.[3] In short, the portfolio manager who watches his credits by watching the tape can be satisfied that financial theory confirms the course upon which convenience sets him.

Shortcomings of Market Capitalization

Intellectual justification for a practice does not, however, guarantee its efficacy. In some circumstances, focusing exclusively on a ratio such as market capitalization to indebtedness could lead to exactly the wrong conclusion. For example, market capitalization rises (and leverage measures derived from it fall) when a company is "put into play" as a potential takeover target. The resulting signal of declining credit risk is deceptive in light of the strong possibility that either a highly leveraged acquisition or a debt-financed takeover defense (such as a stock repurchase) will result. More generally, a rise in the stock price frequently reflects in part a wealth transfer from bondholders to shareholders, implying an increase, rather than a decrease in default risk. Leverage calculations based on market capitalization can also go awry because while stock price changes are communicated instantaneously, investors cannot be certain of a company's total debt balance at any given time. By drawing down its credit lines subsequent to the end of a quarter, an issuer can render its quarterly financial report obsolete by the time it reaches investors.

Admittedly, problems of this nature arise only occasionally, and should have little impact on a well-diversified portfolio. A more fundamental problem with over-reliance on the equity market to gauge credit quality is that empirical research clearly shows that stock prices do not tell the entire story. For example, in Altman's Zeta score model the five-year average ratio of market value of equity to total capitalization is just one of seven variables used for predicting bankruptcy. Since the Zeta model is an objective weighting device constructed to maximize predictive success, we can infer that Altman would not have included the other variables unless doing so achieved greater accuracy than the market-based leverage ratio alone.

Even if it were demonstrable, however, that stock prices always provide a true picture of credit quality, we would still have to ask whether watching them enables the portfolio manager to gain an edge over the competition. On the face of it, that proposition seems unsupportable, simply because stock quotations are so accessible. The more widely information is disseminated, the less valuable it becomes. If every other high yield investor is watching the tape as well, the portfolio manager will find that bids and offers have invariably adjusted to the rise or fall in the stock price by the time he lifts the telephone receiver to act on the news. Although he may occasionally pick off an unwary dealer who was blinking when the stock price change hit the screen, he will probably earn a low payback on this labor-intensive activity. To gain materially from credit-related trading, the portfolio manager must have information that provides a clue to the *future* value, rather than the current value of a security. This is the point on which equity prices fall shortest as a credit-monitoring device, for despite the popular impression of their predictive value, stock prices are far from infallible guides to the future.

Yesterday's News Today

The truth, inculcated in many of us since childhood, that the stock market leads the economy, fosters the notion (which is not a logical consequence) that an individual company's stock price movements dependably foreshadow changes in its profitability. This misconception is reinforced by the definition of a firm's equity valuation as the present value of its future dividend stream, in turn a function of future earnings. In reality, a company's stock price is a consensus of what investors *think* its future earnings will be. To derive these forecasts of future earnings, analysts, who cannot see into the future, extrapolate—often inaccurately, as it turns out—from the present. The shocks that are likely to have the greatest influence on future earnings, such as the rise and fall of governments, currencies and cartels, are unknowable at the time these forecasts are made. In short, stock prices are not truly forward-looking, but instead akin to the futurological novels of a century ago, which were comically incapable of escaping the prejudices of their own era.

Some readers will protest, in the face of these rational arguments, that they have nevertheless witnessed the stock market's uncanny ability to anticipate company-specific news. Often, the true believers will say, a stock price falls for no apparent reason and then a few days later a bombshell hits; in some mysterious way, the market "knows" what will happen. We do not deny that such incidents occur, but we can point to several ready explanations, not one of which involves supernatural forces. First of all, inside information sometimes gets into the hands of a few investors before being officially disseminated, causing a stock to move "before the news is out." Regrettably, Ivan Boesky was not the first nor are his accomplices likely to be the last to profit from illicit information. The illusion that The Market is omniscient can similarly arise from corporations' efforts to dampen the volatility of their stocks by "telegraphing" earnings surprises. An investor relations officer may, in informal discussions, suggest to Wall Street analysts that their outstanding quarterly earnings forecasts are too high or too low. The analysts will then revise their forecasts and alert their salespeople, who will in turn solicit orders that begin to move the stock, days before the news of "unexpectedly" high or low earnings crosses the tape. While this process has a rational explanation, the market's anticipation of the official earnings announcement may look like magic to those who are not in the loop.

Onlookers' wonderment will be especially pronounced if they rely on newspapers for their market intelligence. The general business dailies and magazines occasionally "break" genuine news but from day to day, their reporters rely heavily on securities analysts, who are under no obligation to speak to the press before conveying their recommendations to their customers. In fact, an analyst has a strong incentive to enlighten the Fourth Estate only after getting his firm's customers into a stock. The later, broader dissemination of his recommendation may cause other firms' customers to buy, giving his own an immediate profit.

Specialized trade magazines and newsletters are another major (but typically unacknowledged) source of ideas for the mass-circulation business publications. An article in the trade press may move a stock well before the appearance of a similar report in the national business media; the later story will be perceived by most investors as the point at which new information becomes available. Last in line is the reader of the local newspaper's business section, at best a tertiary source on many stories, since its reporters do much of their research in the national business press.

In summary, the notion that stock prices move in advance of fundamental changes is a myth. That belief is simply the perception of the poor souls who are the last to hear the news.

Do Trends Continue?

Granting this point, might not a high yield manager nevertheless adopt a strategy of selling when the stock price falls and buying when it rises? After all, a generalist cannot stay in continuous contact with every issuer or read every trade journal, and is prohibited from trading on inside information. As long as stock price fluctuations provide reliable signals, why not act on them instead of worrying about their origin?

Ironically, proponents of this leap of faith are often the same people who ridicule the notion of accepting guidance from the rating agencies. Why, they ask, should portfolio managers turn over their credit decisions to faceless committees? As an alternative, they recommend that portfolio managers turn over their credit decisions to an anonymous mob of stock speculators. With rating agencies one can check the analysts' credentials; it is indeterminable whether the small investors who get their ideas from *Wall Street Week* and how-to-get-rich books have any qualifications at all. In our view, investors should use whatever outside resources they find helpful, but must ultimately exercise due care and take responsibility for their credit decisions.

Nevertheless, blindly obeying the tape is defensible if stock quotations supply reliable information about future stock prices. This is a controversial assumption, to say the least. Efficient Market Hypothesis adherents believe (and have voluminous research to document) that securities price movements are entirely random. By this reasoning, there is no basis for inferring that a rising stock price will continue to rise or that a declining market capitalization-based leverage ratio implies still better credit quality in the future. Our own research indicates that at least in certain circumstances, the case is worse than that, i.e., rising stock prices may be predisposed to *fall* in future periods. Therefore, the portfolio manager who interprets a drop in market-capitalization leverage as a buy signal may achieve, not a neutral, but a negative effect on performance![4] We assert this possibility on the strength of two analyses we have made on equity price data.

Our first analysis utilizes data collected by Gary A. Benesh and Pamela P. Peterson for an article entitled "On the Relation Between Earnings Changes, Analysts' Forecasts and Stock Price Fluctuations" in the November/December 1986 issue of *Financial Analysts Journal*. That article identified for selected years the 50 best performers and 50 worst performers from a sample that included 380 stocks in 1980 and 384 in 1981.[5] Exhibits 6–1 through 6–4 (pages 86-89) list the top 50 and bottom 50 in each year, along with their annual price changes and returns. The 13 stocks marked with asterisks in Exhibit 6–1 (best performers of 1980) were also among the worst performers of 1981, listed in Exhibit 6–4. As explained in the Technical Note at the end of this chapter, only about six or seven would be expected to fall to the bottom 50 in the second year if all year-to-year ranking changes were random. Instead, statistical analysis indicates that the best performers were 1.36 times as likely as other companies to be worst performers in the subsequent year. (The 50 worst performers, on the other hand, did not appear to be disproportionately inclined to rise to the top 50 the next year.)

For the second analysis, we collected price data on the NASDAQ stock market index, including the National Market from 1982 onward, a sample consisting generally of smaller-capitalization companies. For each year 1980 through 1985 we identified the 25 biggest gainers and 25 biggest losers (Exhibits 6–5 to 6–16, pages 90-101). We then tested whether these extreme performers showed a propensity to diverge from the market trend in the next year. For example, 19 of 1980's 25 biggest gainers remained in the sample in 1981.[6] Of those 19, only two, or 10.5% of the total, advanced in 1981 even though 38.9% of all companies in the sample advanced that year. In every year except 1982 this pattern was repeated, i.e., the preceding year's premier issues were less likely than the other companies were to advance. As in our first analysis, statistical methods establish that this pattern does not reflect mere chance. The data also show that each year's worst performers were more likely than other companies were to decline in the following year.

Conclusion

The evidence from our two analyses raises serious doubts about basing credit decisions solely on stock price movements (or ratios derived from them) without investigating the underlying causes of the movements. Companies that appear by such measures to be the best and brightest one year have a statistically significant propensity to do worse than their less heralded counterparts the next, and even to be among the down and out by then. Buying bonds of companies that do exceptionally well in the stock market is a risky strategy.

This is not to say that watching stock prices has no utility. The worst performers did not display a corresponding tendency to rebound to the top ranks. Like the top performers, they were more likely than other companies to decline the next year. Accordingly, a strategy of selling bonds of companies that do exceptionally poorly may have some merit for a portfolio manager who lacks the wherewithal to analyze numerous holdings in depth.

Most important is the finding that a ratio such as debt-to-market-capitalization does not reliably predict future credit quality. By this measure, dramatically falling leverage, the consequence of a skyrocketing stock price, may very well signal sharp deterioration. One cannot even use such ratios as counter-indicators, since a rising market-based leverage ratio frequently prefigures still further erosion of credit quality. As we have argued above, risk measures, however precise, will not produce superior performance in an efficient market unless they have predictive value. Stock prices, although alleged to be forward-looking, fail this test. As much as portfolio managers might appreciate having a reliable device for controlling credit risk with a minimum expenditure of time, there is still no substitute for direct, fundamental analysis of the issuers. Putting credit decisions up to a vote of equity investors will sometimes result, as our democratic system occasionally does, in election of the most glamorous but ultimately least attractive candidates.

Exhibit 6–1
Fifty Best Performing Stocks of 1980 (Large Capitalization Data Base)

Company	Change in Price (%)	Return (%)	Company	Change in Price (%)	Return (%)
Carlisle*	246.4	256.6	Pioneer Corp. Texas	76.9	82.4
Western Co. NA	191.7	193.4	Tracor	79.1	81.9
United States Home	142.0	150.3	Cooper Industries	76.6	81.2
Burlington Northern	129.4	136.0	EG&G	78.5	80.8
NL Industries	121.4	126.9	Sealed Air	75.7	80.0
Union Pacific*	118.0	123.6	Murphy Oil*	76.5	78.7
Shell Oil	114.7	122.5	Nucor	75.2	76.7
Waste Mgmt.	108.5	111.8	Inexco Oil	71.5	72.6
Standard Oil Indiana*	102.5	110.0	CBI Industries*	67.3	72.3
Zenith Radio	100.0	109.6	Mountain Fuel	61.2	71.3
Mark Controls*	103.6	107.3	McGraw Hill	63.0	71.0
Dover	97.6	101.8	Standard Oil Ohio*	63.2	67.4
Teledyne	101.5	101.7	Bausch & Lomb	62.6	66.9
Halliburton*	96.5	100.1	Overseas Shipholding*	63.0	66.0
Schlumberger*	87.2	89.4	Atlantic Richfield	59.1	64.9
Norton	81.8	89.0	Wolverine World	58.5	63.7
Foster Wheeler*	84.9	88.7	Combustion Engineeering	57.4	63.7
Tymshare	88.4	88.5	Martin Marietta	56.2	63.1
Hughes Tool	85.8	88.5	Barry Wright	59.8	63.0
Marriot	85.8	87.5	Pogo Producing	59.7	62.2
Smith International*	84.6	87.3	AMF	50.4	61.9
United Sts. Leasing	81.5	86.8	Montana Power	48.1	61.1
Standard Oil Leasing	76.5	84.6	Foxboro	55.8	60.8
Kollmorgen	81.7	84.1	United Energy Resources	54.1	60.5
Amerada Hess*	77.9	84.0	Barnett Banks Florida	53.2	60.4

* Among 50 Worst Performing Stocks of 1981.

Sources: Benesh, Gary A. and Peterson, Pamela P. "On the Relation Between Earnings Changes, Analysts' Forecasts and Stock Price Fluctuations." *Financial Analysts Journal* (November/December 1986) pp. 29-39.

Exhibit 6–2
Fifty Worst Performing Stocks of 1980 (Large Capitalization Data Base)

Company	Change in Price (%)	Return (%)	Company	Change in Price (%)	Return (%)
Owens Corning Fiberglas	-6.1	-1.9	Frank B. Hall & Co.	-12.0	-6.9
Minnesota Pwr. & Lt.	-13.1	-2.0	John Blair & Co.*	-11.8	-6.9
Kentucky Utilities	-13.8	-2.1	Dayton Pwr. & Lt.*	-18.1	-7.0
Houghton Mifflin	-7.1	-2.2	Armstrong World	-13.6	-7.0
Koppers	-7.4	-2.2	Overhead Door	-13.1	-7.1
Crown Cork & Seal	-2.6	-2.5	Midland Ross	-13.2	-8.3
Emery Air Freight	-9.0	-2.7	Southwest Gas	-17.8	-8.3
Bank Virginia*	-11.7	-3.3	North American Coal	-11.0	-9.4
Champion Spark Plug	-11.1	-3.4	Beneficial	-17.8	-9.6
CBS	-9.1	-3.8	Nashua	-15.0	-10.1
Sealed Power	-9.8	-4.1	Northwest Air	-14.0	-11.2
United Telecommunications	-12.7	-4.4	Wm. Wrigley Jr. Co.	-16.6	-11.2
Gifford Hill	-9.2	-4.5	Jefferson Pilot	-15.8	-11.3
Capital Holding*	-10.1	-4.6	Great Western Financial	-15.3	-11.3
Inland Steel	-11.9	-4.6	INCO	-14.2	-11.7
Grainger	-7.7	-4.8	Corroon & Black	-19.0	-12.7
Puget Sound Pwr. Lt.	-15.8	-4.9	Stanley Works	-16.4	-13.1
Pennwalt	-12.2	-5.1	Murray Ohio Manufacturing	-19.6	-13.8
Amax	-9.6	-5.1	Hanna Mining	-18.9	-14.2
Central Illinois Light	-16.9	-5.8	Squibb	-21.9	-18.6
Northern Indiana P.S.	-16.4	-5.8	Airborne Freight	-23.6	-18.9
Nevada Power	-15.1	-5.9	Snap-on Tools	-26.0	-23.3
Avon Products	-13.3	-6.1	Gleason Works	-28.1	-25.2
Polaroid	-10.7	-6.9	American Broadcasting	-31.5	-27.9
American Can	-14.7	-6.9	Bally Manufacturing	-36.1	-35.9

* Among 50 Best Performing Stocks of 1981.

Exhibit 6–3
Fifty Best Performing Stocks of 1981 (Large Capitalization Data Base)

Company	Change in Price (%)	Return (%)	Company	Change in Price (%)	Return (%)
Piedmont Aviation	114.2	116.2	Oak Industries	37.2	38.4
Standard Motor Products	95.0	101.4	Pacific Lighting	23.9	38.0
Warnaco	72.8	79.8	American Home Products	29.8	37.4
Cluett Peabody	57.9	67.0	Rohm & Haas	31.5	37.3
Hershey Foods	53.2	61.2	Dennison Manufacturing	28.1	36.3
Anheuser Busch	48.2	52.5	Bank of Boston	28.1	36.1
Easco	42.6	50.9	Axia	28.2	36.0
Fort Howard Paper	45.3	50.1	CTS	30.7	35.6
Wachovia	43.4	49.9	New England Electric	20.0	34.6
Rochester Telephone	38.0	49.7	Missouri Public Service	21.6	34.4
Palm Beach	41.5	48.7	Allegheny Power	17.3	34.3
Thomas Industries	40.9	47.0	Baldor Electric	31.4	33.1
John Blair & Co.	38.7	45.5	Capital Holding	25.4	32.8
Centel	35.2	45.2	Transamerica	24.7	32.2
Kansas City Southern	40.9	44.9	Mercantile Texas	27.7	32.1
Spring Industries	35.3	44.0	Aetna Life & Casualty	24.4	31.7
Diebold	40.7	42.9	Baltimore Gas & Electric	17.1	31.5
Tucson Elec. Power	28.6	42.5	First Chicago	23.2	31.4
Dayton Pwr. & Lt.	23.2	41.4	Potomac Electric Power	17.2	31.3
Southern New England	27.3	41.2	Illinois Power	15.4	31.1
Whirlpool	31.8	40.5	Borg-Warner	24.0	30.9
Rochester Gas & Electric	24.0	40.1	Kimberly-Clark	23.5	30.7
Flight Safety International	38.9	39.4	Bank Virginia	20.4	30.6
Pepsico	33.5	39.1	Northeast Utilities	14.1	30.2
Ferro	32.5	38.9	Gillette	20.5	28.9

Exhibit 6–4
Fifty Worst Performing Stocks of 1981
(Large Capitalization Data Base)

Company	Change in Price (%)	Return (%)	Company	Change in Price (%)	Return (%)
BankAmerica	-29.8	-25.3	Global Marine	-36.5	-36.1
Watkins Johnson	-27.5	-26.2	Halliburton	-37.6	-36.2
Alcan Aluminium	-30.8	-26.2	Murphy Oil	-38.5	-37.2
Rowan Companies	-26.7	-26.4	Noble Affiliates	-37.7	-37.4
Newpark Resources	-27.6	-27.1	Louisiana Land & Expl.	-40.8	-37.7
Koppers	-32.0	-27.2	Asarco	-40.5	-38.1
Phillips Petroleum	-31.1	-27.2	Mark Controls	-39.7	-38.5
Schering Plough	-30.9	-27.2	Foster Wheeler	-40.3	-39.0
Schlumberger	-28.4	-27.4	NCR	-41.8	-39.3
Smith International	-28.7	-27.6	Standard Oil Ohio	-42.4	-39.5
Kaiser Alum. & Chem.	-33.0	-28.3	Morrison Knudsen	-42.1	-40.0
Texas Eastern	-33.8	-29.1	Sabine	-41.1	-40.6
Milton Bradley	-32.5	-29.2	Valero Energy	-41.2	-40.7
Carlisle	-31.5	-30.1	General Dynamics	-42.7	-41.2
Tenneco	-35.1	-30.5	Overseas Shipholding	-42.5	-41.5
Bucyrus-Erie	-34.0	-30.8	Amerada Hess	-44.4	-42.1
CBI Inds.	-33.2	-31.0	Ocean Drilling & Exploration	-44.2	-43.0
Standard Oil Indiana	-34.9	-31.7	Dravo	-47.4	-44.9
Texas Instruments	-33.3	-31.9	GCA	-46.5	-46.2
SPS Technologies	-33.7	-32.0	Boeing	-49.0	-46.4
Union Pacific	-34.0	-32.1	Enstar	-47.8	-46.5
Manville	-39.9	-33.3	Tosco	-48.6	-48.6
Morse Shoe	-37.6	-35.0	Airborne Freight	-51.9	-49.1
Honeywell	-37.5	-35.2	National Medical Care	-52.2	-50.8
Quaker State Oil Refining	-38.5	-35.3	Fairchild Industries	-62.7	-60.9

Exhibit 6–5
Twenty-Five NASDAQ Best Performers 1980

Company Name	Closing Price 1979	Closing Price 1980	Percentage Increase	Closing Price* 1981	Percentage Increase
Intercontinental Diamonds—Wts.	1/4	5	1900.0	Deleted	
Advanced Monitoring Systems	5/8	8 1/4	1220.0	10	21.2%
United American Energy—Wts.	1/2	5 3/8	975.0	2 7/8	(46.5)
Poly Company of America	7/16	4 1/2	928.5	Deleted	
Continuum Company	6 3/4	62	818.5	23 1/2	(62.1)
Omnimedical	2 3/4	25 1/4	818.1	10 1/4	(59.4)
Pope, Evans and Robbins	2	17	750.0	10 1/4	(39.7)
Radiation Technology	2	17	750.0	10 1/4	(39.7)
Networks Electronics	2 1/8	16 7/8	694.1	7 7/8	(53.3)
Elscint	5	39 1/2	690.0	21	(46.8)
Specialized System—Wts.	2	15 3/4	687.5	3 3/8	(78.6)
Florida Water & Utilities	5/8	4 3/4	660.0	Deleted	
Beehive International	4 3/4	35 1/2	647.3	7 7/8	(77.8)
Clinical Sciences	2 1/2	15 1/4	510.0	5	(67.2)
SFE Technology Manufacturing Co.	4 1/4	25 1/2	500.0	14 1/4	(44.1)
Specialized System—Wts.	4 5/8	26 1/2	472.9	Deleted	
Federal Investors-Class B	9 3/4	53	443.5	Deleted	
EMC Energies	1 7/16	7 3/4	439.1	1 1/2	(80.7)
Datametrics—Wts.	3/4	4	433.3	5/8	(84.4)
Sykes Datatronics	7 1/4	38 1/2	431.0	28 1/2	(26.0)
United Telecontrol	1 1/4	6 1/2	420.0	6 3/4	3.8
Barringer Resources	1 1/2	7 3/4	416.6	4 3/4	(38.7)
Time Sharing Resources	3 1/4	16 3/4	415.3	9	(46.3)
Gemco National	7/8	4 1/2	414.2	Deleted	
Midland Southwest	4	20 1/2	412.5	9 3/4	(52.4)

Number Advanced in 1981: 2
Number Declined in 1981: 17

* Deleted = Dropped from NASDAQ System. Issues that traded on NASDAQ one year and on another exchange in the following year were not deleted.

Exhibit 6–6
Twenty-Five NASDAQ Worst Performers 1980

Company Name	Closing Price 1979	Closing Price 1980	Percentage Decrease	Closing Price 1981	Percentage Decrease
First National Cp. of Louisiana	120	6 1/4	94.7	5 1/2	(12.0)
Network One	3 1/2	3/8	89.2	Deleted	
Art's Way Manufacturing	26	4 3/8	83.1	3	(31.4)
Cavanaugh Communities	6	1 3/8	77.0	Deleted	
National Railway	4	1	75.0	Deleted	
Tobin Packing	3 1/2	7/8	75.0	Bankruptcy	
Houston Complex	3 7/8	1 1/8	70.9	Deleted	
Medcor	4	1 1/4	68.7	Bankruptcy	
Passport Travel	4 3/4	1 1/2	68.4	2	33.3
Leisure Dynamics	5	1 5/8	67.5	1 1/8	(30.8)
Word-Tronics—Uts.	3	1	66.6	Deleted	
TRV Minerals	31 3/4	11	65.3	3 3/4	(69.3)
Financial Industries	6	2 1/8	64.5	3 3/8	58.8
American Home Shield	3 3/4	1 3/8	63.3	3/4	(45.5)
Camelot International	5 3/4	2 1/8	63.0	2 1/2	17.7
Computer Communications	6	2 1/4	62.5	7/8	(61.1)
Advanced Patent Technology	7 1/8	2 3/4	61.4	Deleted	
Astrocom	3 1/2	1 3/8	60.7	15/16	(34.5)
Q-1 Inc.	9 1/2	3 3/4	60.5	1/4	(93.3)
Colorado Gasahol	3	13/16	60.4	11/32	(83.3)
De Tomaso Industries	3 3/4	1 1/2	60.0	1 1/16	(28.0)
King International	6 3/4	2 3/4	59.2	1 1/4	(54.5)
Kettering Industries	4 1/4	1 3/4	58.8	1 5/8	(7.1)
Texas Vanguard Oil	4 1/8	1 3/4	57.5	1/4	(85.7)
Geos	4	1 3/4	56.2	3/4	(57.1)

Number Advanced in 1981: 3
Number Declined in 1981: 16

Exhibit 6–7
Twenty-Five NASDAQ Best Performers 1981

Company Name	Closing Price 1980	Closing Price 1981	Percentage Increase	Closing Price 1982	Percentage Increase
Digital Switch—Uts.	2 ⅝	14 ¼	442.8	71	398.3
Morgan Restaurants	1 ¾	8 ½	385.7	10	17.6
Micro Z Cp.—Wts.	1 ¼	5 ⅝	350.0	Deleted	
Digital Switch	2 ¼	9 ⅛	305.5	38 ¼	319.2
Southwest Leasing	1 ¼	4 ¾	280.0	5	5.3
Orbit Instrument—Wts.	1 ¼	4 ⅝	270.0	10 ¼	121.6
Cumo Resources	2	7 ⅜	268.7	2 ¼	(69.5)
Delta Queen Steamboat Co.	3 ⅛	11 ⅛	256.0	11	(1.1)
Micro Z Cp.—Preferred	11	38 ½	250.0	5 ½	(85.7)
Lynden Transport Inc.	9 ½	31 ½	231.5	20 ¼	(35.7)
Micro Z Cp.	2 ⅜	7 ⅞	231.5	1	(87.3)
Government Employment Insurance	3 ⅝	12	231.0	14 ½	20.8
Amtec Industries Inc.	2 ¾	9	227.2	9 ¼	2.8
Central National Financial Cp.	10 ¾	35 ⅛	226.7	Deleted	
Unifi Inc.	4 ⅝	15	224.3	10 ⅛	(32.5)
Zenith Labs—Class B	2 ½	8	220.0	20	150.0
Midwestern Distribution—Class A	4	12 ⅝	215.6	35	177.2
National Micronetics	7 ⅜	23 ¼	215.2	17 ½	(24.7)
Comdial—Warrants	1 ¼	3 ⅞	210.0	17 ¼	345.2
SI Handling Systems	5	15 ½	210.0	13 ½	(12.9)
Biospherics	2 ⅝	7 ¾	195.2	7 ½	(3.2)
Enzo Biochem	5 ½	16	190.9	26 ½	65.6
Ocean Research Equipment	1 ¼	3 ⅝	190.0	Deleted	
Communications Cp. of America	3	8 ½	183.3	13	52.9
Sterner Lighting Company	2 ⅛	6	182.3	7 ¼	20.8

Number Advanced in 1982: 13
Number Declined in 1982: 9

Exhibit 6–8
Twenty-Five NASDAQ Worst Performers 1981

Company Name	Closing Price 1980	Closing Price 1981	Percentage Decrease	Closing Price 1982	Percentage Decrease
FSC	3 3/4	1/8	96.6	Bankruptcy	
FSC—Preferred	10 5/8	3/8	96.4	Bankruptcy	
Basic Earth Sciences Systems—Wts.	4 3/4	3/16	96.0	1/16	(66.7)
Reserve Oil & Mineral	30 1/4	2	93.3	1 3/8	(31.3)
Q-1	3 3/4	1/4	93.3	5/32	(37.6)
20th Century Energy	7 1/4	1/2	93.1	7/32	(56.2)
Sci Pro	11	13/16	92.6	Deleted	
Reliable Investors	6 3/8	1/2	92.1	1/4	(50.0)
X-Cor International—Class A	10	7/8	91.2	5/8	(28.6)
Automated Medical Labs—Wts.	6 3/4	5/8	90.7	1	60.0
Compact Video—Wts.	13 3/8	1 1/4	90.6	Deleted	
Altex Oil—'83 Wts.	3 7/8	3/8	90.3	1/16	60.0
Explosive Fabricators	5	1/2	90.0	5/16	(40.0)
Omni Resources	3 1/8	5/16	90.0	3/16	(47.0)
Bronco Oil & Gas	31 1/4	3 1/4	89.6	7/16	(87.7)
American Educational TV Network—Uts.	3 5/8	3/8	89.6	Deleted	
Numex	6	5/8	89.5	Deleted	
First Coinvestors—Wts.	4 5/8	1/2	89.1	1/2	N.C.
Gilman Services	13 1/2	1 5/8	87.9	Bankruptcy	
Microsonics	3	3/8	87.5	1 1/2	300.0
Dash Industries	3 3/8	7/16	87.0	13/32	(7.3)
Anchor Petroleum	8 1/2	1 1/8	86.7	Deleted	
Pacific Cypress Minerals	4 1/2	5/8	86.1	3/8	(40.0)
General Energy (Vancouver)	4 1/2	5/8	86.1	1/8	(80.0)
Meta Systems	13 1/8	1 13/16	86.1	Deleted	

Number Advanced in 1982: 3
Number Declined in 1982: 15

Exhibit 6–9
Twenty-Five NASDAQ Best Performers 1982

Company Name	Closing Price 1981	Closing Price 1982	Percentage Increase	Closing Price 1983	Percentage Increase
Advanced Energy	1	16 ½	1550.0	3 ½	(78.8)
Integrated Electronics	¼	3 ⅝	1350.0	Deleted	
Insitutform of North America—Wts.	5⁄16	3 ½	1020.0	1 ⅞	(46.4)
Genetic Systems—Wts.	15⁄16	9 ¼	886.6	Deleted	
Sunrise Savings & Loan Assoc. of Florida	1 ⅛	10 ⅛	800.0	Deleted	
Millicom	1 13⁄16	15	725.5	9 ½	(36.7)
Cerberonics—Class A	3	24 ½	716.6	11 ¼	(54.1)
American Solar King—Wts.	3 ½	26 ¼	650.0	Deleted	
Carhart Photo—Class A	1	7 ½	650.0	7 ¾	3.33
Mayfair Supermarkets	1 ⅞	13 ¾	633.3	14 ¼	3.6
PHH Group	5 ¼	38	623.8	21 ½	(43.4)
Equinox Solar	⅝	3 13⁄16	510.0	1 ⅛	(70.4)
DSC Communications—Wts.	5 ⅛	30 ¾	500.0	Deleted	
Griffin Technology	3	18	500.0	7 ½	(58.3)
Globus Growth Group	¾	4 ¼	466.6	2 ¾	(35.3)
Quest Medical—Wts.	1 1⁄16	5 ⅞	452.9	3 ¼	(44.7)
Boonton Electronics	2 ⅜	13	447.3	7 ½	(42.3)
Globus Growth Group—Uts.	1 ⅜	7 ¼	427.2	Deleted	
Chronar	4 ½	23 ½	422.2	19	(19.1)
Suncoast Plastics	⅝	3 ¼	420.0	4	23.0
Ampol-American Israel—Class A	¾	3 ¾	400.0	Deleted	
Lasermetrics	1 ⅛	5 ⅝	400.0	3	(46.7)
DSC Communications—Uts.	14 ¼	71	398.2	Deleted	
International King's Table	2	9 ⅞	393.7	19 ⅜	96.2
Auxton Computers Enterprises	5 ⅜	25 ½	374.4	17 ½	(31.4)

Number Advanced in 1983: 4
Number Declined in 1983: 13

Exhibit 6–10
Twenty-Five NASDAQ Worst Performers 1982

Company Name	Closing Price 1981	Closing Price 1982	Percentage Decrease	Closing Price 1983	Percentage Decrease
Nucorp Energy—Wts.	10	1/32	99.6	Bankruptcy	
Nucorp Energy	10 3/4	13/32	96.2	Bankruptcy	
Fisher Oil & Gas	3 3/8	1/8	96.2	Deleted	
Geophysical Systems	24 1/4	1 1/16	95.6	Bankruptcy	
Energy Sources	4 1/8	3/16	95.4	Deleted	
Toltec Royalty	4 1/2	1/4	94.4	Deleted	
Zenith Energy	3 1/8	3/16	94.0	Deleted	
Detection Systems—Wts.	3 1/2	1/4	92.8	Deleted	
Amarex	18 3/4	1 3/8	92.7	7/8	(36.4)
Saxon Oil Company	10 1/4	3/4	92.6	Deleted	
Advanced Fuel Systems	5	3/8	92.5	Deleted	
Consolidated Petroleum Industries	3	1/4	91.6	Deleted	
Grove Exploration	4 1/8	3/8	90.9	5/16	(16.5)
International Westward Development	3 3/4	3/8	90.0	1/4	(33.3)
Invesco International	3 3/4	1/2	88.6	Bankruptcy	
Life Imaging	3 3/4	7/16	88.3	9 1/4	2,014.3
Kenal—Wts.	4 1/4	1/2	88.2	1/8	(75.0)
Brajdas	7 7/8	1	87.3	Deleted	
Energy Resources of Dakota	13 3/4	1 3/4	87.2	1 1/4	(28.6)
ND Resources	3 3/8	7/16	87.0	9/16	28.5
BPI Resources	6 1/8	13/16	86.7	1 1/8	38.5
Southern Biotech	3 3/4	1/2	86.6	Deleted	
Sterling Pipe & Supply	9 3/8	1 1/4	86.6	Deleted	
Turbo Resources	3 3/4	1/2	86.6	Bankruptcy	
Bronco Oil & Gas Co.	3 1/4	7/16	86.5	Deleted	

Number Advanced in 1983: 3
Number Declined in 1983: 10

Exhibit 6–11
Twenty-Five NASDAQ Best Performers 1983

Company Name	Closing Price 1982	Closing Price 1983	Percentage Increase	Closing Price 1984	Percentage Increase
Dento-Medical Industries	½	12 ¾	2450.0	6 ¼	(50.9)
Mountain States Overthrust O & G	¼	4 7/32	1587.5	Deleted	
Equilink	⅞	14	1500.0	Deleted	
Marathon Office Supply	½	6	1100.0	Deleted	
John F. Lawhon Furniture	5/16	3 ½	1020.0	2 ⅞	(17.9)
Marathon Gold	½	5 ¼	950.0	1 5/16	(75.2)
Chesapeake Industries	⅜	3 ½	833.3	2 ¼	(35.7)
Geos	⅝	4 ¾	660.0	Deleted	
R.V. Weatherford	1 ⅜	9 ½	590.9	3	(68.4)
D.O.C Optics	1 ⅞	12 ¾	580.0	6 ¾	(47.1)
UNIOIL Cp.	1 ⅝	10 ⅛	523.0	15/16	(91.1)
Sorg Printing Co.	4	24 ½	512.5	8 ⅞	(63.8)
Dresher Inc.	1 ¾	10 ½	500.0	9 ½	(9.5)
Golden Nuggget Inc.—Wts.	9	54	500.0	19	(64.8)
Recoton	1 ¾	10 ⅜	492.8	5 ⅝	(45.8)
Life Sciences	1 ½	8 ⅞	491.6	2 ¼	(74.7)
Helionetics Inc.—Wts.	2 ¾	15 ½	463.6	1 ¼	(91.9)
STV Engineers	1 ¾	9 ½	442.8	6 ½	(31.6)
Veronex Resources	¾	4 1/16	441.6	3 15/16	(4.9)
Minstar	4 ⅜	23 ½	437.1	19	(19.1)
DMI Furniture	2 ¼	12	433.3	10	(16.7)
Integrated Barter International—Uts.	1 ¼	6 ⅜	410.0	Deleted	
Paul Harris Stores	3 ⅜	16 ⅜	385.1	13	(20.6)
Winn Enterprises—Wts.	¾	3 ⅝	383.3	13/16	(77.9)
First Lincoln Financial	4 ⅛	19 ¼	366.6	Deleted	

Number Advanced in 1984: 0
Number Declined in 1984: 19

Exhibit 6–12
Twenty-Five NASDAQ Worst Performers 1983

Company Name	Closing Price 1982	Closing Price 1983	Percentage Decrease	Closing Price 1984	Percentage Decrease
Computer Devices	11 ½	½	95.6	Bankruptcy	
Quick Print of America	3 ⅝	5/16	91.3	Deleted	
MFG Oil	3 ¾	11/32	90.8	Deleted	
Big Bite	13 ½	1 ⅞	86.1	1 ½	(20.0)
Omnimedical	13	2	84.6	Bankruptcy	
Vector Graphic	12	2	83.3	3/16	(91.7)
Video Station	6 ⅜	1 ⅛	82.3	3/32	(91.6)
Biochem International	16 ⅜	3	81.6	⅞	(70.8)
National Data Communications	9 ¾	1 ⅞	80.7	½	(73.3)
Patlex Cp.—Wts.	3 ¾	¾	80.0	Deleted	
Ambassador Group	6 ¾	1 ½	77.7	Bankruptcy	
General Genetics Cp.	3 ¾	⅞	76.6	½	(42.9)
Veta Grande Companies	12 ¼	2 ⅞	76.5	5/16	(89.6)
Private Screening—Uts.	3	¾	75.0	½	(33.3)
Midland Southwest	3	¾	75.0	¼	(66.7)
Great Southwest Industries	3	¾	75.0	¾	N.C.
Teva Pharmaceuticals	8	2 ⅛	73.4	1 7/16	(32.9)
Orthomolecular Nutrition Institute	3 ¼	⅞	73.0	Deleted	
Universal Voltronics	6 ½	1 ¾	73.0	1 9/16	(10.7)
Flame Industries	4 ⅝	1 ¼	72.9	Deleted	
BPI Resources	4 ⅛	1 ⅛	72.7	1	(11.1)
Restaurant Entertainment	4 ⅛	1 ⅛	72.7	⅛	(88.9)
David Minerals Resources	3 ⅝	1	72.4	13/16	(18.7)
Tocom	9	2 ½	72.2	1	(60.0)
TU International	10	2 13/16	71.8	⅖	(85.8)

Number Advanced in 1984: 0
Number Declined in 1984: 19

Exhibit 6–13
Twenty-Five NASDAQ Best Performers 1984

Company Name	Closing Price 1983	Closing Price 1984	Percentage Increase	Closing Price 1985	Percentage Increase
Endo-Lase—Wts.	½	8 ¼	1550.0	7	(15.2)
Profit Technology—Wts.	¼	3 ¼	1200.0	1 ⅞	(42.3)
Staar Surgical Company	1 ¼	9	620.0	10 ⅛	12.5
Technogenetics—Wts.	½	3	500.0	⅝	(79.2)
Panatech Research & Development—Uts.	2	11	450.0	1	(90.9)
Universal Trading Exchange—Class A	1 ¾	9 ½	442.9	6 ¾	(30.0)
Endo-Lase	1 ½	8	433.3	6 ⅞	(14.1)
Panatech Research & Development	⅞	4 ⅝	428.6	4 ½	(2.7)
Endo-Lase—Uts.	6 ⅜	31 ¾	398.0	Deleted	
Benihana National—Wts.	1 ⅞	9 ¼	393.3	13 ¼	43.2
Flexible Computer—Class A	2	8 ⅞	343.8	4	(54.9)
Medical Sterilization	3 ⅜	14	314.8	7 ¾	(44.6)
The Computer Store	⅞	3 ⅝	314.3	⅝	(82.8)
Multi Solutions Inc.—Wts.	2	8 ¼	312.5	3 ⅝	(56.1)
Multi Solutions	1 ⅜	5 ⅝	309.1	2 ½	(55.6)
The Computer Store—Uts.	6 ½	26 ½	307.7	4	(84.9)
Multi Solutions Inc.—Uts.	7 ¾	30 ¼	290.3	13	(57.0)
Environmental Tectonics	2 ¾	10 ½	281.8	4 ¾	(54.8)
Dixson	⅞	3 ¼	271.4	2 ½	(23.1)
Enzon	1 ½	5 ½	266.7	4 ⅛	(25.0)
Tofu Time	3 ¾	13 ⅝	263.3	Deleted	
Exovir	3	10 ⅝	254.2	14 ⅛	32.9
Enzon—Uts.	6 ¾	23 ½	248.1	18 ½	(21.3)
Cardio Pet	3 ½	12 ⅛	246.4	7 ¾	(36.1)
Profit Technology	1 ¼	4 ¼	240.0	3 ½	(17.7)

Number Advanced in 1985: 3
Number Declined in 1985: 20

Exhibit 6–14
Twenty-Five NASDAQ Worst Performers 1984

Company Name	Closing Price 1983	Closing Price 1984	Percentage Decrease	Closing Price 1985	Percentage Decrease
Air One	4 1/2	1/8	97.2	Deleted	
A.T. Bliss & Company—Ptd.	6 1/4	3/16	97.0	Deleted	
Applied Solar Energy—Wts.	4 1/8	1/8	97.0	Deleted	
The Petrie	5	1/4	95.0	Deleted	
Optimum Holding	4 7/8	1/4	94.9	1/2	100.0
Peoples Restaurants	7 3/8	3/8	94.9	Deleted	
Electronic Financial Systems	7	3/8	94.6	Deleted	
Vitality Unlimited	4	1/4	93.8	2 7/8	1,050.0
The Good Taco	4 7/8	5/16	93.6	29/32	191.4
Eagle Computer	7 1/2	1/2	93.3	1/4	(50.0)
Columbia Data Products	11	3/4	93.2	Bankruptcy	
Paragon Communication Systems	3 1/2	1/4	92.9	Deleted	
American Family Pizza	5	3/8	92.5	5/16	(16.5)
Biostim	5 3/4	7/16	92.4	Deleted	
Helionetics—Wts.	15 1/2	1 1/4	91.9	5/16	(74.9)
National Health Care Systems	5 3/4	1/2	91.3	1/4	(50.0)
Central Mortgage Realty Trust	8 1/2	3/4	91.2	5/8	(16.7)
PKS/Communications	8 3/4	13/16	90.7	Deleted	
Unioil	10 1/8	15/16	90.7	1	6.7
Cambrian Systems	5 1/4	1/2	90.5	1/4	(50.0)
American Family Pizza	3 7/8	3/8	90.3	3/16	(50.0)
Magnetic Information Technology	3 3/4	3/8	90.0	1/16	(83.3)
Clubmart of America	5 1/2	9/16	89.8	Deleted	
NRD Mining	3 1/16	5/16	89.8	1/4	(20.0)
PM Industries	3	5/16	89.6	Deleted	

Number Advanced in 1985: 4
Number Declined in 1985: 10

Exhibit 6–15
Twenty-Five NASDAQ Best Performers 1985

Company Name	Closing Price 1984	Closing Price 1985	Percentage Increase	Closing Price 1986	Percentage Increase
Rocking Horse Child Care of America	1/4	4	1500.0	6 3/8	59.4
Satellite Music Network—Wts.	3/8	4	966.7	Deleted	
American Cytogenetics	7/16	4 1/8	841.8	1 1/8	(71.9)
Insitutform of North America—Wts.	5/8	5 7/8	840.0	Deleted	
Span-American Medical Systems	3 1/8	22 3/4	628.0	6 1/8	(72.9)
Fairfield-Noble	1 1/2	10 3/4	616.7	13	20.9
Aca Joe	1 1/16	7 1/2	606.2	2 1/2	(66.7)
Insitutform Group—Wts.	1 1/4	8 5/8	590.0	7 3/4	(10.7)
Silver Hart Mines	1 1/4	8 1/2	580.0	3	(64.7)
Universal Medical Buildings	2 5/8	17 3/4	576.2	16 1/2	(7.0)
TRC Companies	2	13 1/4	562.5	14 3/4	11.3
Nova Pharmaceutical—Wts.	1 1/16	6 7/8	547.4	13	89.1
Emery Energy	1/2	3	500.0	Deleted	
TCBY Enterprises	4	23	475.0	17 5/8	(23.2)
GenCorp	5 3/4	32 1/2	465.2	36 1/4	11.5
Possis Corporation	7	37 3/4	439.3	23 1/2	(37.7)
Environmental Diagnostics—Uts.	1 7/16	7 11/16	434.6	Deleted	
Zenith National Insurance	3 1/4	16 7/8	419.2	22 1/2	33.3
USPCI	5 3/4	29 1/2	413.0	31 3/4	7.6
Franklin Resources	12 1/4	62 1/2	410.2	35 3/4	(42.8)
Cambridge BioScience	1 3/8	7	409.1	5 3/8	(23.2)
Endotronics	3 3/4	19	406.7	20 3/4	9.2
Environmental Systems Company	5	25 1/4	405.0	Deleted	
API Enterprises	5/8	3 1/8	400.0	3 1/4	2.3
Richton International	1 1/2	7 3/8	391.7	4 1/8	(43.4)

Number Advanced in 1986: 9
Number Declined in 1986: 11

Exhibit 6–16
Twenty-Five NASDAQ Worst Performers 1985

Company Name	Closing Price 1984	Closing Price 1985	Percentage Decrease	Closing Price 1986	Percentage Decrease
Oxoco—Pfd.	18 3/4	5/8	96.7	Bankruptcy	
Folks Restaurants	7 3/8	1/4	96.6	1/4	N.C.
American Educational Computer	9	7/16	95.1	9/16	28.6
Gulf Broadcast Company	15 3/8	3/4	95.1	1/2	(33.3)
Nordic Ltd.	3 1/2	1/4	92.9	Deleted	
Art Explosion—Uts.	3 1/4	1/4	92.3	Deleted	
Hale Systems	5 5/8	7/16	92.2	3/16	(57.1)
Eagle Telephonics	9 1/4	3/4	91.9	1	33.3
Strata Corporation—Class A	4 3/8	3/8	91.4	1/16	(83.3)
CME-SAT	4 3/8	3/8	91.4	1/2	33.3
Oxoco	3 1/2	5/16	91.1	Deleted	
Marquest Resources	3 1/2	5/16	91.1	Deleted	
Pharmakinetics Laboratories	7 1/2	13/16	89.2	5/8	(16.9)
Sebrn	3 1/4	3/8	88.5	1 3/16	216.7
National Gold Distributors	3 7/8	15/32	87.9	Deleted	
National Gold Distributors—Uts.	9 3/4	1 3/16	87.8	Deleted	
DMI Furniture	10	1 1/4	87.5	1 3/4	40.0
The Computer Store—Uts.	26 1/2	4	84.9	Deleted	
American Monitor	3 7/8	19/32	84.7	Deleted	
Sebrn—Uts.	6	15/16	84.4	2 11/16	186.7
Rynco Scientific	16	2 3/4	82.8	15/16	(65.9)
The Computer Store	3 5/8	5/8	82.8	Bankruptcy	
Alamo Savings Association of Texas	11	2	81.8	Deleted	
Computer Depot	5 1/2	1	81.8	Bankruptcy	
Pharmakinetics Laboratories—Uts.	34 1/2	6 1/2	81.2	6	(7.7)

Number Advanced in 1986: 6
Number Declined in 1986: 9

Technical Note on Analysis of Exhibits 6–5 to 6–16
By Carlos P. Lima

The first data set consists of returns over the year 1980 for the stocks of 380 companies, and over the year 1981 for the stocks of 384 companies. Given the method of sample selection one might proceed on the assumption that most companies in the 1980 sample would again be represented in the 1981 sample. As it turns out, our conclusions can be amply established without this assumption.

We will concentrate on the changes of performance of the 380 companies in the 1980 sample from 1980 to 1981, as indicated by membership in the group of 50 top performers and 50 worst performers in both years, performance being measured by total calculated stock returns.

The initial observation was that, in this sample of companies, 13 out of the 50 best performers in 180 ended up among the 50 worst performers in 1981; four out of the 50 worst performers in 1980 were found among the 50 best performers the following year.

These numbers are striking, since they are not what would be expected if the performance ranking one year were independent from that of the previous year, or if the ranking one year tended to follow to some extent that of the previous year. In fact, assuming "no effect" of the ranking of one year upon the other, one would expect somewhere around 50 × (50/380), i.e., six or seven companies, to switch from the top to the bottom group, and a comparable number to take the opposite route; and if the rankings tended to resemble each other, we would expect to see fewer such extreme changes of fortune.

What these observations seem thus to be saying is that being a disappointing performer does tend, if anything, to discourage top performance the following year, which is not surprising; but the data say as well, and much more clearly, that top performance in one year also has a negative effect on the prospects for good performance the following year. On reflection this is understandable, but the possibility is more easily overlooked.

Using a hypergeometric model, a test of "no effect" versus high best-to-worst crossover, based on the data of 13 and four guaranteed crossovers, gives an attained significance of 0.65%. This is strong data analytical evidence for higher than chance best-to-worst crossover. At the customary 5% significance level, the data are consistent with a selection scheme in which the probability of being among the worst in 1981 is at least 1.36 times higher for 1980 top performers than for others.

The evidence for lower than chance worst-to-best crossover is weaker (attained significance 17.7%) and about the same for both effects simultaneously (attained significance 18.3%).

These conclusions are not significantly affected by the possibility of some 1980 firms being absent from the 1981 sample, since that circumstance is much more likely to bias the observed crossover frequencies against our main conclusion than in favor of it.

Staying with the first data set, we have more information available, e.g., the number of firms that remained in the top performance group, and the number of firms that remained in the worst performance group from one year to the next. If we neglected the possible effect of absences in the 1981 sample of firms included in the 1980 sample, the following frequencies would obtain (for firms in the 1980 sample):

	1981			
	Best	Other	Worst	Totals
Best	0	37*	13	50
Other	46*	198*	36*	280
Worst	4	45*	1	50
Totals	50	280	50	380

* Calculated by fixing the marginal totals.

This would constitute clear evidence (attained significance 1.75%) of the tendency of extreme performers, both good and bad, to "regress to market norm" (or drop out of sight?). It would be reasonable to hypothesize that this is the main principle actually at work here. Even though it would be interesting to confirm and quantify this, the other data analyzed here are more directly oriented to the detection of performance reversals.

The conclusions reached with the first data set needed some independent confirmation. Without it, it could be argued that we might be dealing with an unusual year (or years), or that the sample selection introduced a bias. It must be noted, however, that even a one-time observation such as that of the first data set speaks clearly for the possibility of good performance one year being a poor predictor of good performance the following year, and should therefore not be overlooked.

The second data set consists of frequency counts of advancers and decliners among best and worst performers in the previous year, for each of the years from 1981 through 1986. The proportions of advancers and decliners in the population from which the extreme performers were taken are also known.

The table on page 105 summarizes the data in the second set.

To simplify the analysis, firms for which the relevant data are not available, and firms in the population that were neither advancers nor decliners, were left out of consideration.

Using a binomial type model, a test of "no effect" versus a lower probability of advance, as compared to the general population, for previous year top performers gives an attained significance of 0.00%, overwhelming evidence of a performance disadvantage for previous year top performers. At the customary 5% significance level, the data support decreased probabilities of advance for top performers over the general population by a ratio of 1:1.6 or worse, on the average. That is, if the population of advancers in a given year is about 48%, we cannot generally expect a previous year top performer to have

Previous Year Top Performers

Year	No.	Advanced	Declined
1981	19	2	17
1982	22	13	9
1983	17	4	13
1984	19	0	19
1985	23	3	20
1986	18	8	10

Previous Year Worst Performers

Year	No.	Advanced	Declined
1981	19	3	16
1982	18	3	15
1983	13	3	10
1984	19	0	19
1985	14	4	10
1986	10	7	3

Year	Population Proportion of Advancers*
1981	38.9
1982	57.2
1983	60.0
1984	32.7
1985	60.2
1986	62.4

* Proportion of advancers among advancers and decliners for the year, in the total population from which best and worst performers were selected.

more than about a 30% chance of appearing among the advancers.

Even if the situation should depend on other factors, so as to make the degree of previous year dependency change from year to year, the conclusions remain strong. Each of four out of the six years analyzed, taken by itself, supplies very strong evidence of the disadvantage of last year's top performers, with probability ratios ranging from 1.3 to 2 (at the 5% significance level). For 1986 the disadvantage is less definitely established, but quite plausible, and for 1982 no advantage or disadvantage can be established with any degree of certainty.

As for the following year performance of poor performers, the data establish quite clearly that they are also unlikely to do well, as one might expect. The disadvantage is, in this case, somewhat more consistent from year to year, but on the whole the two groups are remarkably alike. This is to some extent an artifact of missing data (poor performers are much more likely to be absent from following year advance/decline counts); but the fact that surviving best and worst performers one year are found comparable to a measurable degree the following year is significant.

Endnotes

[1] Edward I. Altman and Scott A. Nammacher, *Investing in Junk Bonds* (New York: John Wiley & Sons, 1987): pp. 78-79

[2] Richard Bookstaber and David Jacob, *The Composite Hedge* (Morgan Stanley & Co. Incorporated: March 1985).

[3] This definitional difference explains why economic models declare a firm bankrupt when its net worth falls to zero, even though many real-world companies continue to operate (and to service their debt) long after their net worth (as defined by the accountants) turns negative. The economists reasonably assume that creditors will demand liquidation once the company's future earnings stream equates to less than the value of its liabilities. For a further discussion of this topic, see "Who's Afraid of Negative Equity?" in this volume.

[4] Equity-related credit measures may not be represented as buy/sell signals by their originators, but some investors are bound to interpret them in

that way. Therefore, however limited the claims made about such ratios, it is appropriate to test their efficacy as predictors of future performances.

[5] Stocks included in the sample had to meet criteria that included a record of earnings forecasts in the Institutional Brokers Estimate System (IBES) data base. In general, these are large-capitalization companies that are suitable vehicles for institutional investors.

[6] Each year, some extreme performers failed to appear in the next year's data, for reasons such as mergers and bankruptcy. The Technical Note concludes that these disappearances do not compromise the validity of our findings.

CHAPTER 7

Overcoming the Fixed Charge Fixation

Without the ability to measure we would not only be materially worse off, but we would probably not even be able to tell when we were doing well. The value of measurement is lost, however, when the measure becomes more important in our minds than the benefit we are measuring. For example, many people pursue the worthwhile objective of reducing their weight by setting a numerical target of pounds to be shed. They then reach the target by adopting fad diets that do nothing more than promote water loss, a process that may defeat the underlying aim of improving one's health.

This same unfortunate tendency to reduce a complex and abstract concept to a single, tangible number manifests itself throughout the financial world. For example, traders' expediency promotes the convenient delusion that M1 is identical to monetary policy's total influence upon economic growth and inflation. Similarly, our ruthless attention to the bottom line fosters the false doctrine that there is no aspect of a firm's financial performance worthy of our attention that is not subsumed by earnings-per-share.

Exclusive focus on fixed charge coverage as a measure of credit quality is another example of this dangerous reductionism and the consequences are particularly severe in the high yield sector. Exhibit 7–1 demonstrates that this single ratio (earnings before interest and taxes divided by interest) falls very far short of capturing a company's credit risk in all its subtlety. The left-hand column ranks six speculative-grade issues according to their observed risk premiums as of late 1985. The Gencorp bond, with the narrowest spread versus Treasuries, has the lowest perceived risk of default, the Republic Steel bond the highest. In the right-hand column, the same issues are ranked by their 1984 "times charges earned," according to Standard & Poor's *Bond Guide*. Given that reference work's widespread use, we can hardly assume that its figures are not "in the market," yet the risk premium rankings correspond poorly to the coverage rankings. Only Republic Steel, with negative coverage in 1984, occupies the same position on both scales. Clearly, a portfolio manager who bases credit decisions solely, or even primarily on reported coverage, will stray far out of line with the market.

Exhibit 7–1
Selected High Yield Issues*

Ranked by Risk Premium Lowest to Highest Basis Point Spread Versus Treasuries		
Gencorp**	12 3/8s	5/1/03
MCI	12 7/8s	10/1/02
Harnischfeger	12s	4/15/04
McLean	12s	7/15/03
Tesoro	12 3/4s	3/15/01
Republic Steel***	12 1/8s	6/1/03

Ranked by 1984 Coverage Highest to Lowest Times Charges Earned in September 1985 Standard & Poor's Bond Guide		
Tesoro	12 3/4s	3/15/01
McLean	12s	7/15/03
Gencorp**	12 3/8s	5/1/03
MCI	12 7/8s	10/1/02
Harnischfeger	12s	4/15/04
Republic Steel***	12 1/8s	6/1/03

* All issues are subordinated.
** Formerly General Tire.
*** Times Charges Earned of Jones & Laughlin Steel.

Some readers will call this test unfair, arguing that we should not compare the coverage of a regulated company like MCI with that of Gencorp, an industrial, or Tesoro, an oil company. That is precisely (although only partially) our point—one cannot measure a heterogeneous group of issuers by a single standard.

Given the obvious inadequacy of fixed charge coverage as a litmus test (many of our readers have probably at some point performed the experiment depicted in Exhibit 7–1, with similar results), its continued preeminence at many financial institutions is surprising. Getting a deal formally approved may require additional documentation, but an acceptable coverage figure, combined with a generous yield (which might be a tipoff of credit problems not revealed by the coverage) can make the buy decision all but a foregone conclusion. If the credit later hits the canvas, the investment committee can at least point to a cold, hard number that originally justified the purchase.

Why Coverage Rules

The basis of fixed charge coverage's supremacy lies in the seemingly unassailable logic of its formula. At the end of the accounting period, after collecting its revenues and paying its operating expenses, the corporation has something left over to pay its interest and taxes. If that residual is less than the interest bill (according to this literal interpretation), the corporation cannot meet its obligations and defaults. Alternatively, the company must borrow to pay its interest, a reprehensible practice in most lenders' opinions, and in their eyes invariably a financial distress signal.

To refute this logic, one has merely to point out that earnings after operating expenses do not necessarily reflect actual cash available to service debt, since most companies report on an accrual basis. Still, the formulaic appeal of fixed charge coverage is strong and is reinforced by the seductive ease of employing it. Bond salesmen generally have the Standard & Poor's *Bond Guide*, mentioned above, at their fingertips and are happy to provide coverage data in support of proposed swaps. As for new issues, the Securities and Exchange Commission has ensured that investors will have coverage numbers to consider. Regulation S-K (Standard Instructions for filing forms under the Securities Act of 1933 and the Securities Exchange

Act of 1934) requires that prospectuses include the ratio of earnings to fixed charges for each of the registrant's last five fiscal years (or for the life of the registrant and its predecessors, if less). The regulation furthermore demands coverage for the latest interim period and provides for capitalized interest, discontinued operations, preferred stock dividends, consolidated and unconsolidated majority-owned subsidiaries, 50%-owned subsidiaries and less-than-50%-owned subsidiaries. (In the last instance, earnings include only dividends received, while losses are excluded unless the registrant has guaranteed the subsidiary's debt.) Since the SEC has obviously thought fixed charge coverage through carefully, investors feel secure in relying upon this officially sanctioned number.

Cracks in the Coverage Foundation

This complacency is gradually being eroded, however. In 1983, the bellwether New York State Insurance Department eliminated fixed charge coverage as a criterion for legal investments for domestic life insurance companies. The rating agencies, although wrongly perceived in some quarters as mere number-crunching robots, recognize the hazards of relying too heavily on fixed charge coverage. According to Harold Goldberg, Senior Vice President of Moody's Investors Services, coverage can be useful for comparing companies that compete in identical markets with nearly equivalent asset mixes. In real life, unfortunately, few such twins exist. Even General Electric and Westinghouse, popularly regarded as clones, have too little overlap in their respective businesses to be held to the same fixed charge coverage standard, in Moody's view. Goldberg acknowledges that comparing a borrower's coverage with its past record can aid in spotting a credit trend. More important, though, is a company's competitive position, which drives all the numbers and which may be enhanced by a distinctive product line or a unique distribution capability. Given its traditional focus on operations, Moody's has never set absolute coverage cutoffs for its rating categories. "We are criteria-averse," Goldberg concludes. Likewise, Standard & Poor's has long understood that although a purely quantitative approach to ratings can be rigorous, hard-nosed and devoid of favoritism, it has one serious defect—it periodically produces absurd results. In 1982, the agency commented:

> "Thus the rating process at S&P is not limited to the examination of various financial measures. Proper assessment of current and future debt protection levels requires that financial statement analysis be performed within a broader context. This involves a thorough review of the industries or business segments in which a company participates, a judgment as to the company's competitive position within that industry, and an evaluation of management. At times, a rating decision may be heavily influenced by financial measures. At other times, analysis of the business risks and other subjective features may dominate."[1]

Other Shortcomings

At this point the reader may interject, "The argument for a more comprehensive credit analysis is persuasive, but impractical. I look at a half-dozen new high yield offerings and leveraged buyout proposals every week. Given all my other responsibilities, I need to boil the credit analysis function down to the essentials. If I have only one number to look at, fixed charge coverage might as well be the one." Our response to this reasonable comment is that fortunately, the investor does not have only one number to look at, and that one cannot hope to obtain good results through blind trust in fixed charge coverage. To begin with, fixed charge coverage is not an exceptional single-variable predictor of financial distress. A 1977 study of actual bankruptcies sized up coverage alongside six other financial indicators: overall profitability, stability of earnings, cumulative profitability, liquidity, capitalization and asset size. Coverage ranked sixth out of seven as a contributor to financial distress by every statistical test employed except one; on that test it ranked seventh.[2] Similarly, a study conducted for the National Association of Insurance Commissioners in 1988 found that "a coverage ratio is not necessary in a model of financial soundness because the concept is better explained by other ratios."[3] Even if history had proven fixed charge coverage an exemplary forecaster of default, however, its employment as a sole proxy for creditworthiness would nevertheless produce periodic misjudgments. Experience demonstrates that once Wall Street gives American corporations a numerical target to aim at, the corporations will pummel the accounting rules until they meet it. The measure quickly overshadows the thing being measured, i.e., creditworthiness. Bookkeeping quirks that enable companies to add noncash items to earnings and subtract interest charges by renaming them become as avidly sought after as the means of genuinely improving economic performance. In such circumstances, the credit analyst who accepts fixed charge coverage as a definitive test of financial quality is akin to a medical examiner who pronounces a man fit after he has tampered with the blood pressure gauge to obtain a normal reading, instead of exercising more regularly and reducing his salt intake. A life insurance company would not approve a policy on that basis and it should not buy a bond on the strength of a similarly flawed test of financial health. (Ditto for mutual funds, trust departments, investment advisers, thrifts, endowments and pension funds.)

Perhaps fixed charge coverage's most serious flaw, though, is the frequent lack of comparability among the credits one wishes to compare—a problem already cited by Moody's Harold Goldberg, above. Company A, with two times coverage last year and earnings that never fluctuate by more than 10% annually, may be a better risk than Company B, with four times coverage last year and repeated, violent earnings swings.

Clearly, an investor requires less of a coverage cushion when the likelihood of earnings taking a nasty fall appears minimal. Similarly, a finance company's liquid asset base can justify narrower coverage than would be acceptable for a heavy equipment manufacturer. Measuring such a mixed multitude by the single standard of fixed charge coverage can produce excesses of both conservatism and liberality. The following two examples should amply demonstrate that certain corporate borrowers diverge so radically from the normal profile as to render meaningless any financial comparisons with the mean of a standard sample.

A False Negative Signal

Let us first consider broadcasting, a business in which no knowledgeable person ever asks the margin by which earnings cover interest charges. Broadcasting's reported earnings, like every other business's, are calculated after deducting depreciation and amortization. Unlike most other industries, however, where these non-cash deductions stand for wear-and-tear of physical assets, the broadcasting business writes off a vast amount of goodwill every year. Rather than declining with age, the economic worth of this goodwill (which represents the value of the franchise) rises over time as advertising revenues grow but available frequencies remain scarce. Analysts therefore normally add back this non-cash amortization item in calculating cash available to cover a broadcasting company's fixed charges.

This emphasis on operating cash flow, rather than earnings, is not broadcasting's only distinguishing characteristic, however. The industry's longstanding, predictable growth record makes prudent investors willing to pay for future earnings to an extent that would be speculative in other ventures. Fixed charge coverages for newly-acquired properties are consequently thin, yet do not signify inordinate risk. Exhibit 7–2 presents a cash flow projection for a mature television station, given certain interest rates for a Single-B borrower and required returns for equity investors in broadcasting properties. We assume a modest 5% annual growth in advertising revenue, matching a projected 2% real expansion in the economy plus a 3% inflation rate. (These revenues have historically kept pace with nominal growth in Gross National Product.) Suppose lenders arbitrarily demand a minimum operating cash flow coverage of 1.3 times for broadcasters. If the acquirer is to meet this test in the first year, while also obtaining his required return on equity (which requires leveraging to lenders' maximum 80%-of-purchase-price level), he can pay no more than seven times trailing 12 months operating cash flow for the station. Unfortunately, stations do not come that way. If they did, the return to equity investors would exceed 40%, far more than their 20-25% requirement. Under the market conditions assumed in this illustration, such a property would fetch 10 times operating cash flow. Exhibit 7–3 shows that investors are not imprudent in paying that multiple, despite the resulting first year operating cash flow coverage of less than 1.0. By the third year, the station generates enough cash to cover fixed charges and by the fifth year coverage rises to 1.21 times. With tax benefits from its book loss, the station generates positive net cash flow from the outset. The lender's confidence (or lack thereof) depends, not on the projected coverage, but on the predictability of growth in broadcasting revenues. This corresponds with the rating agencies' emphasis, described above, on industry and company fundamentals.

Cash flow analysis, by the way, has strong analytical appeal beyond the confines of the broadcasting industry. In leveraged buyouts, where management's critical task is to generate sufficient cash from operations (and possibly from asset sales) to service debt, investors are keenly interested in cash flow coverage, as calculated in Exhibits 7–2 and 7–3. The emphasis is on the projected figures, since numbers based on pre-LBO financial statements have little relevance after a company has radically restructured itself. Analysts typically use EBDIT (earnings before depreciation, interest and taxes) as the numerator of the fraction. For the denominator they may choose either total interest expense or cash interest expense. The latter is pertinent in cases where issuance of deferred-interest bonds or payment-in-kind securities results in a significant component of total interest expense (at least in the LBO's early years) that represents amortization of debt discount or issuance

Exhibit 7–2
Cash Flow Projection—Mature Television Station
Constraint: Cash Flow Coverage of 1.3 Times in Year 1

Required pretax return to equity investor	20-25%
Typical total debt to total capital employed	80%
Interest rate	14 ½%
Annual growth in revenue	5%
Cash expenses as percentage of revenue	60%
Capital expenditures as percentage of revenues	8.4%
Trailing 12 months cash flow	$3.6 million

Projections assume sale at end of Year 5 at 10 times operating cash flow, based on expected future multiples implied by current transaction prices. All net cash flow is applied to pay down debt

($MM)

	Year 1	Year 2	Year 3	Year 4	Year 5
Revenue	9.5	10.0	10.5	11.0	11.5
Cash Expenses*	5.7	6.0	6.3	6.6	6.9
Operating Cash Flow	3.8	4.0	4.2	4.4	4.6
Interest Expense	2.9	2.8	2.6	2.5	2.3
Cash Flow Coverage	1.31x	1.43x	1.62x	1.76x	2.00x

* Excludes depreciation, amortization and deferred taxes.

Purchase price required to obtain figures shown: $25.2 million = 7 times trailing cash flow. Actual return to equity investor: 44.1%

Exhibit 7–3
Cash Flow Projection—Mature Television Station
Cash Flow Coverage Constraint Removed
(Assumptions same as in Exhibit 7–2)

($MM)

	Year 1	Year 2	Year 3	Year 4	Year 5
Revenue	9.5	10.0	10.5	11.0	11.5
Cash Expenses*	5.7	6.0	6.3	6.6	6.9
Operating Cash Flow	3.8	4.0	4.2	4.4	4.6
Interest Expense	2.9	2.8	2.6	2.5	2.3
Cash Flow Coverage	0.90x	0.98x	1.05x	1.13x	1.21x

* Excludes depreciation, amortization and deferred taxes.

Purchase price required to obtain figures shown: $36.0 million = 10 times trailing cash flow. Actual return to equity investor: 23.4%

of new securities, rather than a cash outlay. To a large extent, projected EBDIT coverage has become the standard of comparison for LBO credits and for high yield issuers in general. While bringing cash flow into the picture makes fixed charge coverage a more valid analytical tool, however, excessive reliance on it is prone to many of the same problems as conventional coverage. Not even the improved version can capture all of the credit information needed to evaluate speculative-grade companies.

A False Positive Signal

In the preceding example, a conventional fixed charge coverage comparison with companies in other industries would have led the investor to reject a sound credit. The opposite error can result from misuse of coverage in analyzing a captive finance company, that is, a company owned by and primarily engaged in financing the sales of a manufacturing or retailing concern. This was the nature of Allis-Chalmers Credit Corporation, which in 1983 was a wholly owned subsidiary of Allis-Chalmers Corporation, a manufacturer of agricultural, material-handling and process equipment. For that year, the Standard & Poor's *Bond Guide* reported times charges earned at Allis-Chalmers Credit of 1.30, a respectable number for a finance company,[4] and an increase from 1.21 in the preceding year. That apparently improving trend was a false beacon, however. An examination of the footnotes to the credit company's 1983 financials reveals that finance income, which was not broken down further in the income statement, included income earned from the parent. This income arose when Allis-Chalmers Corporation waived all or part of the normal finance charges to induce retail sales, reimbursing Allis-Chalmers Credit for the amounts waived.

In 1983, $103.2 million, or 57% of the credit subsidiary's total finance income of $179.7 million represented amounts earned in this way. A lender to Allis-Chalmers Credit might well have asked whether Allis-Chalmers Corporation was good for the money.

In fact, the waivers were large enough to throw Allis-Chalmers Corporation into a consolidated loss for 1983, a year for which Standard & Poor's reported times charges earned of 3.34 for the enterprise. The credit company's improved coverage offered little reassurance as the parent reeled under the effects of the federal government's Payment-in-Kind acreage reduction plan and severe price discounting of lift trucks. In 1983, Allis-Chalmers Corporation exhausted its covenanted capacity to incur long-term indebtedness and, having suspended common dividends in 1981 and preferred dividends in 1982, was obliged to restructure its debt in 1983. Bond ratings paralleled the deteriorating situation, dropping from A/A- to B3/B- between 1981 and 1984. (Recognizing the inseparability of the parent and finance subsidiary for credit analysis purposes, the agencies rated the two identically, notwithstanding the subsidiary's irreproachable fixed charge coverage.)

The denouement to Allis-Chalmers Credit's story is especially instructive in this discussion of fixed charge coverage's frequent irrelevance. In March 1985, battered by continued losses, Allis-Chalmers Corporation sold its agricultural equipment business, along with Allis-Chalmers Credit, to Kloeckner-Humboldt-Deutz (KHD), a financially healthy but non-rated West German equipment manufacturer. Standard & Poor's suspended its bond rating when KHD indicated that it did not care to appear before the agency for a financial review. Moody's indicated that it would continue to rate Allis-Chalmers Credit, whether or not the new parent agreed to cooperate, with the subsidiary's rating dependent in large measure on its intended role within the prosperous KHD organization. In any event, the finance company's creditworthiness going forward had but little to do with the fixed charge coverage it had recorded during its previous incarnation as part of the foundering Allis-Chalmers Corporation.

Conclusion

Despite a lack of correlation with market yield premiums and evidence that other ratios provide clearer signals of financial distress, acknowledging the temptation of corporations to manipulate their income statements to meet a predetermined ratio, and notwithstanding two examples in which traditional fixed charge coverage has a negligible bearing on creditworthiness, we do not contend that calculating coverage never facilitates the assessment of financial strength. We would neither banish it from prospectuses nor altogether discourage its use by investors. We do, however, urge portfolio managers to consider not only the number itself, but also all the attendant caveats, as well as other quantitative and qualitative information. Elevating fixed charge coverage to an exclusive determinant of investment suitability lowers credit analysis from an art to a dogma. Investors who would generally describe themselves as pragmatic, rather than dogmatic, must realize that pragmatism in this instance entails not a labor-saving shortcut, but rather examination of sufficient evidence to make an informed decision.

Endnotes

[1] "Credit Overview: Corporate and International Ratings," *Standard & Poor's*, 1982.

[2] Edward I. Altman, Robert G. Haldeman and P. Narayanan, "Zeta Analysis: A New Model to Identify Bankruptcy Risk of Corporations," *Journal of Banking and Finance* (1977): I.: pp. 24-54.

3 Barron H. Putnam, "Preliminary Discriminant Test Results for Measuring Financial Soundness of Manufacturing Companies," report prepared for the National Association of Insurance Commissioners, New York (December 1, 1988).

[4] For example, Double-A CIT's coverage for the same year was slightly lower at 1.28.

CHAPTER 8

Who's Afraid of Negative Equity?

As leveraged recapitalizations have gained in popularity, investors have begun to see something new on balance sheets—negative net worth. Well, not completely new. In years past, a few major corporations managed to lose so much money year after year that they eventually wiped out their retained earnings and showed deficits in their equity accounts. Unless they reversed their profit trend, with or without some help from Uncle Sam, such companies were not investments for the fainthearted. The typical negative net worth company of today has a much different history, but still manages to unnerve a lot of investors. Many simply find it difficult to reconcile their notions of creditworthiness with a company that, according to its financial statements, is worth less than nothing.

Ironically, many institutions probably own credits that are demonstrably weaker than others they reject on the grounds of sub-zero equity. This irrational behavior stems from a quirk in generally accepted accounting principles (GAAP). In brief, it is possible for two transactions—a stock buyback and a leveraged buyout (LBO)—to have economic consequences that are the reverse of what the balance sheet says about their comparative impact on credit quality.

To illustrate, suppose Tooze Company (Exhibit 8–1) repurchases 40% of its stock on January 1, 1988, paying a 175% premium over book value, as required by current market conditions. The company borrows the $44 million required for the buyback and, in accordance with GAAP, reduces its

Exhibit 8–1
Stock Repurchase—Tooze Company
($MM)

	December 31, 1987	January 1, 1988
Assets:		
Current Assets	20.0	20.0
Fixed Assets (Net)	80.0	80.0
	10.0	10.0
Liabilities:		
Current Liabilities	10.0	10.0
Long-Term Debt	50.0	94.0
	60.0	104.0
Stockholders' Equity	40.0	(4.0)
	100.0	100.0
Debt/Total Capital	55.6%	104.4%

stockholders' equity by the amount of the repurchase. Underlying this accounting treatment is the notion that a company cannot own part of itself. Consequently, reacquired shares are treated as unissued stock and must be recorded as a reduction in equity, rather than an acquisition of an asset. The result is that Tooze Company's equity falls to -$4 million and its debt-total-capital ratio increases to 104.4% (from 55.6% one day earlier).

Tooze Company's capital structure looks much different if instead of repurchasing stock it enters into a leveraged buyout transaction (Exhibit 8–2). Tooze Acquiring Corp., organized by senior management and a major investment bank, acquires the 80% of Tooze Company stock not owned by management, paying a 175% premium to book value, as in the stock repurchase scenario. Senior management contributes its 20% stake, plus cash of $8.8 million. To finance the balance of the purchase, Tooze Acquiring Corp. borrows $79.2 million. Unlike the stock repurchase, the LBO does not result in negative net worth. Provided the transaction satisfies certain criteria, which in essence establish that there has been a change in Tooze

Exhibit 8–2
Leveraged Buyout
($MM)

	Tooze Company December 31, 1987	Tooze Acquiring Corp. January 1, 1988
Assets:		
Current Assets	20.0	20.0
Fixed Assets (Net)	80.0	138.0
	100.0	158.0
Liabilities:		
Current Liabilities	10.0	10.0
Long-Term Debt	50.0	129.2
	60.0	139.2
Stockholders' Equity	40.0	18.8
	100.0	158.0
Debt/Total Capital	55.6%	87.3%

Note: Current liabilities include no short-term debt.
Tooze Acquiring Corp.'s equity is composed of:

Managment's Cash Contribution	8.8
Management's Basis in Tooze Company	10.0
	18.8

Company's controlling interest, the accounting rules permit a writeup of assets to substantially reflect the premium to book value paid in the transaction. As a result, Tooze Company's total assets continue to exceed its now increased total liabilities, and stockholders' equity remains positive at $18.8 million. The company's debt-to-total-capital ratio is 87.3% (versus 104.4% in the buyback scenario). Stepping back from the accounting, something is clearly wrong here. Judging by the conventional book leverage ratio, the LBO appears to result in higher credit quality than the stock repurchase, even though it adds $35.2 million more debt to the balance sheet, with no offsetting benefit. The source of the paradox is that the accounting value, but not the

Exhibit 8–3
Financial Comparison
($MM)

Income Statement	Stock Repurchase Tooze Company 1988	Leveraged Buyout Tooze Acquiring Corp. 1988
Revenues	38.5	38.5
Operating Expenses	23.1	23.1
	15.4	15.4
Depreciation Expense	6.2	7.1
Interest Expense	11.3	15.8
Pretax Income (Loss)	(2.1)	(7.5)
Income Tax (Expense) Benefit	0.7	0.0*
Net Income (Loss)	(1.4)	(7.5)

Balance Sheet	December 31, 1988	December 31, 1988
Assets:		
Current Assets	20.7**	20.0
Fixed Assets (Net)	77.8	134.9
	98.5	154.9
Liabilities:		
Current Liabilities	10.0	10.0
Long-Term Debt	93.9	133.6
	103.9	143.6
Stockholders' Equity	(5.4)	11.3
	98.5	154.9
Key Financial Ratios:		
Operating Cash Flow/*** Interest Expense (x)	1.4	1.0
Debt/Operating Cash Flow (x)	6.1	8.7

* In accordance with Accounting Principles Board Opinion No. 11, since the realization of net operating loss (NOL) carryover is not assured, no income tax benefit is recorded.

** Includes an Income Tax Receivable of $ 0.7 resulting from the NOL carryback.

*** Operating Cash Flow=Pretax Income+Depreciation and Amortization economic value, of the assets is higher in the LBO scenario than in the stock repurchase scenario.

Exhibit 8–3 reinforces the impression that accounting differences distort the perceived credit impact of financial restructuring. Whether Tooze Company buys back stock or enters into an LBO, its operating earnings will be $15.4 million in 1988. The LBO, however, results in a heavier debt burden and higher interest expense. The key financial ratios calculated in Exhibit 8–3 confirm that contrary to what the balance sheet leverage ratios indicate, credit quality is superior in the stock repurchase scenario. Repurchase results in 1.4 times operating cash flow coverage of interest expense, versus 1.0 times for the LBO, and a debt-to-operating-cash-flow ratio of 6.1 times, versus 8.7 times. These ratios reflect actual dollars of inflows and outflows, rather than arbitrary asset values that change at GAAP's behest.

The above illustration forces us to conclude that a leverage ratio based on book value is meaningless in the context of highly leveraged transactions. (Indeed, the ratio is fundamentally flawed in all situations, although its faults become glaring only when the economic value of assets diverges sharply from book value.) High yield analysts can and should bypass this measure when evaluating LBOs and recaps. A leverage ratio based on market capitalization (i.e., the market value of all outstanding shares) may be a better indicator of financial risk, but is not available for privatized, LBO companies. Moreover, equity prices may at times give anomalous or exaggerated signals about credit quality.[1] In terms of objectivity and comparability, no financial ratio surpasses cash flow coverage of interest charges, although even that measure is imperfect, as explained in the preceding chapter, "Overcoming the Fixed Charge Fixation."

Conclusion

Rational investors will base their decisions on economic reality, rather than on accountants' imperfect portrayal of it. When analysts cut through the bookkeeping, they will find that many issuers with negative net worth are relatively strong credits within the speculative-grade universe. This is not to say that such recapitalized companies are without risk or are comparable to Double-A credits. By the same token, an investor who understands the accounting for LBOs and stock repurchases realizes that negative equity does not automatically rank a company below all issuers that have positive net worth.

Endnotes

[1] See Chapter 6, "How Useful Are Stock Prices in Monitoring Credit Quality?"

PART II

Segmenting the Market to Find Value

CHAPTER 9

A Dispassionate View of the Rising (?) Stars

One of the most intrinsically appealing strategies in the high yield market is the notion of buying the "rising stars" to capture both high yields and capital gains. This group consists of relatively small companies that carried subinvestment-grade ratings when they first came to market. A rising star stands in contrast to a "fallen angel," a one-time investment-grade issuer that has entered the high yield category through downgrading. We also distinguish between rising stars and divisional buyouts,[1] the latter being spinoffs of larger companies. Although the divisional buyout firms also come to market for the first time as speculative-grade companies, they differ from rising stars in typically having long-established track records in mature businesses.

Implicit in their very name is the expectation that the rising stars[2] will mature into major industrial concerns. Led by dynamic entrepreneurs motivated by substantial equity stakes, these firms are expected to overtake larger, old-line competitors that have grown flabby.

The bondholder, in this telling of events, shares in the issuer's success via the business life cycle (Exhibit 9–1), a concept that parallels Nature's great drama of growth, decay and rebirth. In the earliest stages of the business life cycle, the start-up and emerging growth phases, a company typically has a voracious appetite for cash, a relatively small capitalization and a limited earnings record—all characteristics that relegate it to the speculative-grade category. As the company gets

Exhibit 9–1
The Business Life Cycle Hypothesis

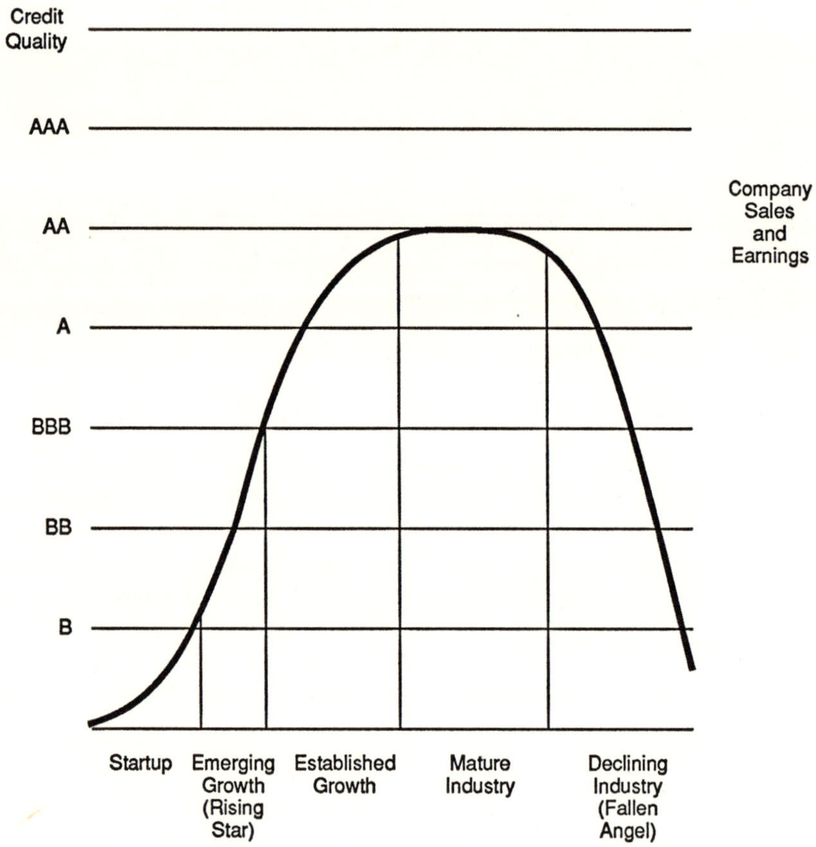

The life cycle hypothesis is a compelling model of an enterprise's development. Companies are not compelled to follow the indicated path, however. One unpictured deviation may occur just as the company is about to reach BBB, as the controlling shareholders releverage in order to withdraw their equity. Similarly, a fallen angel's downgrading is not irreversible; many "declining" companies have rejoined the investment grade ranks through operational and financial remediation.

larger, its growth rate begins to decline but it finances an increasing portion of its cash needs internally. Having by now survived a competitive shakeout in its industry, the firm enjoys a firmly established earnings base and its profile fits the investment-grade category. Finally, the company reaches maturity. Its market saturated, the mature firm posts real revenue increases in line with population growth. In time profit margins begin to narrow and bond ratings slip from the high to the low end of the investment-grade category. If the company fails to find new opportunities for growth and profits, it eventually recedes to the Double-B category or lower, joining the ranks of the fallen angels. At that point the company again becomes interesting to high yield investors, who long ago took their profits following the company's upgrade to investment-grade and reinvested the proceeds in other rising stars. By repeatedly rolling over their funds into companies bound for the high-grade world, shrewd investors can supposedly earn significant capital gains on top of the lofty yields available on low-rated bonds.

Since everyone likes to root for the underdog, there is an inherent attraction in a strategy oriented toward investment in rising stars. These companies also offer greater excitement than the large leveraged buyouts and recapitalized companies. Serious investors, however, must set aside such emotional considerations. Instead, portfolio managers must ask whether the payoffs from upgrading of rising stars to investment-grade occur frequently enough to have a meaningful impact on portfolio returns. If not, the pursuit of capital gains through investing in the companies of tomorrow should be regarded as a sideline, rather than a central focus of portfolio strategy.

The Cold, Hard Facts

Instead of allowing the rising star premise to remain widely accepted on the strength of its superficial plausibility, we decided to test it against the facts. Using Standard & Poor's corporate bond data base, we counted the number of original issue high yield companies[3] with straight public debt for each year from

1976 to 1986 (Exhibit 9–2). In this period, the ranks of such companies rose from 49 to 328 as new issuance of speculative-grade debt soared.

We next recorded, year-by-year, the number of companies that first came to market as speculative-grade issuers, then later rose to investment-grade. As shown in the "upgrades" column, on a weighted average basis just 1.8% of the rising stars made it to investment-grade annually during the period. In some years, the portfolio manager seeking an upgrading gain was looking for the proverbial needle in a haystack; the rate was a mere 0.3% in 1986 and not one company in the S&P data base made it to investment-grade in 1978.

Advocates of the rising stars might respond to these statis-

Exhibit 9–2
Credit Performance of the Rising Stars

		Upgrades** to Investment Grade		Defaults	
Year	Outstanding*	Number	%	Number	%
1976	49	4	8.2	2	4.1
1977	67	2	3.0	5	7.5
1978	165	0	0.0	0	0.0
1979	190	4	2.1	1	0.5
1980	212	4	1.9	1	0.5
1981	212	5	2.4	2	0.9
1982	232	8	3.4	9	3.9
1983	265	5	1.9	8	3.0
1984	314	4	1.3	4	1.3
1985	259	4	1.5	11	4.2
1986	328	1	0.3	18	5.5
Total		41	—	61	—
Average	208.5	3.7	1.8	5.5	2.6

Sources: Standard & Poor's, Morgan Stanley & Co. Incorporated.
*Number of companies that were rated lower than BBB- when they first issued straight public debt.
** To avoid double counting, affiliated companies were counted as a single observation.

tics with a shrug of their shoulders. So what if the buyer strikes gold only on rare occasions? The periodic bonanzas are nice nonetheless and in the meantime the investor has the patriotic satisfaction of lending to the entrepreneurs who are restoring America's economic vigor. Unfortunately, portfolio managers render this service at considerable risk to their performance. Exhibit 9–2 also shows the annual default experience among original issue high yield companies and it is higher (2.9% weighted average for 1976-86) than the rate of upgrading to investment-grade. (Equity ownership, while certainly a strong managerial motivator among the rising stars, is no guarantor of solvency. Malcom McLean held 90% of McLean Industries when it defaulted in 1986.)

In terms of impact on returns, the figures in Exhibit 9–2 translate as follows: For a passively managed portfolio consisting of all original issue high yield companies, the order of magnitude of expected annual incremental return from upgrades into the investment-grade category is 50 basis points. Defaults, on the other hand, may be expected to reduce returns by an amount on the order of 135 basis points. (For the assumptions underlying these estimates see the Technical Note at the end of this chapter.)

Admittedly, a skilled portfolio manager may achieve better credit experience than the market average. It is realistic to hope to avoid most of the defaults (although not all of the preceding price deterioration) through close monitoring of the credits and a strong selling discipline. Still, it is daunting to realize that far from riding an inexorable tide of improving credit quality, the buyer of small companies with high operating risk is in reality swimming against a current in which the cost of defaults is more than twice the reward for upgrades to investment-grade. Why, after a decade of brisk high yield new issuance, have not greater numbers of rising stars followed the script by reaching the Triple-B tier?

The Spirit is Unwilling

At least part of the explanation is that many of the entrepreneurs who control these companies have no interest in obtaining investment-grade ratings. If their companies grow to a scale that could justify upgrading from Double-B, their instinct is to take out their equity, possibly to sink it into some new venture. This is the mentality of the real estate developer and the oil wildcatter (which are in fact the backgrounds of many of today's foremost corporate raiders). Their strategy is to use "other people's money" aggressively, to borrow against a successful current project to fund the next one, and to leverage scarce capital as much as possible.

Since the beginning of 1987, there has been ample evidence that the mindset of many high yield issuers is far removed from working patiently toward entering the ranks of high-grade companies. Despite much talk of "equitization," releveraging has been in vogue and, if anything, has become more tempting since the October 19, 1987 stock market debacle made shares cheaper to reacquire. During 1988, for example, AMC Entertainment and Bally's Grand launched major stock buybacks. Prominent firms such as Triangle Industries and International Controls initiated going-private transactions, while Stone Container leveraged up to acquire Southwest Forest Industries.

The rising stars' unfortunate tendency to view balance sheet strengthening as a temporary condition in need of amelioration is no novelty, however. Even the modest upgrading rate shown in Exhibit 9–2 overstates the extent of entrepreneurial aspirations to high credit quality. Of the 41 companies that Standard & Poor's elevated to investment-grade over 11 years, 15 (or 37%) rose as a direct consequence of being acquired by higher-rated companies, rather than through their own efforts. (One company, Warner Communications, accounted for two of the upgradings, having relapsed to speculative-grade in 1983 after first reaching investment-grade in 1979.)

Rebounding Angels

A further indication that many small companies care little about rising to investment-grade is the contrast that their record presents with the experience of the fallen angels (Exhibit 9–3). Although on average there were three times as many original issue high yield companies as fallen angels with debt outstanding during 1976-86, the number of fallen angels that recovered to investment-grade in those years nearly equaled in absolute terms the number of successful rising stars. On a weighted average basis, 5.2% of fallen angels annually straightened out and flew right back to investment-grade, versus just a 1.8% success ratio for the rising stars. This is surprising since according to the business life cycle hypothesis, the rising stars, with their bright prospects and their lean, hungry managers, should have found it easier to reach investment-grade than the fallen angels, which supposedly had their best years behind them.

The difference between the two groups' success was apparently not a matter of potential, but rather of desire. We can hypothesize that the fallen angels' managers, having been associated with the companies prior to downgrading, viewed ownership of an investment-grade rating as the normal state of affairs. Restoration of an investment-grade bond rating (a prerequisite for selling commercial paper to most institutions) was a key element in many companies' turnaround plans. Original issue high yield companies' managers, on the other hand, had never suffered the indignity of banishment from the elite ranks of investment-grade issuers. For these bootstrappers, deleveraging meant tying up more personal wealth in exchange for moderately cheaper access to the capital market (which they required only very occasionally). On the whole, there was little in the rising star psyche to cause a yearning for investment-grade ratings, an impression affirmed by the 1976-86 experience.

Exhibit 9–3
Credit Performance of the Fallen Angels

		Upgrades** to Investment Grade		Defaults	
Year	Outstanding*	Number	%	Number	%
1976	15	1	6.7	0	0.0
1977	14	4	28.6	3	21.4
1978	77	2	2.6	2	2.6
1979	72	4	5.6	0	0.0
1980	81	2	2.5	2	2.5
1981	72	1	1.4	0	0.0
1982	70	1	1.4	3	4.3
1983	76	5	6.6	1	1.3
1984	80	5	6.3	2	2.5
1985	72	5	6.9	1	1.4
1986	89	7	7.9	7	7.9
Total		37	—	21	—
Average	65.3	3.4	5.2	1.9	2.9

Implications for Investors

Although the statistics we have presented may shatter some illusions, they do not in any sense undermine the rationale for investing in the high yield sector as a whole. The market has been efficient over the long term in providing returns (including capital gains on upgrades to investment-quality) commensurate with risk (defined as volatility, which includes default losses).[4] There are, however, implications in the data presented for choices of securities within the high yield universe.

One key implication is that an investment in a rising star must be fully justified on the basis of yield to maturity, with additional gains viewed as potential windfalls. It is quite speculative to factor into projected returns an expectation of a sizable gain through upgrading to investment-grade. A portfolio manager can, however, take into account the possibility of more modest profits deriving from improved short-term earnings prospects, events that would not warrant significant upgrading.

The credit experience of rising stars further suggests that an investment organization must take a hard look at its own research resources when it comes to considering small issuers that are not actively covered by Wall Street analysts. If there were truly an upward bias in the credit quality of the rising stars, as the business life cycle hypothesis suggests, then it might be defensible to go after the premium yields available on relatively obscure companies, even if it meant stretching research capabilities to the limit or slightly beyond. That strategy is not justified by the facts, however. In the bond market, unlike the world of fairy tales, when you wish upon a star—even a rising star—your dream does not always come true. Like a bolt out of the blue, releveraging may regrettably undo credit quality improvement just as upgrading to investment-grade appears imminent. Defaults, in contrast, will generally not occur quite so unexpectedly, but avoiding them (or even the sharp price deterioration that usually precedes them) requires regular, thorough credit reviews of each name in the portfolio.

For many institutions, the labor costs of that vigilance may exceed the yield advantage available on obscure rising stars. Where this is the case, it is advisable to give up some yield and concentrate on the inherently less research-intensive core holdings, i.e., the most soundly financed of the large, diversified leveraged buyout/recapitalization names, which are actively followed by a number of Wall Street credit analysts.

For investment organizations that have sufficient research capabilities, however, the relative lack of Wall Street coverage creates opportunities in the smaller companies. Similarly, price movements in these issues are likely to show pronounced volatility, since they do not have multiple market makers. This can lead to sizable trading profits for investors who can keep abreast of credit changes. (Wide bid/asked spreads somewhat limit this profit potential, to be sure.)

Portfolio managers who wish to leverage analytical expertise to exploit opportunities in rising stars should recognize the importance of taking profits when an issue has had a good run. As shown by the data presented above, there is no assurance that an improving trend will continue to the maximum payoff that results when a company reaches investment-grade, which dramatically broadens the universe of potential buyers and therefore sharply narrows the issuer's spread versus high-grades.

Technical Note on Assumptions for Return Calculations

Calculation of Expected Impact on Returns of Rising Star Upgrades to Investment-Grade and Defaults

Average Coupon of S&P High Yield Universe	10 ⅞%[1]
Average Maturity of S&P High Yield Universe	10 years[2]
Beginning Yield to Maturity	14.50%[3]
Beginning Price	81.176[4]
Yield Following Upgrade to BBB	10.25%[3]
Price Following Upgrade to BBB	103.844%[4]
Price Following Default	38.9[5]

Portfolio Impact of Upgrades to Investment-Grade

Capital Gain × Percentage of Portfolio Upgraded = Percentage Increase in Value of Portfolio

$$\left(1-\frac{103.844}{81.176}\right)\times 1.8\%^{6}$$

$$= 27.9\% \quad \times 1.8\% \quad = 0.50\%$$

$$= 50 \text{ basis points}$$

Portfolio Impact of Defaults

Capital Loss × Percentage of Portfolio Defaulted = Percentage Decrease in Value of Portfolio

$$\left(1-\frac{38.985}{81.176}\right)\times 2.6\%^{6}$$

$$= 52.0\% \quad \times 2.6\% \quad = 1.35\%$$

$$= 135 \text{ basis points}$$

[1] Rounded to nearest eighth.
[2] Rounded to nearest year.
[3] Based on market level at time of study.
[4] At yield to maturity indicated.
[5] Average for 1974-1986.
[6] From Exhibit 9–2.

Endnotes

[1] See Chapter 10, "Divisional Buyouts: Why Purchasers and Sellers Can Both Win."

[2] This subsector is sometimes labeled "emerging growth," a misappropriation of nomenclature in our opinion. Not all firms that initially borrow as high yield companies are enjoying rapid growth in sales. We further object to indiscriminate use of the term "emerging growth" on the grounds that it has a positive connotation for investors. Dennis G. Sherva, writing in *The Financial Analyst's Handbook* (Dow Jones-Irwin, 1987), sets fairly stringent criteria for characterizing emerging growth companies as desirable equity investments, to wit:

- Earnings per share growth rate of at least 20% per annum over the next five years.
- High operating or pretax profit margins.
- High return on shareholders' equity so that as much growth is internally financed as possible.
- Clean balance sheet with little or no debt.
- Conservative accounting practices.
- Leadership position (number one or two) in the industry, product or market served.
- Exceptional management to handle sustained, rapid growth.
- Annual sales of $10 to $100 million.

Precious few original issue high yield companies meet each of these standards. "Rising star" is no less value-loaded than "emerging growth," but we have chosen to use the term for the very reason that we intend (as the punctuation mark in our chapter title suggests) to question whether the companies' rise is as irresistible as the label suggests.

[3] Defined as companies (as opposed to individual issues) that were rated below BBB- when they first issued public debt.

[4] For confirmation that the high yield sector is not below the capital market line, see Martin S. Fridson and Michael C. Heaney, "High Yield Bonds versus Common Stocks: Risk Adjustment and Inter-Market Valuation," *High Performance* (June 1987): pp. 4-9.

CHAPTER 10

Divisional Buyouts: Why Purchasers and Sellers Can Both Win

The issuers of high yield bonds have diverse origins. At one time, investors thought of the market as being composed of just two subsectors—"rising stars" and "fallen angels." As high yield bonds became the financing vehicle of choice for megamergers, a distinct new category of issuer developed. Too large and too well-established to be classified as rising stars and, unlike the fallen angels, downgraded to speculative-grade because of changes in capital structure rather than deteriorating profits, the leveraged buyout and recapitalized firms quickly won favor because of the large float and liquid markets their bonds enjoyed. Yet another category of high yield issuer was created by high-stakes litigation, which the plaintiffs' bar had perfected by the early 1980s. Companies embroiled in health-related class action suits, or facing massive claims in cases involving patents or disputed contracts, could suddenly find themselves rated below investment-grade solely because of legal risk, even though both their profits and their balance sheets remained strong. Finally, there is a subsector of the high yield market that, while it has not been as widely recognized or publicized, is differentiable in several important ways from the other groups we have enumerated—divisional buyouts. A divisional buyout occurs when a corporation sells a business unit to an investor group that typically includes the unit's senior management.[1] In some cases, a major new company is created as the investment group simultaneously purchases operations in the same or related businesses from several corporations.

Divisional buyouts display some of the other high yield categories' most favorable characteristics, without sharing all of their shortcomings. Like a rising star company, the typical divisional buyout is led by managers who have a large, direct ownership stake in the firm's profits, and therefore a strong motivation to be more aggressive and harder-working than they would as hired hands within larger corporations. Unlike some rising stars, however, divisional buyouts are generally not cash-hungry operations in high-growth, low-predictability industries. Instead, they tend to arise from the desire of large corporations to divest mature, non-core businesses that do little for their stock prices, yet generate stable cash flow capable of supporting highly leveraged capital structures. In a similarity with leveraged buyout firms, managers of divisional buyouts are free of the short-term pressures of the public equity market, and therefore able to make decisions that best serve their firms over the long term. (Admittedly, many of these companies urgently need to generate cash in the early years to pay down debt, but they have no reason to produce artificial accounting profits through economically unsound decisions.) While divisional buyout bonds generally do not enjoy the same degree of secondary market liquidity as bonds issued in the larger leveraged buyouts and recapitalizations, this disadvantage is offset by higher yield.

Appealing as these characteristics may be, however, divisional buyouts raise one fundamental doubt. If the division's management is buying the operations from a large corporation at an attractive enough price to permit servicing of a heavy debt load, as well as an attractive return to the equity investors, why is the large corporation selling? Perhaps high yield buyers are being tricked into lending to perennial cellar-dwellers being cast off by their parents.

It is certainly conceivable that some division-sellers are trying to palm off on gullible lenders the problems they have failed to unload to other corporations or through initial public offerings. The plausibility of this scenario, however, merely reaffirms the importance of selectivity, a principle that applies in all sectors of the high yield market. It makes no more sense to invest in any and every divisional buyout than it does to lend to every oil wildcatter who struts into town or every steel mill operator with a proud past and empty pockets. However, just as those industries—even at their lowest points—contained some viable companies, divisional buyouts often prove highly profitable to fixed income investors. This does not occur only when a wily investor group outwits a major corporation at the bargaining table. In reality, there are several reasons why corporations can benefit from divisional selloffs that leave something on the table for the acquirers and their lenders. The reasons involve trends in American corporations that place overriding strategic importance on certain divestments. While the sellers are not indifferent to getting fair value for their assets, other, more fundamental corporate objectives may dominate their negotiating stances.

Centrifugal Force in Corporate America

Since the early 1980s, while the newspapers and politicians have variously heralded and decried the explosion of mergers and acquisitions (Exhibit 10–1) U.S. corporations have, with much less fanfare, concurrently stepped up the pace of divestments. (Exhibit 10–2). Is it mere chance that companies are discarding businesses with greater frequency, or can we discern fundamental economic causes which impel them to the separation?

Paradoxically, perhaps, the surge in merger activity is itself a contributor to the divestment boom. With more of their stock in the hands of impatient, performance-driven institutional money managers, and with the Justice Department taking a relatively benign view of mergers, major corporations have increasingly realized that they could become targets of hostile tenders.

Exhibit 10–1
Mergers and Acquisitions

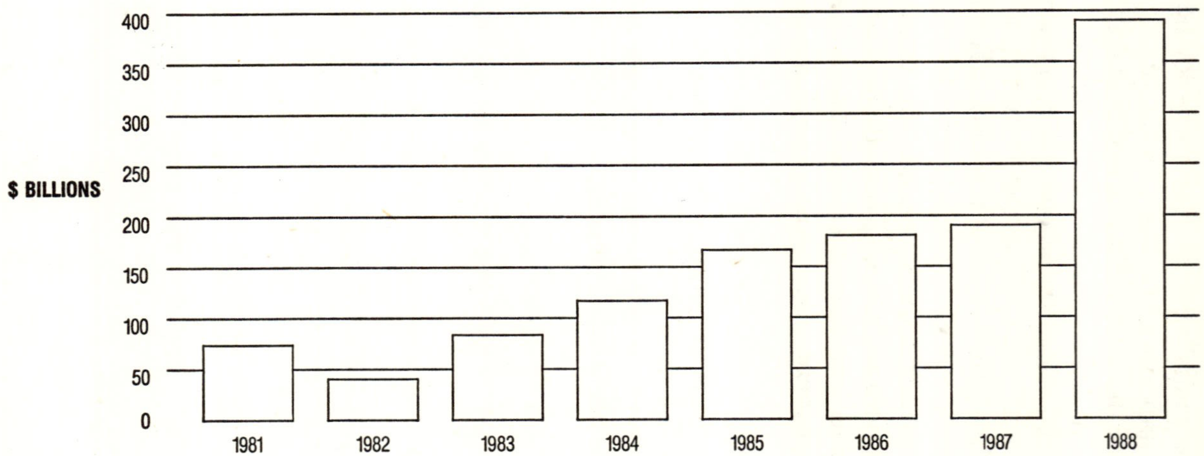

Source: Morgan Stanley & Co. Incorporated
Based on announced deals having an aggregate value of $35 million or more

As corporations have gobbled up one another at an increasing rate . . .

Exhibit 10–2
Announced Manufacturing Divestments

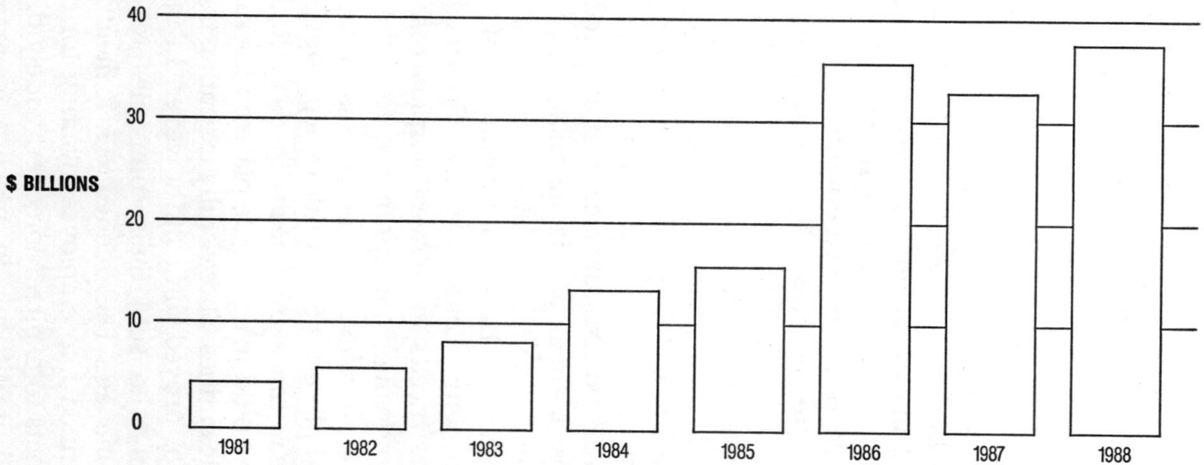

Source: Morgan Stanley & Co. Incorporated

. . . they have also stepped up their selling of non-strategic operations.

Whether to preempt or to foil takeovers, many companies have taken defensive steps that lead directly to divestments. The potential victim may, for example, defend itself by making a major, debt-financed acquisition of its own. By increasing its size, the company reduces the number of bidders capable of attacking it, while also eliminating unutilized debt capacity that a raider could use to finance a takeover. If an acquisition of exactly the desired size is not readily available, the defense may entail a bigger purchase (and more borrowing) than is needed to get out of danger, followed by a sale of non-core operations to raise cash for debt retirement. Alternatively, a company worried about hostile tenders may try to beat the bust-up artists to the punch by divesting units that are not operationally linked to core operations. An even more emphatic response to the threat of takeover is to preclude the possibility entirely by going private in a leveraged buyout. To bring down debt following an LBO, a company may sell businesses that, while readily separable from the rest of the corporation, have produced satisfactory profits and would not be sold in the absence of a financial restructuring.

Divestments are not only side effects of mergers and antitakeover defenses, but also symptoms of investors' disenchantment with conglomerates. Spawned by mature manufacturers' needs to reinvest surplus cash flow, widely diversified companies once promised to make two plus two equal five for shareholders. The premise was that the stock market would place a higher value on a portfolio of companies, selected so as to cancel out one another's cyclical earnings patterns, than it would in aggregate place on the same companies as stand-alone entities. Successfully executing this theoretically sound concept proved difficult, however. In many cases, the entrepreneurs who sold their companies to conglomerates stayed on to manage. They tended to lose their zeal when they were transformed into employees waiting for their non-compete agreements to expire. Moreover, widely diversified companies found it difficult in practice to manage disparate operations effectively. Neither a small staff with decentralized decision-making nor extensive controls (and attendant overhead) at headquarters produced the promised synergy. Eventually, the conglomerates found Wall Street valuing the whole as less than the sum of the parts. If the bust-up artists did not get to them first, they narrowed their focus through divestments.

Vertical Vertigo

The divestment boom can be viewed as an unwinding not only of conglomeration, but also of an older business strategy—vertical integration. Like a conglomerate, a vertically integrated company makes sense on paper. By producing its own raw materials, the reasoning goes, a manufacturer can reduce its costs by the amount of its former outside suppliers' profit margin. Likewise, a producer of intermediate goods can guarantee a captive outlet by acquiring a producer of end products. Just as many logically conceived conglomerates failed to live up to their promise, however, vertical integration has in many instances become an outmoded strategy.

Eliminating the middleman's profit helps a manufacturer only if there is in fact a profit to be eliminated. Nowadays, many raw material and intermediate product industries are mature, low-barrier-to-entry businesses with excess capacity. Manufacturers that years ago bought out suppliers in hopes of obtaining a competitive edge in material costs now find themselves with hundreds of millions of dollars trapped in operations that drag down their overall return on assets. In aluminum, which developed as an integrated industry, Alcoa now finds it attractive to concentrate in higher-value-added fabricated products, relying increasingly on others to supply ingots, which carry thin margins.

Vertical integration can also prove counterproductive when a manufacturer's employees are covered under a master labor contract. In the 1987 auto industry bargaining, Ford benefited from having boosted its reliance on outside components suppliers. The number-two automaker was able to grant increased job security to workers in its assembly operations, while still benefiting from aggressive cost-reduction efforts by its parts suppliers. General Motors, which produces a larger portion of its own components, had a more difficult time in the negotiations. In the end, the company accepted sizable wage increases in exchange for flexibility in divesting parts plants that make the automaker high-cost if they remain under master contract restrictions.

Parenthetically, labor contracts have been a key factor in another type of corporate fragmentation, the creation of short-line railroads from portions of the larger trunk lines. Freed from highly restrictive work rules, the short lines have some hope of competing with the trucking industry.

As for the captive market strategy, manufacturers often find that their management skills do not extend to retailing. Some leading computer producers have launched—only to abandon—efforts to sell directly to consumers through computer stores. Southland, a convenience store retailer with substantial gasoline sales, tried to back-integrate into petroleum refining by buying a state-of-the-art refinery with capacity below that of its 7-Eleven stores' gasoline volume. The company reasoned that it could keep the refinery perennially running flat out, thereby reducing the refining business's notorious cyclicality, and buy its excess requirements from others. Unfortunately, refining margins were subsequently squeezed to such an extent that high capacity utilization was not enough to prevent losses. Southland found that during a glut, a captive supply is a liability, rather than an asset.

But Why Sell to Management?

It should by now be clear to the reader that the corporations contributing to the divestment boom have powerful economic motives for selling. They are saddled with acquisition debt, scorned by equity investors who assign low multiples to conglomerates, and determined to dismantle outmoded vertical integration strategies. With such strong impetus behind the sellers, it is not surprising that the buyers can negotiate attractive terms.

What is not apparent from the foregoing discussion, however, is the rationale for selling to management. One might think that the divesting corporation could obtain a higher price by putting its unit up for competitive bids from other, well-heeled corporations. Alternatively, taking a division public is a way to get a good price if there are no obvious buyers in the corporate sphere.

While these options may be preferable in some instances, a sale to management has advantages that make it the best choice in others. Michael R. Vetsuypens, Assistant Professor of Finance at the Edwin L. Cox School of Business of Southern Methodist University, suggests several benefits of the divisional buyout as a mode of divestment.[2] First, the value created by the divestment is likely to be greater if decision-making authority is transferred to a group of managers in close touch with the marketplace, and able to respond quickly to business opportunities, rather than to another remote corporate headquarters. In addition, giving operating managers a more direct equity stake in the performance of their unit increases their incentive to perform, an effect that is not achieved by selling the unit to another multidivisional corporation. In contrast to the public offering option, the divisional buyout provides benefits through equity participation by third-party investors who specialize in such transactions. These investors have a strong incentive to monitor management closely and prod it to good performance, since any debt-servicing problems that arise will damage their reputation with lenders and impair their future dealmaking capability. Furthermore, buyout specialists can add value by introducing skilled managers with whom they have worked in previous transactions as advisors to the newly independent firm.

In view of the advantages enumerated by Vetsuypens, it is reasonable to conclude that in some cases, a divisional buyout will create a more efficient firm than will a sale to another corporation or to the public, and will therefore permit a higher price to be paid to the divesting firm. (Vetsuypens's study, by the way, finds no evidence that sales to management result in stock price losses for divesting company shareholders, despite the relative absence of the arms-length bargaining that characterizes sales to other corporations. If anything, divesting company shareholders experience modest stock price gains in such circumstances.)

Picking up on Vetsuypens's point about the value of introducing managerial expertise into a firm, we perceive the impact of increased merger activity on senior executive employment as a catalyst for divisional buyouts. When two competing firms merge, one chief operating officer, one chief financial officer and one head of marketing are likely to become redundant. Indeed, one important motive for industry consolidation is to achieve economies of scale in corporate overhead. The resulting availability of proven managers with many productive years ahead of them facilitates the creation of new firms from divisions of several large corporations.

In this type of multiple-division transaction, the buyouts can create value by effecting an industry consolidation that would not otherwise occur. Suppose, for example, that a particular chemical is produced by divisions of several major chemical companies. Assume further that no producer has more than a small share of the market and that industry capacity significantly exceeds demand. With no firm in a position to exert price leadership, price competition is intense and returns are below what the producers earn on their other product lines. Prevailing antitrust guidelines would permit some consolidation, i.e., a combination of the divisions of certain firms, which would lead to firmer pricing. Unfortunately, no firm desires to increase its investment in this product line, which has only modest growth potential. On the other hand, no firm is willing to alleviate the overcapacity problem by simply shutting down its operations, which would necessitate a substantial writeoff. All producers are consequently destined to continue earning unsatisfactory returns unless something breaks the impasse. That something can be the formation of a new company to acquire the divisions of two or more competitors. As long as the sellers receive prices equivalent to the depreciated value of the assets (which may be far below replacement cost), they avoid writeoffs and increase their average return on investment. As the agent of consolidation, the buyer can look forward to better profitability than existed when the industry was more fragmented. Moreover, a private firm is less concerned about reported earnings than a public company, and therefore is in a better position to relieve overcapacity by shutting down redundant facilities, even if a writeoff is required.

Opportunity Knocking

The divisional buyout's prospects may be improved further if there are investment opportunities that the previous owner has not chosen to exploit. If, as we have assumed, a division has only modest growth potential, a public company driven by pressure to produce steady earnings-per-share increases will view it as a source of funds, rather than an area for reinvestment of cash. Funding of high-growth, cash-hungry divisions will take precedence over outlays for cost improvement or incremental capacity additions at a mature division. As a freestanding operation, however, the same low-growth division has an incentive to capitalize on marginal profit opportunities. The private equity holders' objective is not to generate earnings-per-share growth, but to pay off debt through cash flow. Essentially, the equity investor in a divisional buyout firm is in a position analogous to that of a homeowner who is paying down a mortgage. As more debt is paid off, the owner's small wedge of equity (the down payment in the homeowner's case) increases. In a divisional buyout, the equity investor liquidates debt through cash generated by the business, and for an original stake of perhaps 10% can ultimately wind up owning 100% of the firm's asset value. Opportunities to increase cash flow at the margin accelerate the debt paydown, and are therefore attractive, even though to the previous corporate owners they were not worth pursuing. The difference between the value of incremental investment opportunities to a multidivisional corporate owner and to a private equity investor is another reason why both buyer and seller can correctly perceive that they have made a good deal in a divisional buyout.

In a similar vein, competitive considerations may prevent a multidivisional corporate owner from exploiting opportunities that a private owner would pursue. For example, a beverage company that produces its own metal containers might be able to fill unused capacity by selling cans to competitors. The firm may feel ambivalent about gearing up a salesforce to seek outside business, however, while engaged in a fierce competitive struggle, requiring all its spare investment dollars, in the beverage business. If the beverage maker concludes that the capital it has tied up in the canning operations could be deployed in a strategically superior way within the core beverage business, it may withdraw its capital via a divisional buyout. The new, private equity holder will feel no reluctance to solicit business from all beverage companies, thereby increasing capacity utilization and cash flow. The seller may, if it so desires, contract with the buyer for supply of its future can requirements so that the benefits of vertical integration will not be entirely lost. A lock-up arrangement of this sort can also be advantageous to the newly formed divisional buyout firm, since it reduces uncertainty about future revenues. Once again, the divisional buyout is a mutually beneficial transaction, rather than a zero-sum game in which one party must get the better of the other.

Accept No Substitutes

Granting, based on the foregoing arguments, that a divisional buyout group can fashion an economically sound enterprise without having to outsmart a large and sophisticated corporate seller, the high yield portfolio manager nevertheless faces a challenge in distinguishing good deals from counterfeits. For instance, there is a difference between a non-core division with unexploited opportunities and a division that has been deliberately milked for cash to the point where it is technologically too far behind its competitors ever to catch up. Likewise, investors should not confuse entrepreneurial buyouts with bailouts of outmoded manufacturing facilities by coalitions of labor unions and local governments motivated primarily by a desire to preserve jobs. The latter sort of venture may succeed, but is inherently riskier than a divisional buyout arranged by professional investors and managers who see a chance to make huge capital gains.

This is not to ignore the benefits of giving middle- and lower-level employees an equity stake in a bona fide divisional buyout. The venture's success may depend on retaining plant managers and skilled workers, which equity participation can facilitate. Bond buyers should ordinarily expect, however, to see no more than 10% of a buyout's stock distributed to all operating employees, with the bulk of the shares concentrated in the most senior managers' hands.

A final analytical issue involves transitional period captive contracts, discussed earlier in the beverage can illustration. The degree of comfort that lenders can derive from such arrangements varies with the specific contract terms. A division setting out on its own may lock in a specified volume of sales to its former parent, thereby assuring a revenue stream and reducing risk to lenders. In addition, the agreement may include ceiling and floor prices, which limit the risk to both buyer and seller. Not all contracts include price limits, however. In any event, the arrangement typically terminates before the divisional buyout bonds mature, so the portfolio manager must be confident that the borrower will ultimately be competitive and able to service its debt without a guaranteed outlet for its goods.

Conclusion

A business operation can have widely dissimilar values in different contexts. It may be worth more when combined with one or more competitors than as a lone player in a highly fragmented industry. It may be worth less to a multidivisional company that has more pressing investment needs than to an entrepreneur eager to exploit all of its profitable opportunities. The business may have greater value with workers who have an equity stake in lieu of a union contract that imposes costly, inflexible work rules.

Investors who understand this principle will recognize value that is invisible to others who operate under the assumption that one side always wins in a negotiation. It is valid, and indeed necessary, to ask about any divisional buyout, "If this is such a good deal for the group that is buying the company, why is the seller willing to sell so cheaply?" There is no shrewdness, however, in dogmatically disbelieving that the answer can ever be that the price is attractive to both parties.

Endnotes

[1] Technically, the business unit may be a subsidiary (i.e., a corporation), rather than a division (a business unit with no separate legal status). Throughout this chapter and the next, we use the term "division" to refer to both types of entities.

[2] Michael R. Vetsuypens, "Management Buyouts of Divisions: Managerial Discretion and Shareholder Wealth," September 1987.

CHAPTER 11

Divisional Buyouts: The Capital Gains Kicker

The preceding chapter discusses certain advantages of the subcategory of high yield bonds known as divisional buyouts. Like the "rising stars" (small, high-growth companies), divisional buyout firms have the favorable characteristic of being run by managers who are motivated by substantial equity stakes. Unlike many rising stars, however, divisional buyouts are not voracious cash-users in volatile businesses, but mature companies with predictable cash flows. In common with leveraged buyouts, privately owned divisional buyouts enjoy insulation from short-term pressure to maximize reported earnings, allowing them to make decisions that best serve investors' long-term interests.

In early 1988 it became apparent that there was one more excellent reason for high yield bond buyers to invest in divisional buyouts—the chance to realize substantial capital gains. During the period there were two dramatic illustrations of the impact of acquisition by a larger, higher-rated company.

Accuride

Formed through a buyout of Firestone's truck wheel and rim operations, this company issued 13 ½% senior subordinated notes due December 1, 1996 on June 30, 1987. On March 7, 1988 the company was acquired by Phelps Dodge, a copper producer then rated Baa2/BB+ that was eager to reduce its commodity price sensitivity by becoming more involved in metal fabrication. After examining its options, Phelps Dodge elected to tender for the Accuride bonds. From 100 at the issue date to the 116 3/8 tender price as of the March 30, 1988 expiration date, the Accuride 13 1/2s provided a total return (nonannualized) of 24.75%. Over the same period, the high yield market as a whole returned 5.70%.

Cain Chemical

The ethylene, high-density polyethylene and ethylene glycol facilities of several major chemical companies composed the assets acquired in this 1987 divisional buyout. On April 14, 1988, less than a year after Cain's inception, Baa2/BBB Occidental Petroleum's offer to buy the chemical producer was accepted. In recognition of the implicit credit support of an investment-grade parent, Moody's upgraded Cain's 12 7/8% senior subordinated notes due June 30, 1997 from B2 to Ba1 on April 28, 1988. Standard & Poor's followed suit on May 12, 1988, raising its rating from B- to BBB-. Investors who bought the 12 7/8s at issue (June 29, 1987 at 100) realized an 18.27 % nonannualized total return through May 2, 1988, when the bonds were quoted at 108 1/4 . The high yield market's return for the same period was 6.24%. Later in the year, Occidental gave Cain bondholders an additional bonus by tendering for the issue at 108.88 and paying $20 per bond to obtain a covenant modification.

Blind Luck or Shrewd Insight?

In our estimation, the large bondholder gains produced by Accuride and Cain Chemical are not simply examples of dumb luck. Rather, the payoffs demonstrate that divisional buyouts have an inherent propensity to produce exceptionally favorable outcomes for bondholders. Not every deal will match the returns of

Accuride and Cain, but a portfolio that emphasizes divisional buyouts stands an excellent chance of outperforming the market. This is so because the preferred end-game strategy of the principals in a divisional buyout is likely to be selling out to a larger (and probably higher-rated) company. In general, this approach has more favorable credit implications than alternative means of cashing out the equity investors, such as releveraging the company, or going public without simultaneously and significantly reducing debt.

Several factors make selling the company a more logical option for divisional buyouts than for other types of high yield companies. For one thing, managers who come out of a large corporate structure may be more willing to reenter one than an entrepreneur, who built a company from scratch, will be to sell to a big firm and stay on as a manager. Furthermore, the equity holders, who include institutional investors and possibly an investment bank, are likely to favor selling out to a larger company, which allows them to take out all of their equity. In contrast, the alternative of an initial public offering (IPO) may enable them to sell only a portion of their stake. The IPO market may be able to absorb only a fraction of the owners' shares, so the investors may have to liquidate their holdings over time, pursuant to Securities and Exchange Commission Rule 144, or wait for subsequent registration statements to be filed covering their resales. A final reason that selling the company is likely to be the end-game strategy is that divisional buyout firms come in more affordable-size pieces ($135 million in Accuride's case and $1.25 billion in Cain's) than the larger leveraged buyouts. Occidental Petroleum, with a $14 billion capitalization, was able to absorb Cain without damaging its bond ratings. In contrast, any of the bigger LBOs would carry such a large price tag and bring so much of its own debt into the equation, that the acquirer would face a high risk of being downgraded, thereby reducing or wiping out any capital gains potential for the divisional buyout debt holder.

A Chance to Participate

One additional reason for portfolio managers to favor divisional buyouts is that they offer a chance to share in the issuer's upside. This is significant because to many buyers, the risk-sharing in a typical high yield financing seems inequitable. Bondholders take a chance that the issuer will default but in the event that the issuer thrives, they can generally look forward to nothing better than getting their money back on schedule. They may even *lose* value if the equity holders cash out through a releveraging.[1] Because divisional buyouts have a propensity to get acquired by larger companies, however, a better outcome is likely for bondholders.

A company that acquires a divisional buyout firm has a limited number of options with respect to the acquired company's bonds. It can assume or guarantee the debt, thereby causing it to be upgraded. As the acquired company's ratings cross the investment-grade/speculative-grade frontier, a dramatic narrowing of yield spreads occurs, producing a substantial capital gain. Alternatively, the acquirer can decline to guarantee or assume the divisional buyout firm's bonds, but even in that case some upgrading will probably result. Standard & Poor's tends to evaluate related companies on a "whole-enterprise basis," often rating an unguaranteed subsidiary at the same level as its parent, even though the subsidiary might not warrant as high a rating on a stand-alone basis. Moody's, too, normally gives some weight to implicit credit support in the absence of an absolute legal obligation. As a final option, the acquiring company can retire the acquired company's debt, possibly in order to cancel restrictive covenants. Assuming the bonds are protected by early redemption restrictions, the acquiring company will have to offer some inducement (i.e., a capital gain) to obtain bondholders' approval.

By whichever of these routes the capital gain comes about, a divisional buyout bond offers fixed income investors genuine upside along with credit characteristics that provide better-than-average downside protection. Over time, that combination represents a reliable recipe for superior performance.

Endnotes

[1] The complaint about uneven treatment may be justified with respect to the structures of some deals. On the other hand, bondholders should acknowledge that their truncated upside is in some measure offset by their power to accelerate debt payments (and effectively force the issuer into bankruptcy) when their equity cushion is dissipated. Thanks to this mechanism for preventing further erosion of assets, bonds have historically recovered to more than 40% of their principal value within a short time after default. Equity holders, in contrast, can in theory lose their entire investment and do in fact sometimes recover only a nominal amount in bankruptcy court. Bondholders may decide that in a particular issue the tradeoff between limited upside and downside protection is unfavorable. As a rule, though, they cannot truthfully claim that they have only downside and the equity holders have only upside.

CHAPTER 12

Does Legal Risk Belong in a High Yield Portfolio?

The scene is a high yield portfolio manager's office. As she sifts through a stack of telephone messages, her eye is caught by the underscored phrase "17.50% yield to maturity" on one slip of paper. Examining the message more closely, she discovers that it concerns an offering of bonds of Amalgamated-United Corporation, a $1 billion-net worth manufacturer that was rated Single-A until last year, when a $2 billion judgment against the company was awarded in a product liability civil suit. Although Amalgamated-United's operating earnings have remained rock solid, the rating agencies have downgraded the company to Single-B to reflect the potential wipeout of its equity.

Intrigued by the yield, some 500 basis points higher than on other Single-B paper she is seeing, the portfolio manager calls the salesman who is showing the bonds. After some good-natured banter, the discussion turns to business, specifically to the risk that the lawsuit might bankrupt Amalgamated-United. The salesman is, as always, well-prepared and sincere. "The market and the rating agencies have overreacted, as usual," he explains. "It's obvious to me that the verdict will be overturned. Amalgamated-United has been cleared of identical charges in a criminal case, so the company will eventually win, based on the same facts, in civil court. Our analyst has calculated that even if the verdict stands, the damages will be reduced to something less than the company's $200 million of insurance coverage. The actual damages suffered by the plaintiffs were clearly nowhere near $2 billion. Sally, I've been selling high yield bonds for 10 years. Take it from an old pro—this one's a layup."

While Joe relates his story, the portfolio manager's mind is racing ahead. "I can't believe there's no risk whatsoever in this situation, but at a 17.50% yield I'll be well compensated. And since I have two seasoned credit analysts working for me, I'll surely be alerted if the situation starts to turn for the worse. Single-B paper is our bread-and-butter—our track record proves that we understand this sector. It looks like Joe has come up with another winner for us. Let me see if I can bid him down a little."

* * *

If the proposed transaction takes place, it may work out favorably for the portfolio manager, but it is questionable whether she has correctly assessed the risk of buying a company that could be bankrupted by a lawsuit. The trap here is in reasoning that because Amalgamated-United is rated Single-B, and the portfolio manager's mandate is to invest in speculative-grade bonds, Amalgamated-United is automatically a candidate for purchase, given sufficiently high yield.

In reality, a speculative-grade rating is about all the fictitious manufacturer has in common with the rest of the high yield universe. Most other sub-investment-grade companies are in the low-rated category because they have either high operating risk (rising stars and fallen angels) or high financial risk (leveraged buyout/recapitalized companies). Experienced analysts are surely competent to assess these risks, since they have previously studied many closely analogous situations. The nature of operating and financial risk, moreover, is that external developments (surging interest rates, declining business activity) tend to foreshadow severe deterioration well in advance of default. Admittedly, not all adverse credit developments are foreseeable, but the portfolio manager can hedge the random risk elements through broad diversification. In contrast, the sample of public debt issuers that have been bankrupted through lawsuits is still rather small, so there are few comparable situations from which to infer reasonable risk premiums. Legal risk, moreover, tends to disprove the adage that "companies do not go bankrupt overnight," a generally true statement in the realm of operating and financial risk.

Diversification potential, furthermore, may not be adequate for many investors' purposes, since at any one time there are few "life-or-death" issuers awaiting legal decisions that will either force them into Chapter 11 or return them to investment-grade. Given these attributes, bonds that are rated below investment-grade solely because of legal risk should be regarded as a subsector entirely distinct from the rest of the high yield sector, and perhaps one to be avoided altogether as a matter of policy.

An investor who understands the portfolio implications of taking legal risk, and nevertheless wants to participate in the sector, should seek better advice than the typical bond salesman can provide. For that matter, the typical credit analyst will not add much value, for he has the same handicap that the salesman has—a tendency to apply common sense to legal proceedings. Anyone who has been personally involved in a lawsuit knows there is no assurance that the obvious, logical and fair resolution will be the outcome. A decision that the layman perceives as a perversion of justice does not necessarily signify that the courts are corrupt or that a fast-talking lawyer has bamboozled the jury. Instead, a paradoxical verdict can be the natural result of legal procedures that have evolved out of centuries of efforts to balance legitimate, contending social needs. Without knowing the full background, the non-lawyer often finds the consequences of courtroom protocol incomprehensible.

The law's curious logic is illustrated by an old joke about a lawsuit seeking a million dollars in damages, alleging that the defendant broke an antique vase loaned to him by the plaintiff. The defendant's lawyer presents three defenses:

1. "My client never borrowed the vase."

2. "The vase was already irreparably damaged when my client borrowed it."
3. "My client returned the vase in perfect condition."

Clearly, if any one of these three defenses is valid, the other two are patently false. Nevertheless, in a lawsuit of this kind, it is quite reasonable to expect all three defenses—as well as others—to appear. The principle of "inconsistent pleading," which allows such carryings on, has little to do with ordinary notions of justice and fair play, but is the staff of life to litigators.

The Wrong Arm of the Law

In the foregoing Amalgamated-United vignette, Joe, the self-styled legal advisor, opined that the facts that cleared the defendant of criminal charges must ultimately exonerate it in the civil trial, too. Had the salesman actually attended law school, he would have learned that the standard of proof is much higher in a criminal case than in a civil case, and thus successfully defending criminal charges is no guarantee of success in the civil forum. In the *Corrugated Container* suit, centered in Houston, Texas during the late 1970s and early 1980s, the primary issue was an alleged price-fixing scheme involving numerous manufacturers and distributors of cardboard boxes. A grand jury was empaneled and criminal indictments were handed down. Many defendants named in the indictments pled out, that is, settled their (criminal) differences with the government. Mead Corporation, however, refused to settle, vigorously defended itself and was ultimately acquitted. Unfortunately, Mead's victory in the criminal case apparently made the company overconfident about its chances in the related civil cases, where a less stringent standard of proof was required for plaintiffs to succeed. Mead again elected to have its day in court while 35 other defendants settled for a total of $300 million. This time Mead lost. In cases such as *Corrugated Container* a defendant is "jointly and several-ly" liable, meaning that Mead could be held accountable for all of the damages caused by its 35 alleged co-conspirators. Furthermore, plaintiffs in antitrust suits are entitled to treble damages. In the debacle, Mead was judged liable for total industry damages of $335 million, trebled to $1 billion, less the $300 million settlement already agreed to by the other defendants. The $700 million net judgment represented about 80% of Mead's net worth at the time. From this greatly weakened position, Mead eventually salvaged a $45 million settlement, far more than it presumably could have settled for before trial.

In a similar vein, Ford Motor Company successfully defended itself against criminal charges that the location of the Pinto's fuel tank in the rear had caused the model to explode on collision. The verdict was of no avail in civil cases, however, and a jury awarded $120 million (later reduced on appeal to $6 million) in damages to the estate of just one victim. Plainly, uninformed advice about the law's peculiar workings can seriously distort an investor's perception of risk.

Incidentally, common sense might indicate that had Ford, subsequent to the Pinto accident but before the trial, redesigned the Pinto by moving the engine to a safer location, the plaintiff could have introduced the redesign as evidence that Ford acknowledged the old Pinto's hazard. Common sense would err, however, for our society has decided that there is an overriding need to avoid chilling a manufacturer's desire to improve the safety of its products as soon as defects become apparent. If such improvements could be used against the manufacturer in a trial, remedial safety measures would come slowly, if at all. By such subtleties, unknown to many who are nonetheless only too eager to dispense free legal advice, does the law overturn commonly held notions of justice.

More Classic Blunders

Returning once more to the Amalgamated-United discussion, we find that the securities analyst, who, unlike Joe, holds a postgraduate degree (although not in jurisprudence) and is a

Chartered Financial Analyst to boot, has run the facts through his HP-12C and concluded that the damages will not exceed $200 million. In December 1984, Wall Street analysts went through a similar exercise, calculating the potential damages arising from Union Carbide's accident in Bhopal, India on the basis of expected lifetime earnings of the victims. By this reckoning, the company's liability appeared to be less than its purported insurance coverage. "A ludicrous overreaction," chorused the analysts when investors chopped Carbide's market capitalization by $300 million. Ludicrous or not, the first three days' response was followed by a further $100 million reduction in market capitalization over the next two days. Accustomed to believing that everything can be quantified and translated into earnings per share, the analysts had gotten the less important part of the story (i.e., the standard for calculating compensatory damages), but neglected the potentially much larger punitive damages. (At least $40 billion of claims were eventually filed on behalf of plaintiffs.) Other examples of amateur malpractice included bald misstatements ("The Bhopal plant is 51% owned by the Indian government.") and erroneous expounding of legal principles ("A parent company's liability is always limited to its equity investment in the subsidiary."). In this crisis, analysts did not inscribe a proud chapter in the annals of securities research. Moreover, there is no assurance that they have learned their lesson and will refrain from venturing beyond their field of expertise in the future.

If salespeople and analysts lack the knowledge to provide reliable research on legal risk, is the solution then to seek the advice of lawyers with long experience in litigation? Unfortunately, even getting good legal advice may not reduce legal risk exposure to an acceptable level, barring the opportunity to spread one's bets over several different companies. The surprise element is such a high factor in the courtroom that the most capable handicappers' prognostications can easily go awry.

This is illustrated by an episode in the criminal trial of former General Motors executive John DeLorean on charges of drug dealing. During the jury's deliberations, one juror asked for a clarification of the correct procedure in the event of the jury's failure to achieve unanimity. The judge merely directed the jury to read his charge (the instructions given at the conclusion of testimony). Unfortunately, while the charge specified that a verdict of either "guilty" or "not guilty" required a unanimous vote, it did not make clear the third possibility—a "hung" (undecided) jury, which results in a retrial. The DeLorean jurors were in fact split, and aware that they could only convict the defendant by a unanimous vote, they returned a "not guilty" verdict. Later, as the judge was entertaining the dismissed jurors in his chambers, a juror asked, "What is a hung jury?" The judge explained that this meant the jury was deadlocked and that the case must be retried. Responded the juror, "That is what we were, but we thought we therefore had to find him not guilty." Stunned, the judge, along with the prosecutor, sought to reconvene the jury, but it was too late and the verdict stood.

No matter how well versed in litigation, an analyst could not have foreseen the DeLorean case's outcome. This sort of unpredictability raises questions about the wisdom of adding a single legal risk issue to an otherwise logically constructed high yield portfolio.

Empty Threat or Empty Bag?

If Joe the bond salesman is reading this chapter, he is probably about to play his trump card. "Despite all your examples, you should not talk my customer out of buying Amalgamated-United bonds," says Joe. "None of the companies you've mentioned went bankrupt. Sure, the nervous Nellies dumped Union Carbide, but the bonds bounced back as they always do. Too risky? Ha! The real risk is in staying out while your competitors load up and wait for the market to come to its senses."

Contrarianism certainly has its merits, but Joe's argument merely shows that 10 years of experience in high yield bonds may be a liability in certain respects. When he entered the busi-

You Be the Judge!

Investors who try to analyze legal risk may be tempted to apply common sense to courtroom proceedings. This can be hazardous, as the following quiz demonstrates.

1. *A jury empaneled to hear a complex case involving unfamiliar corporate law is ordinarily permitted to take notes and to carry a copy of the judge's instructions into the jury room.*

   True_____ False_____

2. *Just as a "not guilty" verdict in a criminal case is inadmissible in a related civil case, a "guilty" verdict in a criminal case has no effect on the outcome of a related civil suit.*

   True_____ False_____

3. *Acme Corp. contracts with Wiley Co. to supply birdhunting equipment, and the contract is dated June 30, 1987. On July 1, 1987 Acme's president writes an internal memo detailing to his staff the terms and meaning of the contract. If Acme and Wiley end up in litigation over the contract, the memo will be inadmissible as evidence to prove the meaning of the contract.*

   True_____ False_____

4. *If the defendant in a criminal case has previously been convicted of a brutal assault, the prosecution is free to introduce this information at the trial.*

   True_____ False_____

Answers at end of chapter.

ness, it was an accurate perception that lawsuits presented little bankruptcy risk. Claims were often astronomical but settlements usually proved minuscule and the bondholder was paid well for keeping a cool head while others panicked over Love Canal and Agent Orange.

The 1978 Bankruptcy Act reform began to alter conditions, however. No longer was insolvency a prerequisite for seeking protection under Chapter 11. Corporations did not change their behavior overnight, but in 1982 Manville filed bankruptcy to escape massive asbestos-related lawsuits. Since then, several other major corporations, including Wilson Foods, A.H. Robins and Texaco, have entered Chapter 11 as a result of litigation. No longer can the battle-scarred veterans complacently invest in companies that are jeopardized by high legal claims, confident that the fainthearted sellers are affording them easy gains.

The Distribution Counts, Too

"All right," says the indefatigable bond salesman at this point, "I may have inadvertently overstated the case when I said lawsuits never put companies out of business. But you have to admit that the market prices this kind of risk inefficiently. At the first whisper of default, certain institutional portfolio managers bail out at any price they can get. Their risk/reward preferences are skewed by irrational compensation plans. If they improve performance by taking more risk, they get a 5% bonus; if they hold a bond that defaults, they get fired. Naturally, this kind of incentive system is sometimes going to make bonds available at unjustifiably cheap prices."

Joe is getting closer to the truth now, but his latest argument can be challenged on two grounds. First, it is impossible to say whether the market prices legal risk efficiently, since the sample size of litigation-related defaults is so small at this point. Second, only a portfolio manager who is comfortable with the distribution of potential returns can consider a bond cheap, no matter how high the yield.

In point of fact, many portfolio managers are likely to be uncomfortable with the probable return pattern of a legal-risk bond. Exhibit 12–1 represents the distribution of one-year returns on a 10-year bond that has an equivalent chance of defaulting, experiencing no change in perceived risk, or passing the crisis and once again being regarded as investment-grade. The analysis assumes that a bond with these characteristics will be priced at a 20% yield to maturity, and filters out any effect of interest rate fluctuations.[1] In the stable scenario, the return (20.00%) is well above the 12.00% going rate on Single-B paper. If the litigation is resolved favorably, the bond returns to its former investment-grade valuation and the bondholder's courage is rewarded by a spectacular 74.35% total return. Total return in the default scenario, -5.07 %, is cushioned by the bond's 34-point discount at the beginning 20.00% yield to maturity, but is nonetheless a highly undesirable outcome. For many portfolio managers, the wide range of potential returns, and the comparatively high probability attached to the worst-case scenario, will outweigh the potential payoff on being right. Buying a single legal risk issue may not be appropriate for such investors. In particular, managers of smaller portfolios will have difficulty with the volatility that is likely to characterize the price behavior of a bond that will either go bankrupt or be upgraded. Whereas 10 core names (i.e., large-capitalization, industry leaders downgraded solely because of financial restructuring) may represent satisfactory diversification and generate acceptably steady returns in a $50 million high yield portfolio, introduction of a legal risk bond that fluctuates five points each time a new motion is filed could produce more excitement than the portfolio manager needs.

If (and it is a big if) there are as many as five "life-or-death" legal-risk bonds in the market at a given time, and they are involved in totally unrelated litigation, the return distribution improves for investors willing to participate in this subsector (Exhibit 12–2). The probability that one issue will default

Exhibit 12–1
Distribution of Expected Returns: One-Bond Legal Risk Portfolio

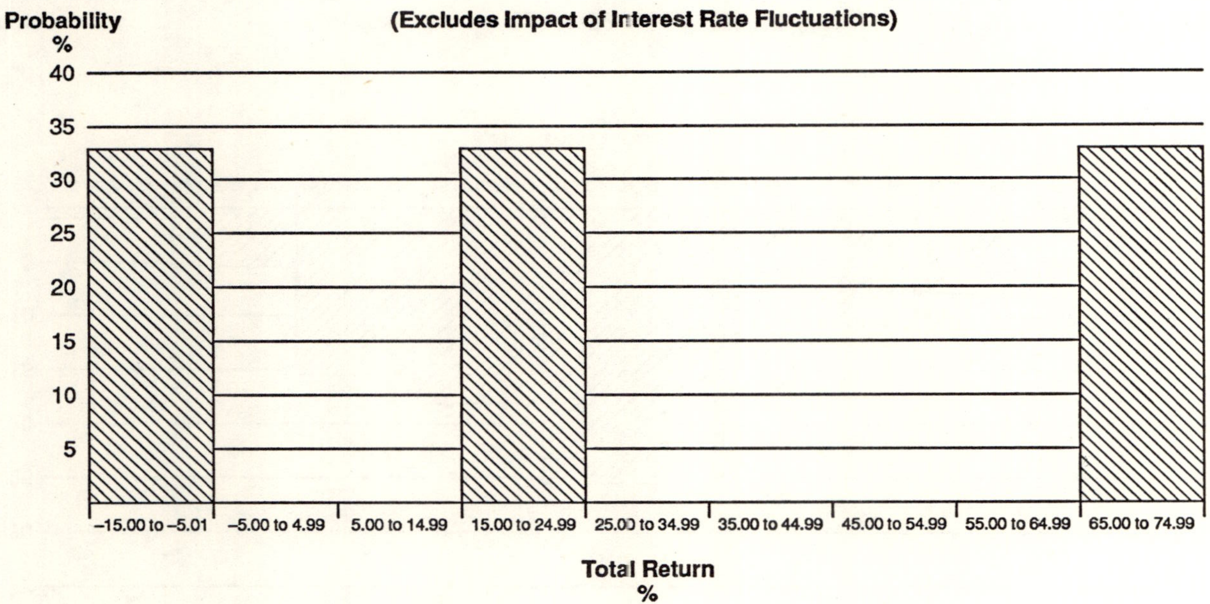

Horizon	One Year
Coupon	12%
Maturity	10 Years
Beginning Yield to Maturity	20.00%
Beginning Price	65.957

Scenario	Ending Yield/Rice	Total Return	Probability
Default	N.M./50.000	-5.07%	⅓
Stable	20.00%/67.211	20.00%	⅓
Improve	10.00%/111.668	74.35%	⅓

Exhibit 12–2
Distribution of Expected Returns: Five-Bond Legal Risk Portfolio

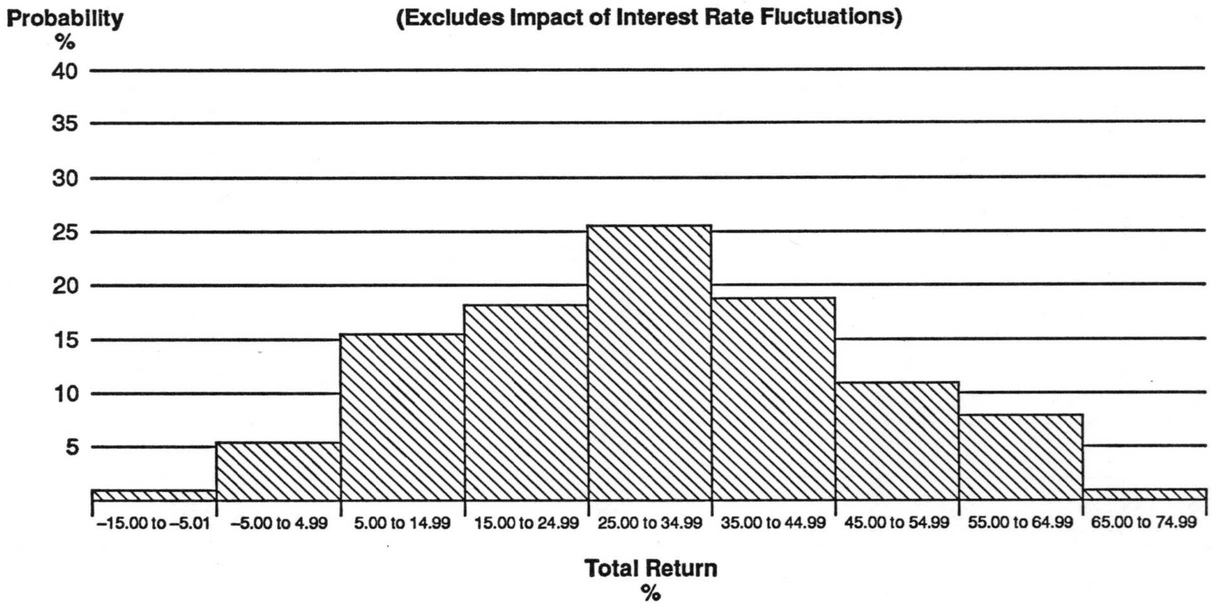

Horizon	One Year
Coupon (each of five issues)	12%
Maturity (each of five issues)	10 Years
Beginning Yield to Maturity	20.00%
Beginning Price	65.957

Scenario	Ending Yield/Rice	Total Return	Probability
Default	N.M./50.000	-5.07%	⅓
Stable	20.00%/67.211	20.00%	⅓
Improve	10.00%/111.668	74.35%	⅓

remains one-third, but the probability that all five issues will default is just 0.5%. Likewise, the best possible outcome, improvement at all five issuers, is extremely improbable. Potential outcomes cluster in the middle ranges; there is a 76% probability that the investor will earn a return in the range of 15.00% to 54.99%.

Although the diversified legal risk portfolio's return pattern is superior, it is also quite hypothetical, since life-or-death situations are comparatively rare. Some portfolio managers will still prefer the return pattern of a more conventional high yield portfolio, depicted in Exhibit 12–3. In this analysis, a diversified portfolio of 10-year bonds begins and ends the period at a 12% yield-to-maturity, a level representative of Single-B issues with "normal" (i.e., not heightened by pending legal claims) default risk. The default losses subtracted from the 12.00% total return that would otherwise result are based on actual 1977-1986 experience. (Each historical year's loss rate is assigned a 10% probability, notwithstanding the fact that past experience may not be indicative of future results.) Investors adopting this strategy can expect an even tighter distribution of returns than the diversified legal-risk approach provides. For many, the conventional high yield portfolio's greater predictability will outweigh its much more limited upside.

Conclusion

Does legal risk have a legitimate place in the typical high yield portfolio? Aggressive investors can make a case that it does, based on Exhibits 12–1 through 12–3. Even an undiversified, single-bond position in the subsector promises to add substantial return to a diversified portfolio, without creating intolerable incremental risk. Starting with a portfolio that would otherwise return 11%, the addition of a 1% exposure to a legal risk issue will (if the assumptions underlying Exhibit 12–1 are correct) reduce overall return to 10.84%, increase it to 11.09% or increase

Exhibit 12–3

Distribution of Expected Returns: Diversified, Non-Legal Risk High Yield Portfolio

(Excludes Impact of Interest Rate Fluctuations)

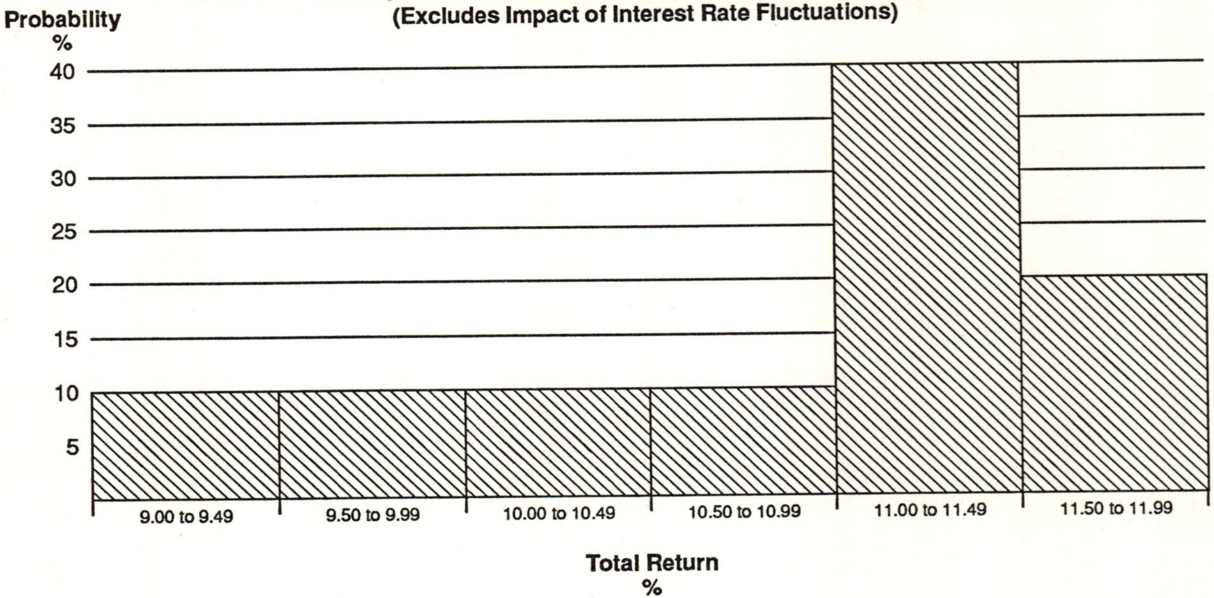

Horizon	One Year
Coupon	12%
Maturity	10 Years
Beginning Yield to Maturity	12.00%
Beginning Price	100.00

Default rates are annual figures reported for 1987-1986 in Edward I. Altman, *The Anatomy of the High Yield Debt Market* (Morgan Stanley & Co. Incorporated, April 1987) p. 15.

Default loss calculation assumes price of 40 post-default and loss of one coupon upon default.

it to 11.63%, all with equivalent probabilities. A five-issue position (if obtainable) with a 5% weighting poses only a 3% probability of cutting the 11% expected return to 10.45% or less, and a 38% probably of raising it to at least 12.29%. Moreover, our colleague Richard Bookstaber has observed that a legal risk bond may represent a desirable diversification for a high yield portfolio, since it will have little covariance with other issues that are vulnerable primarily to business cycle and industry-specific dangers.

The potential rewards of investing in legal risk bonds are not without costs, however. Unlike the slow deterioration that afflicts most eventual corporate bankrupts, issues that default because of litigation may file Chapter 11 suddenly, with no evidence of imminent insolvency to warn investors. The trigger may be nothing more than a board of directors meeting convened to explore alternatives presented by counsel. Investment committees may take a dim view of portfolio managers who step into immediate catastrophes, notwithstanding fancy rationales involving return distributions and risk/reward optimization. Portfolio managers may even be judged imprudent if found, subsequent to sustaining a bankruptcy, to have been ill-equipped to analyze the special category of risk responsible. As demonstrated by the numerous examples cited above, few investment organizations (buy or sell side) are competent to assess legal risk, nor will even qualified attorneys necessarily succeed in predicting the outcome of a particular trial. In short, the decision to dabble in legal risk should rest on more than a tempting yield and the well-intentioned advice of a poorly informed salesman or analyst.

Answers to Quiz

1. ***False.*** *Some judges permit note-taking nowadays, but the old rule, which still widely applies, prohibits it on the reasoning that a juror might become confused and copy testimony incorrectly*
2. ***False.*** *A defendant who is convicted of a criminal charge is "collaterally estopped" (prevented) from disputing his guilt in any civil suit involving the same nexus of facts.. The judicial system long ago decreed that if one is found guilty*

under the more stringent criminal standard, legal resources will not be wasted in relitigating the same issue under the easier civil standard.

3. ***True.*** *The Parol Evidence Rule provides that except under certain enumerated circumstances, a court may not look further than the four corners of the contract itself to ascertain the meaning of its terms.*
4. ***False.*** *The prosecution can introduce evidence related to a defendant's previous misdeeds only if the defendant elects to testify*

Endnotes

[1] Readers should not infer that the 33 ⅓% probability assigned to each of the three scenarios is based on a rigorous empirical study. As already mentioned, the sample size of companies that have defaulted as a result of litigation is small. Despite this limitation, the analysis underlying Exhibits 12–1 and 12–2 should provide a sense of the range and predictability of returns in this subsector.

CHAPTER 13

LDC Debt's Diversification Effect On a High Yield Portfolio

Securitizing commercial banks' loans to less-developed countries (LDCs) is an idea with tremendous appeal to a number of financial intermediaries. For the banks, transforming problem LDC loans into marketable securities would enable them to reduce their exposure by selling assets to risk-oriented institutional investors. Already, there is some capability for commercial banks to trade LDC debt with one another, but without bringing new players into the game, they can at best redistribute the various countries' loans within the same universe of lenders. Investment banks, too, see an attraction in LDC debt. Having profited substantially in recent years from underwriting and trading other kinds of securitized assets, they perceive a vast new opportunity in opening up the institutional market to direct sovereign loans. With over $300 billion of Third World debt outstanding, it is not surprising that Wall Street has already invested considerable time and effort in attempting to overcome barriers to the development of this market.

Obstacles to Securitization

The barriers are formidable, as evidenced by the lack of emergence to date of a securitized LDC loan market, despite protracted speculation in the press.[1] For one thing, some of the sovereign borrowers argue that if their debt is to trade at a discount, they—rather than speculators—ought to capture the discount. Moreover, the debtor government's ability to call its creditors together to negotiate a rescheduling may be reduced if its debt is dispersed among many institutional investors, rather than concentrated in a syndicate of commercial banks. These objections can be critical, since securitization cannot in all probability proceed without cooperation of the borrower, as well as other bank lenders. In the latter case, the objection is that sovereign issuers might be inclined to preserve their reputation in the capital markets by staying current on securitized loans even when compelled to defer interest on their remaining bank debt. Holders of unsecuritized bank loans could then find themselves effectively subordinated.[2] A final obstacle involves commercial banks' regulatory accounting. Unless a bank has already fully reserved for or charged off its loans, selling them can result in a hit to earnings. Because of such constraints as capital requirements, a bank may not be in a position to sell LDC loans when it would be most advantageous, from a market standpoint, for it to do so.

What Will Investors Say?

Assuming that Wall Street's resourcefulness can eventually overcome these obstacles, the final challenge will be gaining acceptance for LDC debt among buyers largely unfamiliar with the product. The most risk-averse fixed income investors are likely to reject the concept out of hand, having read about Third World threats of debtors' cartels and defaults. In some cases, institutional memories are long enough to encompass previous waves of actual—rather than merely threatened—sovereign defaults.[3] As a result, the market for securitized LDC loans will on the first cut be narrowed to institutions that either dabble in or actively invest in high yield corporate securities. Even among these "qualified prospects," moreover, some investors will probably not leap at the opportunity to grace their portfolios with Peruvian and Yugoslavian obligations.

In some cases, institutions' charters will preclude their participation in the securitized LDC debt market. A perusal of high yield mutual fund prospectuses, though, suggests that this large group of buyers will generally not be barred from owning debt of foreign issuers. Some prospectuses are silent on the subject, while others authorize foreign holdings of between 5% and 25% of total assets. High yield funds have in fact been active at times in the volatile Australian-dollar-pay sector, including Australian government securities. Commercial banks and pension funds likewise invest in foreign sovereign credits, as do life insurance companies, subject to "basket" constraints. Thrifts appear to be involved on a more limited scale.

Merely being legally empowered to buy foreign bonds does not automatically result in a portfolio manager's participation. Some investors may allow their knee-jerk xenophobia to override rational economic considerations. (We are reminded in this connection of the backwoods Congressman who, upon being informed during the 1979 energy crisis that a single electric power plant in his district was consuming 100 billion British thermal units daily, indignantly demanded to know why the utility could not instead burn American fuel.) Other portfolio managers may hold off due to their fears of innovation, at least until a few deals have been floated, allowing the "bugs" to be exposed and the secondary market to be tested.

These objections are unlikely to be universal or long-lived, but there is another that will seriously challenge underwriters of securitized LDC debt, namely, investors' self-acknowledged lack of expertise in sovereign credit analysis. Is it prudent, they will rightly ask, to invest in speculative-quality issues without having in-house analysts capable of assessing default risk? Mastering sovereign analysis is not simply a matter of learning a new set of ratios, of looking at external debt as a percentage of Gross Domestic Product instead of calculating cash flow coverage. Rather, one must study the cultural and social context of the unfamiliar numbers, and make judgments about political stability for which one's education and prior experience may be meager preparation. Moreover, a corporate credit analyst newly designated as the house sovereign specialist would probably be operating in an intellectual vacuum; the same individual, if suddenly assigned the retailing industry, might have as a colleague a retailing equity analyst or a one-time retailing credit specialist now serving as a portfolio manager.

LDC Benefits

All of these arguments are valid from the standpoint of fiduciary responsibility. One can counter them, it is true, by pointing out that countries—like corporations—act in their own self-interest, so that they must submit at some level to basic economic analysis. Ultimately, though, there is only one conclusive rebuttal to LDC aversion, namely, that the benefits of owning securitized LDC loans justify the expense of obtaining reliable sovereign credit information, even if that means hiring an experienced sovereign risk analyst.

Just such an economic argument overcame the initial resistance of some high yield investors to electric utilities when, in 1983, that industry began to represent a significant portion of the speculative-grade sector as a result of downgradings. Some fund managers argued that the utilities' continued solvency would be decided in the political arena, rather than in the marketplace. Since their expertise was in the latter venue, they felt unqualified to make credit judgments on the likes of Public Service of Indiana and Consumers Power. As the speculative-grade utility segment grew, however, and yields rose in consequence of several companies reaching crisis points, it became costly to ignore the group. By the middle of 1984, electric utilities were approaching 20% of the high yield universe and were outyielding groups such as basic industry and energy by 175 basis points. In the battle to sell mutual fund shares, waged largely on the basis of current yield, this was too big an edge to concede to the competition, whatever philosophical reservations one might have about nuclear utilities at the mercy of elected officials.

While these economic arguments were sufficient to overcome high yield buyers' qualms about the exotic new variety of securities known as utility bonds, the numbers will have to be even more compelling to entice portfolio managers into the still more exotic LDC sector. It is generally believed that to be salable, securitized Third World loans will have to be priced at a substantial yield pickup to the speculative-grade corporate market. The reasoning is that they will be inherently riskier than conventional high yield bonds. We are unaware of any proof of this premise, but suspect that at least initially it will be widely accepted as investors mistake their own fear of the unknown for objectively demonstrated danger. In these circumstances, LDC bonds may offer excellent investment value, for one of their greatest virtues—their diversification benefit within a corporate portfolio—is likely to be overlooked. This benefit is the positive side of sovereign debt's lack of resemblance to conventional high yield debt. More than that, diversification value may provide the margin that justifies the expense of acquiring expertise in sovereign risk analysis.

By "diversification benefit" we do not mean simply that an institution with 50 high yield holdings can lessen the potential impact of a default by splitting up its funds among 10 additional names. A more rigorous definition involves the salutary effect of reducing portfolio volatility without sacrificing return. Exhibit 13–1 illustrates the basic concept. Securities A and B display a similar degree of price fluctuation, but their price movements follow dissimilar patterns. The different patterns might reflect the fact that the two issuers' earnings are not sensitive to the same economic indicators. By combining the two securities in a portfolio, the investor can benefit from the offsetting impact of their price fluctuations and achieve a comparatively stable principal value (Line A + B). Exhibit 13–2 shows that this idealized portfolio, with securities that exactly cancel out each other's price fluctuations, produces return midway between the returns on Security A and Security B, but with lower volatility—an indisputable benefit.

In contrast to this happy result, combining Securities C and D (Exhibit 13–3) offers no diversification benefit. When C's price rises or falls, D's rises or falls at the same time and by the same amount. Putting the two together produces the same pattern as either security alone produces, so that volatility (Exhibit 13–4) is not reduced as it was in Exhibit 13–2.

Portfolios A + B and C + D represent theoretical extremes on a spectrum from maximum to minimum diversification benefit. In the real world, one does not find securities with perfectly offsetting or perfectly matching price movements, but rather securities that either more closely or less closely track one another's fluctuations. Clearly, though, the rational investor will strive to achieve an effect closer to maximum diversification (Exhibits 13–1 and 13–2) than to minimum diversification (Exhibits 13–3 and 13–4).

The question is whether that objective will best be served by augmenting a U. S. corporate bond portfolio with more U.S. corporate bonds—subject to the same economic and competitive environment as, and issued by, companies that may be suppliers or customers of the companies already represented in the existing portfolio. Alternatively, can diversification be better achieved by adding foreign government bonds, the credit quality of which will be determined by a very different set of factors?[4] Common sense suggests the latter, i.e., that the more effective means of reducing swings in principal value is to buy LDC debt.

There is just one minor obstacle to proving what common sense tells us in this instance—the unfortunate circumstance that there are almost no speculative-quality sovereign bonds trading in today's public market. As a consequence, institutional investors will have to rely on limited and indirect evidence of the diversification benefit of LDC debt if and when they are offered the opportunity of buying it. Our analysis of the available data, however, suggests that acquiring the research needed to support an investment program in Third World

Exhibit 13–1
The Diversification Effect

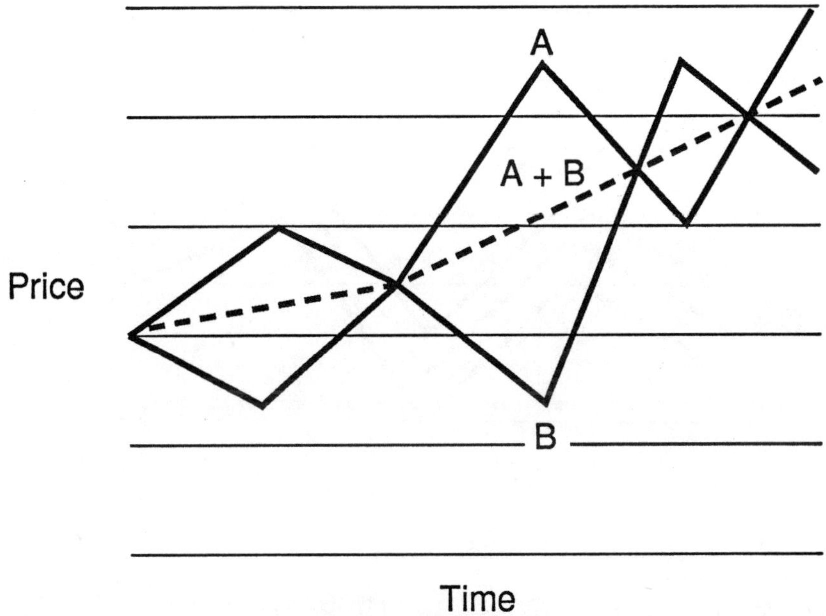

Exhibit 13–2
The Benefit of Diversification

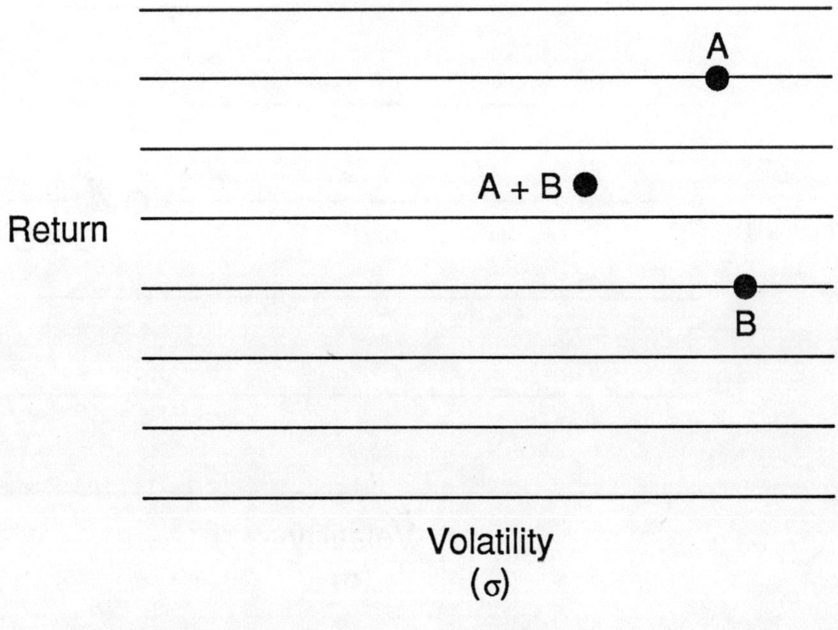

Exhibit 13–3
Non-Diversification

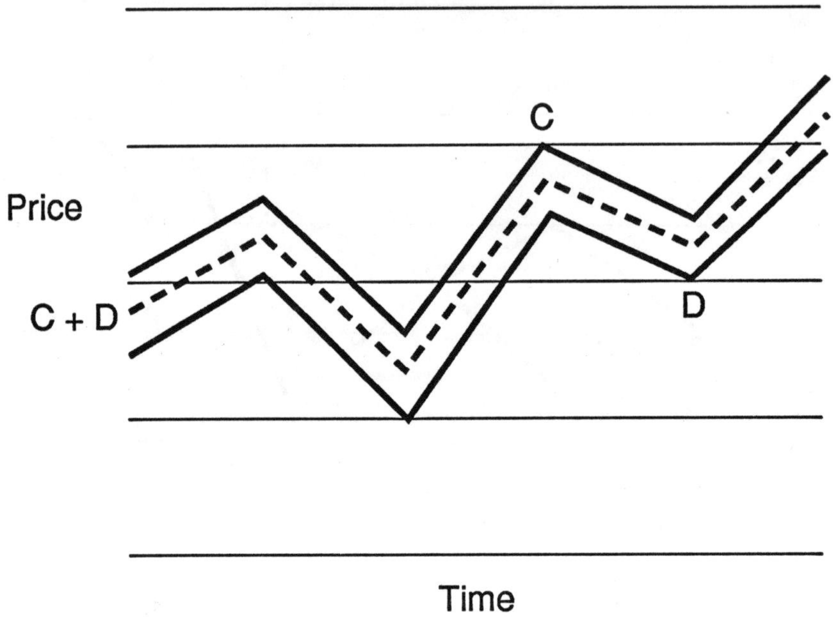

Exhibit 13–4
The Cost of Non-Diversification

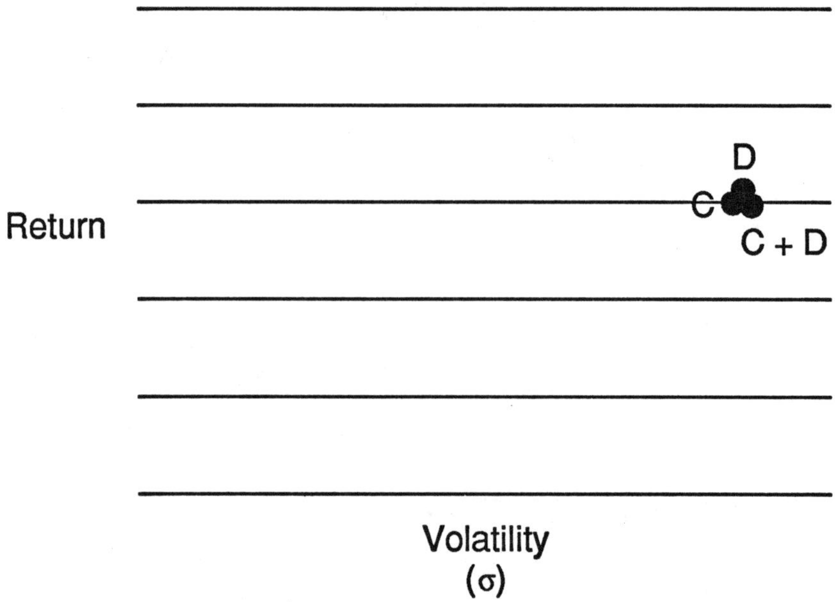

bonds may indeed be economically justifiable in terms of reduced portfolio risk.

Evidence from Bank Loans

The first of two experiments we conducted to test this proposition utilized price data from the secondary market in LDC bank loans.

Banks have for some time been swapping unsecuritized loans among themselves, with several motives in mind. Some banks have wished to rationalize their portfolios, for example, to eliminate small positions that consume large amounts of analytical resources, and to consolidate their holdings into a few core positions. Other swaps have arisen from banks' differing perceptions of risk. Many European banks, for example, have traded their Latin American loans for debt of Poland, with which they feel more comfortable. In addition, banks may take into account their own institutional strengths, ancillary business and political factors. Financial reporting may also play a role in the secondary market for LDC loans. A U.S. bank does not have to disclose its exposure to a particular country unless its loans to that country equal or exceed 0.75% of the bank's assets. Therefore, if one bank has a 1% exposure to Argentina and 0% to Brazil, and another has 0% to Argentina and 1% to Brazil, the two can effect a swap resulting in each having 0.50% exposure to Argentina and 0.50% to Brazil, none of which they will be required to mention in their annual reports.

Exhibit 13-5 lists the countries for which monthly price ranges—expressed as a percentage of face amount—were available for 1986 and 1987. Ranges for December 1987 are shown to provide the flavor of the depth of discounts observed during the full period.

If, as we hypothesize, prices on LDC debt respond to different factors than speculative-grade corporate bonds, then the price changes on an equally weighted index of all 10 countries in our sample should have a low correlation with a representa-

Exhibit 13–5
Sovereign Credits Quoted In Secondary Bank Loan Market

Country	Price Range December 1987*
Argentina	35-38
Brazil	45-47.5
Chile	60-63
Ecuador	34-38
Mexico	51-54
Peru	2-7
Poland	41-43
Romania	81-83
Venezuela	49-52
Yugoslavia	53-55

* Percentage of face value.
Source: Shearson Lehman Hutton.

tive index of lower-related corporates. We tested this surmise by creating a 20-bond high yield corporate portfolio, widely diversified by industry (Exhibit 13–6). Each issue carried a speculative rating throughout the test period and none defaulted. We then regressed the sovereign index's monthly prices (the sums of the medians of the constituent countries' monthly ranges) against the prices of the corporate portfolio (the sums of the medians of the constituent bonds' beginning-of-month and end-of-month prices). As shown in Exhibit 13–7, price changes of the sovereign and corporate portfolios had a correlation (R^2) of 46.2 %, a result that was shown to be statistically significant.This finding supports the hypothesis of a diversification benefit for LDC debt, since by definition any R^2 of less than 100% means that the two samples will to some extent cancel out each other's price movements. What we are more interested to know, however, is whether adding LDC debt provides more diversification benefit than can be achieved by supplementing a high yield corporate portfolio with additional high yield corporates—a strategy that requires no new analytical skills. To this end, we split the corporate portfolio in Exhibit 13–6 into two subsamples, 1 and 2,

Exhibit 13–6
Diversified Portfolio of 20 High Yield Corporate Bonds

Subsample 1

Company	Issue	Industry
Amax	14 ½% Notes due 12/1/94	Metals/Mining
Arrow Electronics	13 ¾% Subordinated Debentures due 3/15/04	Technology
Blair (John)	13 ⅝% Subordinated Debentures due 1/15/98	Media
Castle & Cooke	12% Subordinated Notes due 9/1/91	Conglomerates
Dart Group	14% Subordinated Debentures due 9/15/95	Retailing
Green Tree Acceptance	8 ¼% Senior Subordinated Debentures due 6/1/95	Financial Services
Long Island Lighting	9 ⅝% General & Refunding due 6/1/06	Electric Utilities
Union Carbide	8 ½% Debentures due 1/15/05	Chemicals
Walter (Jim)	10 ⅞% Subordinated Debentures due 5/1/08	Building Products
Western Union	13 ⅝% Notes due 3/15/94	Telecommunications

Subsample 2

Company	Issue	Industry
ANR Pipeline	11 ¾% Debentures due 11/15/97	Gas Utilities
Bethlehem Steel	9% Debentures due 5/15/00	Metals/Mining
General Development	12 ⅝% Subordinated Debentures due 9/1/05	Real Estate/ Construction
Harte-Hanks Communications	14 ⅜% Subordinated Debentures due 11/15/00	Media
MCI Communications	9 ½% Subordinated Notes due 8/1/93	Telecommunications
MGM/UA Entertainment	10% Senior Subordinated Notes due 4/15/93	Leisure
Middle South Energy	15 ⅜% First Mortgage due 5/1/00	Electric Utilities
Pan American World Airways	13 ½% Senior Debentures due 5/1/03	Transportation
Triangle Industries	11 ½% Subordinated Debentures due 9/1/03	Packaging
Wickes Companies	15% Subordinated Notes due 5/1/95	Conglomerates

taking care to maintain industry diversification within each subsample. The results (Exhibit 13–8) are again consistent with our hypothesis. Since the two high yield corporate subsamples show a higher correlation ($R^2 = 68.7\%$) with each other than the LDC index does with the full corporate sample ($R^2 = 46.2\ \%$, above), it appears that LDC debt offers greater potential for diversification of an existing high yield corporate portfolio.

Comparability Questions

Encouraging though these findings may be for proponents of LDC loan securitization, we must qualify our conclusions due to questions of comparability between the instruments being regressed against each other. The high yield corporates in our experiment are actual, seasoned securities. In contrast, the bank loan index is merely a proxy for the securities that portfolio managers will have the choice of purchasing if securitization becomes a reality. Price changes on the LDC debt could show a low correlation with the high yield corporates simply because of structural differences—including dissimilar liquidity and maturities—between the secondary market for bank loans and the secondary market for corporate bonds. Furthermore, as LDC loans are securitized, their maturities and covenants may be altered to conform more closely to the high yield corporate market's norms, and their floating rates fixed, in order to enhance their marketability. Therefore, the instruments that will actually be available in the future may be more similar to, and trade more like, high yield corporates, resulting in a smaller diversification benefit than Exhibits 13–7 and 13–8 imply.

Notwithstanding these valid questions, comparability concerns should not cause the evidence derived from our experiment to be dismissed, for there are mitigating factors.

First, the problem of structural differences between the two markets is not as crippling as it would be if, for example, we were comparing loans to local mom-and-pop businesses, which are not ordinarily sold by the originating banks, and

Exhibit 13–7
LDC Loans versus 20-Bond High Yield Corporate Portfolio
Correlation of Monthly Price Changes: 1986-1987

R^2	0.462
Number of Observations	24
Degrees of Freedom	22

Significant at 99% Level

Exhibit 13–8
Subsamples of 20-Bond High Yield Corporate Portfolio
Correlation of Monthly Price Changes: 1986-1987

R^2	0.687
Number of Observations	25
Degrees of Freedom	22

Significant at 99% Level

U.S. Treasury securities, the market for which represents the ultimate in liquidity. Relative to other types of bank assets, LDC loans have a well-developed, organized market. Admittedly, the quotations often represent "workout prices," and incidents such as Citicorp's $3 billion writedown of its LDC portfolio in May 1987 can temporarily cause liquidity to evaporate. Workout prices and episodes of reduced liquidity (e.g., immediately following disclosure of the Boesky affair in November 1986) likewise characterize the high yield bond market, however. Accordingly, the transfer, through securitization, of LDC debt from the secondary loan market to the public bond market may not change price patterns as greatly as would a migration between two more radically dissimilar markets.

The second mitigating factor that legitimizes our comparison of loans to bonds is that maturity differences are not as serious a problem as might be the case in other subsectors. Consider once more the extreme contrast between local mom-and-pop loans and U.S Treasury securities. The maturity differences between those two debt categories is clearcut. A small bank loan in good standing with a stated maturity of four years can be straightforwardly regarded as a four-year obligation for valuation purposes. Likewise, a 10-year Treasury's term is fairly unambiguous (provided we leave duration out of the discussion) and at the same time critical to its evaluation, since there is usually some slope to the yield curve. Accordingly, if the values of a four-year mom-and-pop loan and a 10-year Treasury failed to move in lockstep, one would have to attribute at least a portion of the discrepancy to the maturity difference, rather than assigning all of it to credit differences.

Once again, though, the objection does not apply so neatly to a comparison of LDC loans and high yield corporate bonds. Whatever their nominal maturities today, LDC loans are surely being evaluated by secondary buyers in the context of the extensions necessitated by the borrowers' difficulty in paying interest, much less retiring principal on schedule. Typical terms on recently renegotiated LDC debt include 20-year maturities, with no principal payments required for the first seven or eight years. In the extreme case, buyers may view LDC loans as perpetuals, in which case current yield alone will determine the discount from face value, and yield to maturity or to average life is irrelevant. As it happens, current yield is also a dominant valuation factor for high yield bonds, despite their explicit maturities. Current income maximizers play a significantly greater role in high yield corporates than in U. S. Treasuries. As a result, two pari passu bonds of a single high yield issuer may trade at the same current yield, notwithstanding different maturities; pure current income maximizers will (at least in theory) arbitrage away even a one-basis-point yield pickup on the longer-term security. In short, high yield issues may trade essentially on a current yield basis only, exactly as they would if they were perpetuals. Since current conditions point to similar treatment for LDC loans, maturity differences do not logically preclude a comparison of the two categories.

Results of one additional test that we ran on the LDC loans and the high yield index lend further support to the view that lack of comparability between the two instruments is not a fatal objection to the conclusions drawn from Exhibits 13–7 and

13–8. We first regressed the previously described LDC portfolio against the price history of a constant-maturity 10-year Treasury[5] and found a correlation of R^2 = 43.8% (Exhibit 13–9). When we regressed the 20-bond high yield corporate portfolio against the same Treasury series, we found a similar correlation: R^2 = 46.1%. LDC loans and high yield corporates, in other words, showed about the same degree of sensitivity to the general level of interest rates, as measured by the Treasury market.[6] This suggests that notwithstanding structural differences between the two types of obligations, they respond similarly to one major determinant of value. Since structural factors do not thwart a common response to a common environmental factor, it is reasonable to conjecture that what is dissimilar in the behavior of the LDC loans and the high yield corporates—i.e., whatever causes the R^2 to be less than 100%—is at least partly related to differences in underlying credit factors, and not solely to structural differences.

Exhibit 13–9
Comparisons with 10-Year Treasury
Correlation of Monthly Price Changes: 1986-1987

LDC Loans versus 10-Year Treasury

R^2	0.438
Number of Observations	24
Degrees of Freedom	22

Significant at 99% Level

20-Bond High Yield Corporate Portfolio versus 10-Year Treasury

R^2	0.461
Number of Observations	24
Degrees of Freedom	22

Significant at 99% Level

Bond Market Evidence

Fortunately, establishing the existence of a diversification benefit in LDC debt does not depend entirely on proving the validity of comparing bank loans and bonds. We were able to derive corroborating evidence from a direct comparison of high yield corporate bonds with a limited amount of LDC debt that is already in the form of a publicly traded bond.

Although the great bulk of LDC external debt at present is in the form of unsecuritized private loans, some issuers, including Mexico, Panama and Venezuela, have outstanding public bonds that are payable in U. S. dollars and are not in default. In most cases, the outstanding amounts are small and pricing histories are too sketchy to permit useful analysis. We did, however, find satisfactory data in *Moody's Bond Record* for the United States of Mexico 8 ⅛% due December 1, 1997. Approximately $21 million of this issue remained outstanding in 1988. It was originally offered to the public in 1972 and is listed on the New York Stock Exchange. Over the period we examined (January 1984 through February 1988), the yields observed for this non-rated issue (12.89% as of December 1987) clearly indicated that the market perceived its credit risk to be in the speculative range.

To test for evidence of a diversification benefit in this sovereign bond, we identified three high yield corporate bonds that were similar in coupon and maturity to the Mexico 8 ⅛% of 1997 (Exhibit 13–10). Correlations between the yields on all four issues should thus have been free—insofar as that is possible—of structural factors and therefore influenced solely by differences in underlying credit factors.

Exhibit 13–11 is a matrix of the individual yield correlations of the Mexico 8 ⅛% with each of the three corporate issues, and of the corporates with one another. Consistent with hypothesis, the LDC issue is less highly correlated with any of the corporates than any corporate is with any other corporate.

As with our findings from the bank loan and high yield portfolio data, these results support the notion that high yield investors can reduce volatility more effectively by adding LDC issues to their existing portfolios than by simply splitting up their holdings among more corporate issues.

For further confirmation, we studied the total return and volatility impact of adding the Mexico 8 1/8% to a portfolio consisting of high yield corporates. Exhibit 13–12 details the results of this final experiment, which studied the period January 1, 1984 through February 1, 1988. During that time, an equally weighted portfolio of the three high yield corporate issues produced a total return of 11.76% and a monthly standard deviation of 0.39. Adding the Mexico 8 1/8% of 1997, also on an equally weighted basis, raised total return to 12.73% while reducing the standard deviation to 0.36. This represents the best possible result—increased return and reduced risk.

Readers should be cautious about extrapolating from such limited data, since it is conceivable that there are individual high yield corporate bonds that would have had a similar impact, by virtue of not following the market's general price pattern. Still, taking into consideration all of the data presented in this article, it is realistic to believe that the chances of finding potent volatility-reducers are greater among the LDC issuers.

Conclusion

Data limitations make it difficult to prove the common sense proposition that high yield corporate portfolio managers can get more diversification benefit by buying sovereign debt than by buying more of what they already have. One of our tests was based on sufficient data but less than perfectly comparable samples, while the other had no comparability problem but less data than we would like. Nevertheless, the findings point in the same direction as our intuition and, considered in their entirety, suggest that LDC bonds will be worth a look if obstacles to their creation can be overcome. Gearing up for a new product is never easy, but with over $300 billion available for securitization, the LDC sector could prove too big and too economically attractive for competitive money managers to ignore.

Exhibit 13–10
Selected High Yield Corporate Bonds
(Approximating Coupon and Maturity of Mexico 8 ⅛% due 12/1/97)

Company	Issue	Industry
Navistar International	8 ⅝% Debentures due 9/1/95	Capital Goods
Sunshine Mining	8 ½% Silver Index Bond due 4/15/95	Metals/Mining
Telex	9% Subordinated Debentures due 11/1/96	Technology

Exhibit 13–11
Mexico 8 ⅛% due 12/1/97 versus Selected High Yield Corporate Bonds Correlation of Monthly Price Changes: January 1, 1984-February 1, 1988

	Mexico 8 ⅛% 12/1/97	Navistar 8 ⅝% 9/1/95	Sunshine 8 ½% 4/15/95	Telex 9% 11/1/96
Mexico 8 ⅛% 12/1/97	1.00			
Navistar 8 ⅝% 9/1/95	0.147	1.00		
Sunshine 8 ½% 4/15/95	0.099	0.455	1.00	
Telex 9% 11/1/96	0.036*	0.583	0.440	1.00

* Not significant.
Figures in matrix represent R^2 for the test period. All results were found to be significant at the 95% level or higher, unless otherwise noted

Exhibit 13–12
Impact of Adding Mexico 8 ⅛% due 12/1/97 to High Yield Corporate Portfolio
January 1, 1984 through February 1, 1988

	High Yield Corporates*	Mexico Bond	High Yield Corporates plus Mexico Bond
Total Return	11.76%	16.41%	12.73%
Monthly Standard Deviation	0.39	0.27	0.36

* Consists of the three bonds shown in Exhibit 13–10.

Endnotes

[1] In speaking of securitized LDC loans, we mean repackaging of loans for sale to institutional investors. We do not refer to "debt-equity conversions," in which discounts on sovereign loans are converted into incentives to make equity investments in the local economy, nor to interbank swaps of loans in their present form. Similarly, we exclude from our definition the swap, organized in 1988 by Morgan Guaranty, of discounted Mexican government bonds for bonds backed by U.S. Treasuries. Indeed, all such credit-enhanced structures are outside the scope of this article, which addresses specifically the notion of bringing institutional investors into the picture as a new category of risk-takers.

[2] Some observers, however, argue that if the sovereign debtor's situation turns truly grim, it will forsake its public holders and concentrate on keeping happy those lenders (i.e., the banks) who are in a position to advance additional funds.

[3] Between 1931 and 1933, every Latin American debtor defaulted, with the sole exception of Argentina.

[4] Admittedly, LDCs' ability to service their debt is not entirely divorced from U.S. economic conditions, since the U.S. is a major trading partner of many of the countries. Furthermore, because LDC debt is typically denominated in dollars and at floating rates, fluctuations in U.S. interest rates have a significant influence on the borrowers' debt-servicing burden. As long as the linkage is looser than the corporate-to-corporate tie, however, LDC debt may have a significant diversification benefit.

[5] Our hypothetical Treasury security was an 8 ½% coupon with a 10-year maturity, priced at the median of the beginning-of-month and end-of-month yield for the benchmark 10-year issue. This mechanism enabled us to regress price versus price, rather than price versus yield.

[6] Readers may find this result surprising, given that the high yield corporates in our sample were all fixed-rate, while LDC bank debt typically floats over the London Interbank Offering Rate (LIBOR). Pricing of the LDC debt may have responded to fluctuating interest rates' impact on borrowers' ability to service or extend existing debt, rather than to the revaluation of coupon that a fixed-rate obligation undergoes.

PART III

Maximizing Performance

CHAPTER 14

A Framework for Forecasting High Yield Performance

Before committing the time required to read an extended essay on maximizing interim performance, the high yield investor will perhaps first ask whether the topic is relevant. After all, high yield bonds' fundamental virtue is their capacity to harness the mighty power of compound interest—a force that, while nearly imperceptible over short periods, overwhelms other investment factors in the long run. Investors with horizons (as distinguished from measurement periods) greater than a couple of years—a group that includes most pension funds, thrifts and insurance companies—can purchase high yield bonds secure in the knowledge that if they can contain default losses within reasonable bounds, the compounding of a yield 400 or 500 basis points above the risk-free rate will take care of returns.[1] As for the high yield mutual funds, are they not primarily vehicles for the income-oriented small investor? Fluctuations in a portfolio's market value ought not to concern the individual whose measure of an investment's success is the size of the monthly check it generates. One might conclude, then, that there is no natural market for a treatise on enhancing interim performance and that the reader will consequently miss nothing of value by skipping over what follows. Besides, even if some investors had valid reasons for trying to beat the averages by actively managing their portfolios, and assuming they could time their trades successfully, they might not obtain any net advantage, given transaction costs in the comparatively illiquid high yield sector.

Notwithstanding these objections, we suspect that most who have proceeded this far will read on, for the reality is that interest in interim performance is intense among high yield investors. On the pension fund side, the ultimate authority for manager selection lies with a corporate chief executive officer who probably got to that position by being a "can do" type. To such a person, recessions and price-cutting competitors are not sufficient excuses for salesmen who fail to meet their quotas, nor are intransigent labor unions and escalating insurance premiums satisfactory explanations from production people who fail to cut costs. Why, then, should a bear market excuse a money manager who fails to minimize the corporation's pension fund contribution? Like it or not, managers of pension money are part of a system that demands that publicly owned corporations produce consistent quarterly performance—a system enforced mainly by (who else?) the pension funds of those same corporations. As for the mutual funds, while their shareholders may say they are looking for income, they select their funds not solely on the basis of advertised yields, but also according to published comparisons of short-term total return. In short, even though the high yield market should by its nature attract investors who are able to take the long view, many participants do not enjoy the luxury of remaining calm in the face of temporary reverses. They must therefore attempt to outperform their peers consistently, recognizing all the while that transaction costs impose a significant handicap.

A Choice of Weapons

Whether resigned to the necessity, or excited by the challenge of attempting to beat the averages, a portfolio manager has only a limited number of ways to succeed. One very effective approach is to successfully avoid an especially large default that depresses everybody else's performance. Unfortunately, one cannot count on such providential calamities to occur frequently enough to confer perennially superior performance on the manager sagacious enough to sidestep them consistently. Interest rate anticipation may be considered by managers who are confident of their abilities in this area, but high yield bonds are not ideal instruments for utilizing these skills, since they do not move in lockstep with the general level of rates over the short term. Arbitrage swapping, to the extent that it is feasible in the high yield sector, is a widely understood technique on which no manager has a copyright. It is therefore unlikely to be profitable enough to produce a major performance advantage over competitors, even though the absolute dollars generated may justify the activity. Similarly, deft flipping of new issues can produce marginal benefits, but is not a unique skill that will vault its practitioners to the top decile. By process of elimination, then, we conclude that asset allocation is the last, best hope for high yield portfolio managers striving to attract new assets through superior performance.

Another chapter in this volume ("Employing High Yield Bonds in a Sector-Swapping Strategy") deals with one variety of asset allocation, namely, the strategic under- or overweighting of industry groups to capitalize on major shifts in the perceived riskiness of broad sectors of the economy. We will discuss here another allocation choice available to the typical high yield manager—the latitude to be fully or less than fully invested in high yield paper.

For institutions such as insurance companies, which are always invested in a variety of financial assets, it is second nature for managers to decide at certain times to be at less than 100% of their limit for low-rated bonds. There is no less of an opportunity for high yield mutual funds to profit by limiting the impact of the sector's inevitable episodes of short-run underperformance, even though their charters direct them to concentrate in speculative-grade issues. The typical high yield fund's prospectus imposes no specific constraints on holdings of investment-grade securities, although some state an intention of investing 80% of assets in low-rated debt. This leeway saves the manager from having to invest cash flow entirely in high yield bonds during periods of scarce supply, when buying them would procure poor value for the fund's shareholders. To illustrate how potent a performance tool this freedom provides, we compared the annualized returns for the first nine months of 1986 of a 10-bond high yield portfolio and a 10-bond Single-A portfolio (Exhibit 14–1). One simple asset allocation decision, a shift from 100% high yield to 75% high yield/ 25% Single-A on January 1, 1986, would have enabled the portfolio manager to outperform the pure high yield portfolio by 128 basis points, before considering transaction costs and the necessity of maintaining a cash reserve.

Description of the Analytical Framework

Investors who are obliged to strive for interim performance, and who agree that manipulating the high yield/investment-grade mix is one of the most likely means of succeeding, face a daunting task. They must forecast the net impact of a myriad of interrelated forces that determine the high yield sector's return over any period. Some of these forces are the result of countless other economic developments, complicated by crosscurrents, as well as new circumstances that render useless any reasoning by analogy with past cycles. To make this chaotic tableau yield to analysis, we must establish some organizing principles. First, lest

Exhibit 14–1
Annualized Total Returns of Selected Portfolios
January 1, 1986 through September 30, 1986

10-Bond High Yield Portfolio	14.44%
10-Bond Single-A Portfolio	19.57%
75% High Yield/25% Single-A	15.72%

Value of Shift from Pure High Yield
to Blended High Yield/Single A:

15.72%
-14.44%
1.28%

our analytical framework become unwieldy, we will not attempt to list every single factor that influences the high yield sector's performance. This will not seriously impair the framework's value, since not every variable is significant. Retrospective analysis of periods in which high yield bonds produced superior or inferior returns generally reveals that just a few factors contributed overwhelmingly to the outcome. Accordingly, we will limit our list of causes to those we believe to have the potential to predominate in future periods. (Even as select a group as this, however, includes some that may be inconsequential in the *current* outlook.) Another organizing principle we have adopted is to treat the high yield sector's performance as largely independent of high-grade returns over short periods. Barring extraordinary swings in the general level of interest rates, we do not believe this approach paints an unrealistic picture. At this point in the high yield market's evolution, many speculative-grade investors can freely move capital into high grades, but relatively few high-grade investors can do the other side of the trade. Therefore, temporary bargains in the low-rated sector will not always be quickly arbitraged away. Empirical research by Bookstaber and Jacob supports our contention that the link between interest rate moves in high-grades and speculative-grades is a loose one.[2] Accepting this feature of the model does not compel the reader to suppose that long-term, secular shifts in Treasury rates, reflecting changes in inflationary expectations, will leave speculative-grade yields unaffected. The relative independence assumption also leaves us free to regard the varying magnitude of the high-grade/speculative-grade yield spread (i.e., the risk premium for speculative-grade) as one factor that will either constrain or stimulate the high yield sector's performance in the period ahead.

Exhibit 14–2 is a rendering of the framework we have devised in accordance with these principles, drawn in the form of a scale. "Supply of High Yield Debt" and "Demand for High Yield Debt" are portrayed as vessels into which dollars are constantly flowing, even as dollars are simultaneously flowing out the other end. A change in the rate of any inflow or outflow, unless offset by some other change in the system, will tip the scale. The scale's arm remains horizontal, with the indicator pointing to "Normal" performance, so long as supply and demand remain in balance. We may define normal performance for the high yield sector as a total return equivalent to the high-grade return plus the promised yield premium, less default losses. Note that there are three cases that produce balance, and hence a normal return:

1. Equivalent Growth, where both supply and demand enjoy net inflows, with neither side growing faster than the other.
2. No Growth, where outflows exactly offset inflows on both the supply and the demand sides.
3. Equivalent Contraction, where supply and demand suffer net outflows, but with neither contracting faster than the other. This case demonstrates the important fact that high yield bonds may produce satisfactory returns even when investors are withdrawing capital from the sector, provided underwriters can close the new issue spigot sufficiently to offset the contraction in demand for high yield debt.

Low-grade bonds produce a "High" return, according to this analysis, when demand grows faster than, or contracts more slowly than, supply. (Note here that demand growing faster than supply does not necessarily imply an acceleration of the inflow of funds into the high yield sector; a deceleration of the outflow will achieve the same result.) If, on the other hand, the growth in supply of high yield debt temporarily overtakes demand, the scale arm tips in the direction of supply and the indicator shifts to the "Low" position, meaning that the high yield sector produces a total return lower than the promised yield premium over high-grades, minus default losses. We expect Exhibit 14–2's greatest value to portfolio managers will be

Exhibit 14–2
A Framework for Forecasting High Yield Performance

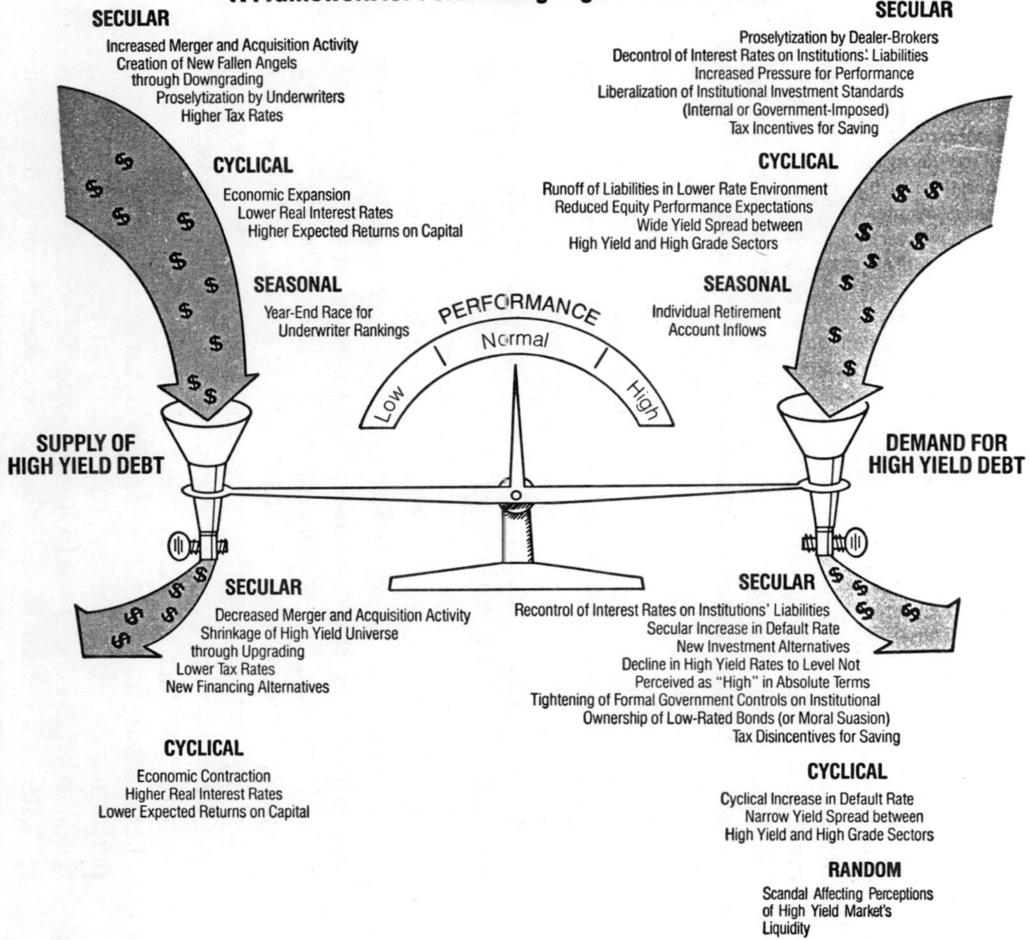

its listing in one place all the major factors affecting prospective returns in high yield bonds. By using this framework, the investor who undertakes to outperform the market by selecting a strategic high yield/high-grade mix can survey all of the relevant variables systematically and in conjunction with one another. Note that the framework does not permit the portfolio manager to weight the variables quantitatively in order to generate a high-confidence level forecast of returns. Indeed, we question whether some of the variables will ever submit to precise quantification. Rather, we envision portfolio managers proceeding by circling in all four quadrants the factors that appear most likely to be major influences over the next few quarters. Visual inspection should then suggest which way the scale is likely to tip and hence whether high, normal or low performance may be expected.

A few other comments on the model will facilitate its utilization. One key point is that the causal factors listed are direct causes only; indirect causes are excluded. Among the potential stimuli to supply, for example, increased merger and acquisition activity could itself be caused by looser antitrust enforcement, a consolidation necessitated by shrinking profit margins, or a number of other underlying forces. Furthermore, the direct causes listed in Exhibit 14–2 may also be indirect causes of other direct causes. For instance, lower tax rates directly reduce the supply of high yield debt by shifting borrowers' preferences toward equity financing, but they may indirectly increase supply by contributing to economic expansion. We can justify neglecting such second-level effects, however, by the fact that they tend to occur after lengthy lags, whereas our framework is designed for maximizing interim performance. Furthermore, the impact of second-level effects tends to be as echoes are to louder, original sounds. Consistency with our earlier stated plan of considering only the most significant factors provides a further rationale for excluding these indirect effects from the analysis proper, even though the investor may wish to consider them in assessing certain direct causes during a particular period.

One final observation that may help users of this framework is that its asymmetry is instructive. For example, the quality spread between high-grade and low-grade bonds appears only on the "Demand for High Yield Debt" side. An investor can shift funds from investment-grade to noninvestment-grade instruments, but an issuer is typically not free to borrow in either sector at a given point in time. This suggests that if over time more institutions begin to exploit variations in this quality spread, the spread will stay within a narrower and narrower band, with no corresponding supply-side phenomenon to inhibit this trend.

Conclusion

There are huge potential benefits to manipulating a portfolio's percentage exposure to high yield, but it follows that the penalties for ill-timed switches are likewise substantial. Clearly, investment managers who plan to use this technique must be thorough in planning their moves. A new economic or regulatory development may appear certain to have a dominating influence until it is viewed in context of many other countervailing forces. Only by considering all of the most important variables in an organized manner can a portfolio manager satisfy the fiduciary requirement of exercising due care.

Endnotes

[1] For demonstration of the dramatic advantages that accrue to high yield bonds over extended periods, see Chapter 20, "The Time Factor in High Yield Market Risk."

[2] Richard Bookstaber and David P. Jacob, "The Composite Hedge: Controlling the Credit Risk of High Yield Bonds," Morgan Stanley & Co. Incorporated (March 1985).

CHAPTER 15

A High Yield Strategy for Investment Advisors

If asked to identify the sector of the fixed income market least suited to their own styles of running money, many investment advisory firms would probably name high yield bonds. Anybody entrusted with pension and endowment assets has to be acutely aware of fiduciary responsibilities; high yield bonds have speculative-grade ratings, characterized by Moody's in language such as, "their future cannot be considered as well assured" and "there may be present elements of danger with respect to principal or interest."[1] Pension managers are typically evaluated on their total return, while high yield bonds' most salient characteristic is their high current income. Furthermore, many investment advisors have played the relative performance game primarily by altering duration according to their interest rate outlooks. High yield bonds are much less responsive to interest rate movements than Treasuries, agencies, mortgage-backed bonds or high-grade corporates, the vehicles typically used to execute rate-anticipation strategies.

Notwithstanding the perceived gulf between their approaches to running money and the nature of speculative-grade bonds, investment advisors are compelled to come to terms with the market's rapid growth. Between 1983 and 1988 the amount of straight public high yield debt outstanding increased five-fold to some $155 billion. Clearly, investment advisory firms' potential client base accounted for a meaningful portion of that growth.

From a strictly defensive standpoint, participation in the high yield market by pension funds means that in order to retain clients, investment advisors must increasingly compete with high yield programs, which provide superior returns in periods of stable interest rates by simply maximizing income.

Viewed in a more opportunistic light, institutional interest in high yield bonds potentially enables an investment advisor to expand its client list. Marketing staffs may, for example, find excellent new prospects among institutions more concerned about current income than quarterly relative performance. As evidenced by 1988's proliferation of hybrid funds (mixing Treasuries and high yield bonds, for example), there is another potential market among sophisticated investors who recognize that high yield bonds, which are relatively non-interest-rate-sensitive, can actually *reduce* the risk of a high-grade portfolio by reducing its covariance.

An analogous diversification benefit exists for the investment advisory firm itself. If the firm's portfolio managers happen to call interest rates dead wrong and wind up in the tenth decile among high-grade funds, the resulting loss of clients may be softened by having produced good results in the high yield portfolios, which have historically been countercyclical. Just as it can make sense for an investment advisor to insulate its revenue stream against large asset reallocations by managing both equity and fixed income, there is logic in further diversifying fees by subcategories within fixed income. (The argument is even stronger for a pure fixed income shop.)

A final reason for an investment organization to venture into high yield is the professional stimulation offered to portfolio managers and analysts. We have observed that many seasoned high-grade managers enjoy the new challenge and the dynamic environment of high yield. Credit analysts find themselves more central to the action the lower down the quality spectrum their firms invest. The "psychic income" that is generated in these ways can pay off handsomely in terms of motivating and retaining talented employees.

Cultural Barriers to Entry

While the benefits of adding a high yield capability are readily recognized, making the requisite mental adjustment is more difficult. Risk, per se, is not the obstacle. Investment advisory firms, after all, are familiar with volatile options and futures and have braved the perils of cross-currency trading. They may nevertheless feel ill-equipped to deal with risk in the form that it takes in the speculative-grade sector. The skills that many investment advisors have developed within their organizations relate to interest rate risk and prepayment risk, not to credit risk.

A common approach to credit risk among such firms focuses exclusively on the yield premium assigned to "the corporate sector" at various points in the business cycle. Based on a forecast of cyclically rebounding Gross National Product, for example, a portfolio manager may shift to a higher weighting in corporates in anticipation of a narrowing of spreads versus Treasuries. The securities chosen to implement this sector bet will probably be highly liquid issues that are thought certain to remain Double-A-rated until the appropriate time comes to reverse the trade. By using only blue chip bonds, the portfolio manager avoids the pitfall of making a correct sector decision, but giving back all of the profits through illiquidity-related transaction costs or the failure of specific issues to track the sector trend.

To firms that manage money in this fashion, there is no value in having analysts tearing apart the financials of thinly traded Triple-B credits that may be undervalued by virtue of not being widely followed. As a result, these firms are unlikely to have in place credit specialists experienced in dealing with the comparatively narrow margins of credit safety encountered in speculative-grade names.

In addition to worrying about essential skills that they lack, investment advisors contemplating expansion into high yield may fear that the skills they have in abundance are inapplicable. Their market-timing talents will be of limited value, since low-rated bonds do not respond as directly as high-grades do to interest rate movements. Nor will their ability to recognize undervalued sectors of the market help them if, as they may have been told, each high yield issue trades on the basis of its unique credit characteristics, with no observable industry group effect. In any case, active management strategies of this sort are not productive in an environment where secondary market-making is sparse and dominated by a single firm, as the common wisdom holds. Seemingly, the only way to add value as a high yield manager is to get big allocations of new issues and ride them up in the aftermarket, an option that will likely be unavailable to a new kid on the block.

Perception versus Reality

Investment advisors are correct in raising all of these issues and in carefully assessing their own capabilities before going after the fees promised by expansion into the high yield sector. In our view, however, none of the concerns enumerated above should bar a well-managed investment organization from incorporating low-rated bonds into its strategy for portfolio management and into its plan for business development. A new entrant can succeed as long as it designs a program that is compatible with its own unique mix of resources. The risk of failure is unacceptably high only if an investment advisor competes against mutual fund organizations and insurance companies on their terms instead of leveraging its own strengths.

High-grade managers who perceive the speculative-grade sector as a hostile environment need to become aware of the huge gap that exists between the perception and the reality of high yield bonds. For instance, the financial press has not adequately reported the reality that over the past few years market share has rapidly been dispersed among several leading underwriters (Exhibit 15–1). While the perception persists among nonparticipants that the high yield secondary market is monopolistic, portfolio managers familiar with the sector know that in order to get bigger pieces of the underwriting pie, the

Exhibit 15–1
Distribution of High Yield Underwriting Market Share

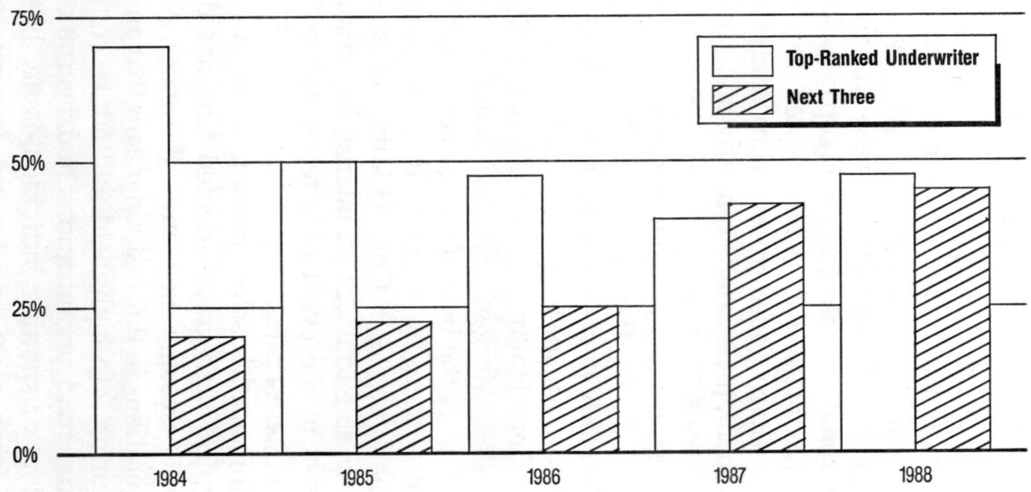

Source: Morgan Stanley & Co. Incorporated.

competitors have had to expand their market-making activities as well.

This is not to deny that for many smaller issues the underwriter is the only firm providing research coverage or making a market. Such bonds represent a subsector of the high yield market in which organizations lacking large in-house credit staffs are indeed ill-equipped to operate. There is another subsector, however, for which many investment advisory firms are well-suited. The "go-gos," large, liquid issues—in many cases created through recapitalizations of major companies formerly rated Single-A or Double-A—are well-adapted to the total return style. With perhaps half a dozen firms analyzing and making markets in them, these bonds typically trade with half-point bid/asked spreads that are good for par amounts of around $5 million. Moreover, by concentrating on the most creditworthy names among the go-gos, a firm can greatly reduce (although certainly never eliminate) the in-house credit resources required to participate in the high yield sector. Exhibit 15–2 lists the Core Holdings as of January 1989. These issues represent the Morgan Stanley Credit Research Department's selection of the best of the go-gos, a list that includes deals underwritten by several different investment banks. Among other criteria, a Core Holding must meet a "stress test" of being able to cover all interest and mandatory principal repayments in the event of a recession and a 300-basis-point surge in interest rates.

It is by focusing on this select portion of the high yield market that the typical high-grade-oriented firm has the best chance of successfully crossing the Double-B frontier. Narrowing the scope of operations in this fashion means that an investment advisor venturing into high yield will not be competing directly with mutual fund organizations and insurance companies that are adept at spotting individual-issuer misvaluations. Instead, an investment advisor can leverage existing skills to carve out a distinctive niche. For example, an especially conservative pension fund may not be willing to allocate even a portion of its assets to a pure high yield program, but may approve a hybrid strategy, combining high yield bonds and Treasuries. The proportions of the two asset classes within the hybrid portfolio can be varied over time, depending on market conditions and relative value. This is an active approach that will lend itself well to skills that are highly developed within many investment advisory firms. Other total return managers can build on their experience in swapping between sectors (e.g., governments, corporates and mortgage-backed securities) to move assets around among various industry subsectors of the high yield market.

Testing for Feasibility

Before ordering the marketing materials from the printer, most money managers will first want to investigate the feasibility of these strategies. We believe there is ample evidence that it is indeed possible to adapt a number of active management techniques from other segments of the fixed income market. Corroborating this claim is the fact that a number of high yield managers are already using them.

At this point, we must emphasize that the following comments on feasibility are subject to the size of the portfolio desired and the speed with which the funds are to be invested. The suggested strategy requires a manager to operate within a select portion of the high yield market; an institution contemplating the creation of a half-billion-dollar portfolio will probably not want to limit its choice of securities too severely. Even a quarter-billion-dollar portfolio is hard to build quickly without heavy reliance on the new issue market. New issues frequently offer excellent value and are therefore well worth considering. Buying them, however, means attending the road shows and analyzing deals that are dependent on asset sales, implying a greater commitment of resources to credit research than the pure strategy outlined below.

With that proviso, let us consider first whether the hybrid portfolio is a viable strategy. As we have already pointed out, the vehicles required for implementation of this approach are

Exhibit 15–2
Core Holdings (As of January 1989)

Company	Coupon	Security	Maturity
American Standard	12 ⅞%	Sen. Sub. Debs.	06/30/00
Burlington Industries	13 ⅞%	Sen. Sub. Notes	10/01/96
Caesars World	13 ½%	Sub. Notes	10/01/97
Carter Hawley Hale	12 ¼%	Sen. Sub. Notes	08/15/96
Coastal Corp.	11 ¾%	Sen. Debs.	06/15/06
Colt Industries	12 ½%	Sen. Sub. Debs.	10/15/01
Container Corp.	12 ⅜%	Sen. Sub. Debs.	09/30/98
Eckerd Holdings	11 ⅛%	Sub. Debs.	05/01/01
First Brands	12 ½%	Sen. Sub. Debs.	09/01/98
FMC	12 ½%	Sub. Debs.	06/01/01
Fort Howard	12 ⅝%	Sub. Debs.	11/01/00
Fruit of the Loom	10 ¾%	Sen. Sub. Notes	07/15/95
Harcourt Brace Jovanovich	13 ¾%	Sen. Sub. Debs.	09/15/99
Holiday Corp.	11%	Sub Debs.	04/01/99
Long Island Lighting Co.	11 ⅞%	General Refund.	04/15/15
Macy (R.H.) & Co.	14 ½%	Sen. Sub. Debs.	11/15/01
Masco Industries	10 ¼%	Sen. Sub. Notes	02/15/97
Owens-Corning Fiberglas	11 ¾%	Sen. Sub. Debs.	11/15/01
Owens-Ilinois	12 ¾%	Sub. Debs.	06/01/99
Phillips Petroleum	14 ¾%	Sub. Debs.	03/15/00
Safeway Stores	11 ¾%	Sen. Sub. Notes	11/15/96
SPTC Holdings	12 ⅛%	Sub. Debs.	10/01/00
Union Carbide	9 ¾%	Sen. Sub. Notes	04/15/94
United Airlines	13%	Sen. Sub. Notes	06/15/98

available. Core issues can serve as proxies for the high yield universe, just as certain very liquid high-grade corporates enable a manager to capture swings in the corporate/Treasuries spread with the lowest possible transaction costs. Clearly, too, the spread between high yield and Treasuries (Exhibit 15–3) is volatile enough to provide worthwhile arbitrage opportunities. The magnitude of potential profits, moreover, is substantial. During 1987, for example, high yield bonds outperformed Treasuries through the first nine months, but were swamped (9.56% versus 1.02%) in the fourth quarter. To quantify the benefits of market timing, imagine a hybrid portfolio with a

Exhibit 15–3
High Yield Spread History

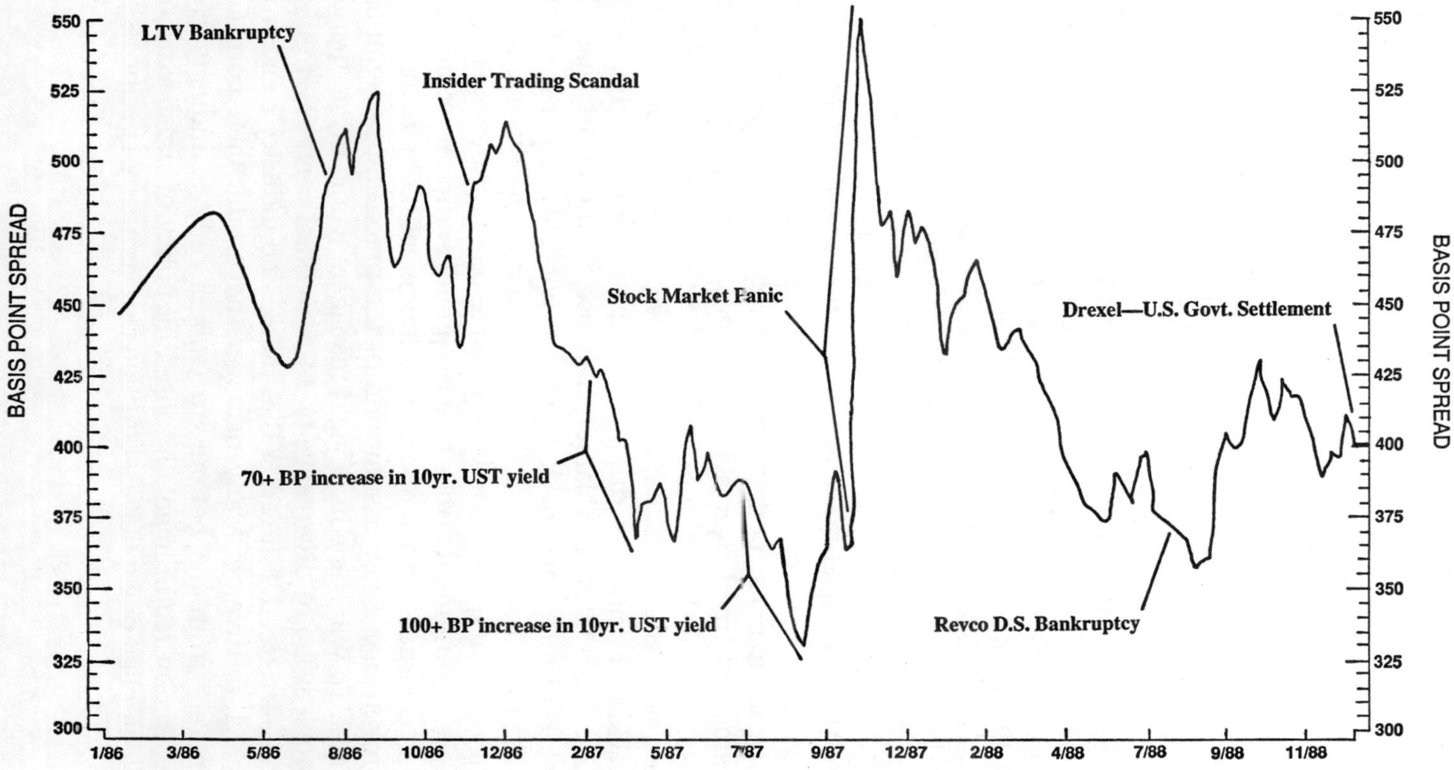

maximum weighting of 50% high yield and a minimum of 0%, with the balance invested in long-term Treasuries. A manager who read the market conditions correctly would have been at the maximum high yield position through September 30 and fully invested in Treasuries for the balance of the year. Allowing one full point of transaction costs on the switch, the hybrid portfolio would have returned 4.85% for the year, a significant improvement over the full year -1.85% return provided by a pure long Treasuries portfolio. The hybrid strategy would also have reduced volatility—instead of a -7.61% quarterly return in the third quarter on long Treasuries, an investor would have earned -4.49% with a 50/50 mix.

Establishing feasibility is more difficult in the case of the industry subsector swapping strategy than for the market-timing strategy.[2] For one thing, a manager would not be able to rely exclusively on 20-odd Core Holdings to implement a strategy of capturing shifts in relative value among (as we divide the universe) 20 different industries. The reason is that any company's performance can easily diverge from its industry's trend over a short period. Therefore, a subsector-swapper must stay informed on the credit quality of at least two or three issuers in each industry in order to minimize the tracking errors introduced by company-specific changes in risk. This implies a larger in-house credit effort than the market-timing approach requires—not only because of the need to follow more names, but because of the closer monitoring of credit quality that is required as one ventures outside the Core. Assuming a firm is able to commit sufficient resources to the enlarged credit research requirement, it remains to be proven that a key assumption of the preceding paragraph is valid. To wit, some high yield managers would argue that the problem is not divergence of an individual company from its industry trend, but rather that there is no industry trend from which to diverge. Many managers have built their portfolios entirely from the bottom up (subject only to industry concentration requirements imposed by policy or prospectus), on the implicit or explicit assumption that company-specific risk is the overriding analytical concern when dealing with speculative-grade issues. In some cases, this approach was adopted out of sheer necessity. Only a few years ago, there were almost no high yield issues with enough liquidity to permit them to be bought as needed in pursuit of a plan of systematic diversification. As a consequence, investors had to buy whichever new issues became available when they had cash, even if that meant excessive concentration in an industry that happened to be in the heavy financing phase of its operating cycle. Other high yield managers bought bonds on an issue-by-issue basis, without much regard to industry mix, simply because they were temperamentally or philosophically inclined in that direction rather than in the direction of top-down management.

Measuring the Rewards

While the bottom-up approach has produced excellent results for many managers, the evidence indicates that a subsector-oriented strategy is quite viable as an alternative means of enhancing performance. Chapter 17, "Is There a Group Effect in High Yield Bonds?" demonstrates that an individual bond's price movements are indeed influenced by the trend of its industry. This group effect represents an opportunity for managers who yearn to get into the high yield game but lack the expertise to compete head-on with organizations supported by first-rank company analysts. Just how attractive the top-down opportunity can be is suggested by an analysis of 1987 total return by industry. Using our 20-industry segmentation of the market, we found subsector returns ranging from 15.08% (Metals/Mining) to -4.12% (Real Estate/Construction). Based on these results, let us suppose a manager had simply identified in advance the industries that constituted the worst-performing quartile. An equally weighted portfolio of the remaining 15 industries would have produced a return of 5.85%, versus 3.81% for the passive 20-industry portfolio.[3] Correctly selecting the top half of the industry universe would have raised the portfolio's return to 8.13%, while concentrating on the top quartile would have earned 11.38%.

(Note that this degree of concentration, 20% in each of five industries, is permissible within the guidelines typically found in high yield mutual fund prospectuses.)

While there is no guarantee of success in picking the right industries, the potential rewards of a top-down approach compare favorably with the likely payoff on security-specific trading. Every year, painstaking credit work on individual issuers turns up a limited number of opportunities to realize 10- and 20-point capital gains. The overall portfolio impact of these "home runs" may, however, be limited by single-issuer concentration restrictions—typically 5% for high yield mutual funds. By the same token, numerous smaller opportunities, both in secondary trading and through buying new issues at concessions to secondary levels, arise over the course of a year. Some managers will trade more actively and some will identify bigger bargains, but it represents perfectly respectable performance to have 100% turnover and net an average profit of one point on all trades—winners and losers. That record would have translated into a 1987 total return of 5.61% (100 basis points above our estimate for the high yield universe), versus the above-mentioned 5.85% that would have been realized by accurately forecasting the five worst-performing industries.

Conclusion

We would never minimize the risks of dabbling in the high yield market without adequate research support. From a fiduciary standpoint, moreover, an investment advisor cannot abdicate responsibility for assessing credit risk. Nevertheless, for investors who see a role for high yield bonds in accomplishing their objectives, the existence of hundreds of small, obscure issuers of dubious quality should not be an insuperable barrier. Focusing on the most liquid and highest-quality issues cuts the credit analysis task down to a size that is manageable for firms that have historically emphasized other functions. Operating within the more tradable and more predictable portion of the high yield universe, total return managers can offset the yield giveup versus the less liquid issues by applying active management techniques they have previously utilized in the investment-grade arena. Albeit by a different path, they can arrive at the same destination as others who have preceded them into the speculative-grade realm—superior long-term returns through intelligent risk-taking.

Endnotes

[1] *Moody's Bond Record,* December 1988, page 1. Note that like the traditionally conceived "prudent man rule," Moody's definitions apply to bonds on a one-by-one basis, rather than to a diversified portfolio. Spreading risk by industry and by issuer is a cornerstone of any high yield investment program and our studies indicate that doing so produces and investment that trades off risk and return much in the manner observed in other segments of the capital markets. See for example, Martin S. Fridson and Michael C. Heaney, "High Yield Bonds Versus Common Stocks: Risk Adjustment and Inter-Market Valuation," *High Performance* (June 1988): pp. 4-9.

[2] While this article focuses on industry subsector-swapping, there are other high yield subsectors that offer arbitrage opportunities. Managers who favor this style may wish to study the relationships between zero/coupons and current coupons, and between the high-end and low-end credits within the speculative-grade universe, to cite just two examples.

[3] Because some high yield issues are not classified among the industries we track, the 20-sector return varies somewhat from the total return that we estimate for the entire high yield universe (4.61% in 1987).

CHAPTER 16

Employing High Yield Bonds in a Sector-Swapping Strategy

As more total return players, particularly pension fund managers, are drawn to the high yield sector, the need for timing-oriented research increases. Investment advisors compete for funds on the basis of annual and quarterly performance and therefore lack the luxury of waiting for compound interest to validate their strategies five years hence. These investors have a natural interest in recognizing when the high yield sector is undervalued and temporarily shifting funds into it. The tools they might use to identify such undervaluation can help other investors, as well. For example, the prospectuses of most high yield mutual funds give managers considerable discretion to invest in other sectors. An effective sector-timing mechanism could enable these managers to outperform competitors who tend to stay fully invested in low-grades.

The following analysis concentrates on just one of many potentially exploitable relationships—long Single-A corporates versus high yield. While useful comparisons with other sectors—Treasuries, mortgage-backed securities, Eurobonds, etc.—are possible, we focus here on devising techniques for exploiting sector relationships and have accordingly concentrated on a single spread. We have further limited our analysis to strategies based on calling the major changes in relative value, rather than the week-to-week shifts of 10 or 20 basis points. The high yield market's degree of liquidity does not provide the necessary ease of entry and exit to exploit this random motion. Above all, we want to avoid creating the impression that high yield bonds track Single-As or Treasuries so closely over the short term that minor spread changes offer worthwhile arbitrage opportunities. At this point, the supply/demand factors in high yield are sufficiently distinct from those in high-grades that the markets can move quite independently over the short term. In no event should an investor who has decided to sell a low-rated bond at a specified yield for credit reasons pull the offering because the Treasury market has ticked up five basis points, causing a minute narrowing of spread.

Playing the Spread

Exhibit 16–1 displays a 10-year history of the spread between a 14-bond Single-A corporate portfolio and a high yield portfolio drawn from a universe of 440 bonds rated BB + or lower by Standard & Poor's during the 1975-85 period.[1] For each year covered by the study, we selected 50 industrial fixed-rate issues and weighted them equally to construct the high yield portfolio. Over the 10-year period, the Single-A portfolio's average coupon was 8.2% and its average maturity 18 years, compared with 10.5% and 15 years for the high yield index.

The simplest way to utilize the data in Exhibit 16–1 is to calculate an average spread for the period and establish a trading rule of going into high yield when it is "undervalued," that is, at a greater-than-average spread versus Single-A, and reverse into Single-A when the spread is narrower than average. Applying this approach retroactively, we calculated an average spread of +180 basis points during the period. Recognizing the high yield market's limited liquidity, we switched sectors only when the spread reached a point 20 basis points wider or narrower than the average. The results obtained by this trading rule appear in Exhibit 16–1. By going into Single-A whenever the spread narrowed to +160 basis points and back into high yield at the +200 signal, an investor would have outperformed the buy-and-hold strategy for both Single-A and high yield. Indeed, over the 10-year period, the

Exhibit 16–1
How the Single A / High Yield Spread Tracks the Business Cycle

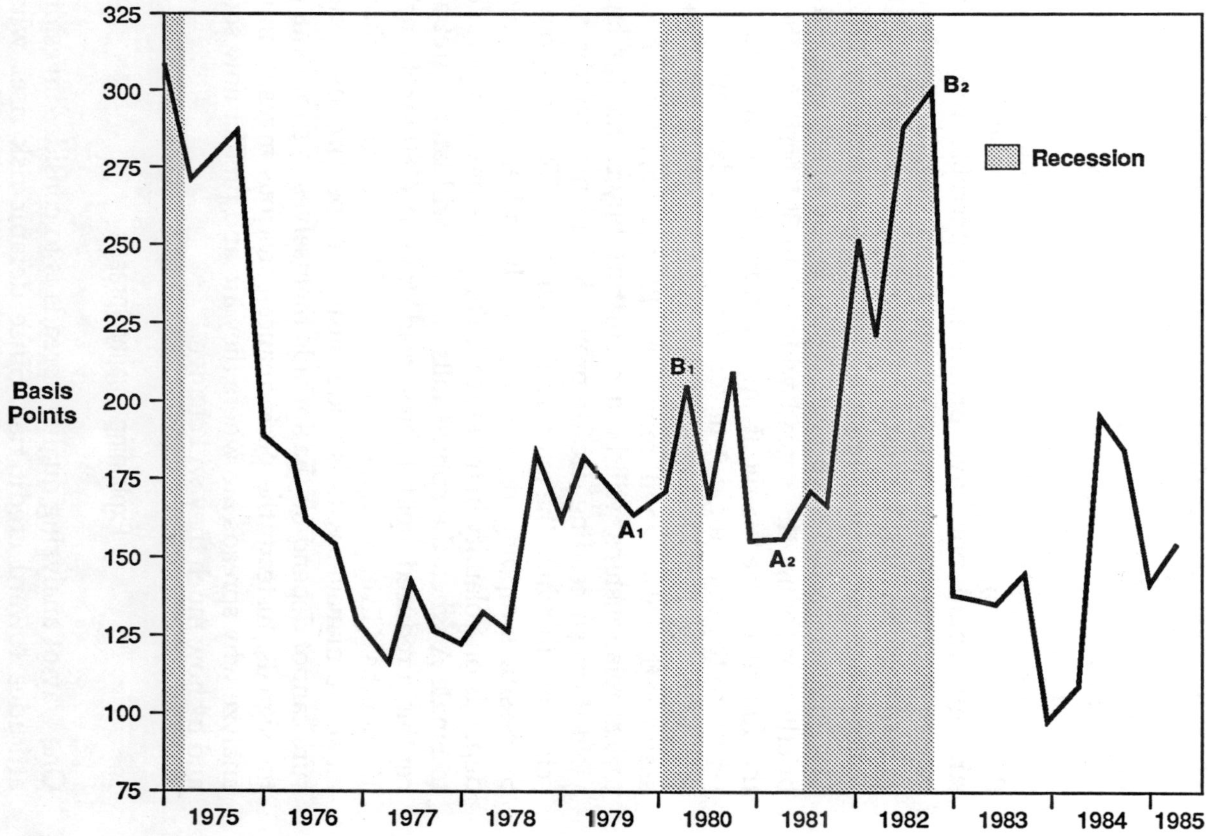

portfolio managed on this principle would have increased by 332%, or 7,500 basis points more than the passive High Yield portfolio and 18,800 basis points more than the passive Single-A portfolio. That difference represents a compound annual total return advantage of 5.6% and 10.8%, respectively, over the passive portfolios.

However impressive one may consider those figures over the decade-long horizon, though, this automatic switching strategy would not have produced impeccable results for money managers who were evaluated on their quarterly or annual performance. For instance, swapping into the high yield sector when the spread breached +200 basis points in 1982's first quarter would have been costly in the short run. After briefly narrowing, the spread widened to 301 basis points in the fourth quarter without any warning to the investor to return to the safe Single-A haven. Another fundamental problem with the historical spread approach is that it implicitly assumes that history will repeat. A +180 spread, based on historical relationships, will be a premature buy signal for high yield if the succeeding decade proves to be a more credit-conscious era in which the average differential is 250 basis points. Successful swapping on the basis of historical spreads also depends on volatility in the spread. The investor who upgrades to Single-A when the spread falls to +180 will later regret accepting a reduced yield if the spread stays at +180 for the next 12 months. Giveup trades work only if they reverse. In short, an active manager who is under near-term performance pressure cannot depend on the spreads themselves to supply all of the signals. Instead, the performance-conscious investor must analyze why spreads are where they are and predict how soon and by how much they will change.

Explaining Quality Spreads

One way of analyzing quality spreads is to consider investors' attitudes toward credit risk. Since default risk rises when economic activity slackens, lenders will presumably be most averse to lower-quality issues during recessions. That increasing aversion should show up as a widening of quality spreads. Looking again at Exhibit 16–2, we can confirm this hypothesis. In general, the shaded periods representing recessions coincided with episodes of widening spread, denoted A_1-B_1 and A_2-B_2.

Another explanation frequently given for quality spread changes is the proposition that spreads widen as the general level of interest rates rises. An alternative form of this argument is that yields (on Single-As, High Yield bonds or whatever) are stable over time as a percentage of Treasury yields. For example, if Double-B bonds consistently yield 125% of the Treasury rate, the Double-B/Treasury spread will be 250 basis points with Treasuries at 10% and 325 basis points with Treasuries at 13%. Exhibit 16–3 shows that the "high rates = wide spreads" hypothesis has not worked well for high yield bonds. In fact, when the general level of interest rates (indicated by the upper line representing long Treasury yields) peaked, in January 1982, the Single-A/high yield spread was just 138 basis points, some 42 narrower than average. Conversely, when Treasury yields plunged by 380 basis points, to

Exhibit 16–2
Results of Swapping by Historical Spreads
April 30, 1975-August 30, 1985

Dates of Swap Signals	Direction of Swap	Buy and Hold Strategies	
		High Yield	Single-A
4/30/75	High Yield	High Yield	Single-A
9/30/76	Single-A	High Yield	Single-A
6/30/80	High Yield	High Yield	Single-A
10/30/80	Single-A	High Yield	Single-A
12/30/80	High Yield	High Yield	Single-A
2/30/81	Single-A	High Yield	Single-A
3/30/82	High Yield	High Yield	Single-A
2/30/83	Single-A	High Yield	Single-A
8/30/85	Unchanged	High Yield	Single-A
Cumulative Total Return:	332.5%	257.3%	144.5%

Exhibit 16–3
Higher Rates Do Not Mean Wider Spreads

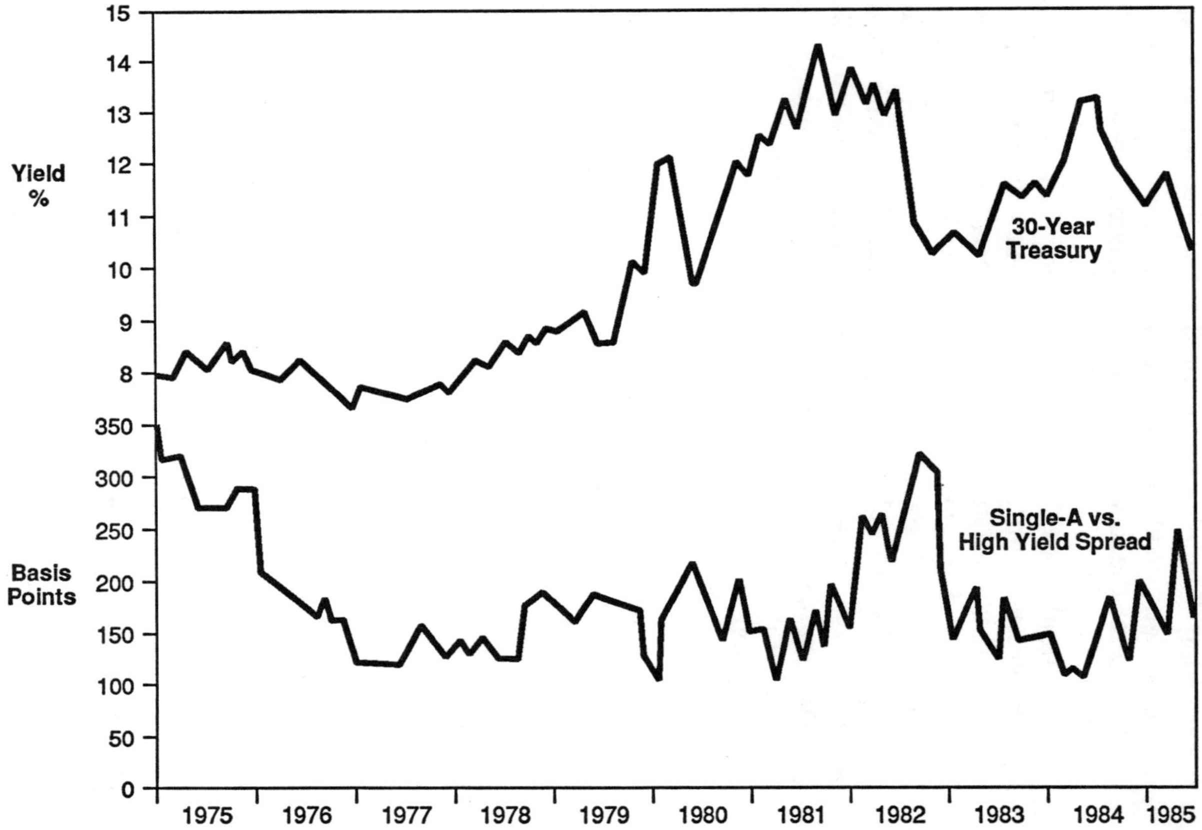

10.30% in November 1982, the Single-A/high yield spread widened to 302 basis points.

Explanations of these "anomalies," which are in fact consistent with the period's overall pattern, are readily available. In a bear market, absolute yield levels on low-grades of 16% or more are likely to attract funds from other sectors, including equities, which may appear less attractive on a risk/ reward basis. Such inflows would tend to cap low-grade yields, causing the quality spread to narrow as yields on Single-A corporates rise along with Treasury yields. Reinforcing this tendency is the unwillingness of speculative-grade companies to float fixed-rated debt at the yields implied by the formula of a constant percentage of the Treasury rate when the Treasury rate skyrockets. At such times, "bells and whistles" such as equity kickers may become more common, enabling coupons to remain low, or borrowers may simply roll over their bank lines rather than fund at oppressively high rates.

Economic Indicators as Swap Signals

If we conclude from our examination of Exhibits 16–1 and 16–2 that the Single-A/high yield spread tracks the business cycle more closely than it tracks the general level of interest rates, we must then select an economic indicator as our signal for timing the high yield/Single-A switch. We know that we want to get out of the high yield sector when the recession begins, but the National Bureau of Economic Research does not tell us that we are in a recession until at least two quarters after it starts—too late to escape the widening of spreads. Accordingly, we tested a number of variables in hopes of identifying one that consistently provided advance warning of major changes in the Single-A/high yield differential. Some that worked well in predicting changes in the direction of interest rates, such as the ratio of personal income to M1, failed to signal spread changes. This reinforced the impression formed by Exhibit 16–2, namely, that high rates do not necessarily coincide with wide spreads. The composites of leading and coincident indicators did better as guides to changes in quality spreads, but were inconsistent, performing particularly poorly during the 1977 economic slowdown. We obtained our best results with the composite of six lagging indicators. (This composite is conceptually tricky, since it is essentially a mirror image of the more familiar leading indicators. An upturn in lagging indicators signals that the economic recovery is ending and that recession is on the way.) Exhibit 16–4 plots the Single-A/high yield spread alongside the year-to-year change in lagging indicators, marked numerically at each point that the series passed through zero. Notwithstanding some spikiness, all points at which lagging indicator series turned negative (numbers 1, 3 and 5), thereby signaling that a recession was ending, were followed by narrowing spread trends, consistent with hypothesis. Following points 2, 4 and 6 (crossover to positive lagging indicators, heralding the end of the recovery), the main trend of the Single-A/High yield spread was invariably a widening.

Having identified lagging indicators as the best signal of spread changes, we then retroactively tested the performance of a portfolio managed according to the following decision rule: Switch into high yield when lagging indicators turn negative and switch back to Single-A when lagging indicators turn positive. Exhibit 16–5 displays the results. On a retroactive basis, the lagging indicator decision rule increased the initial portfolio's value by 336% over approximately 10 years, bettering the 332% gain produced by the historical spread decision rule (Exhibit 16–1). Of particular interest to managers who are measured by their short-term returns, the lagging indicator decision rule achieved these results without sacrificing intermediate term performance. As Exhibit 16-6 illustrates, this approach outperformed the historical spread method in five out of 11 periods, matched it in three and slightly underperformed it in only three. As such, keeping an eye on lagging indicators can potentially enhance the performance of sector-swapping managers who recognize the pitfalls, described above, of responding solely to deviations from historical average spreads.

Exhibit 16–4
Lagging Indicators Tag Spread Changes

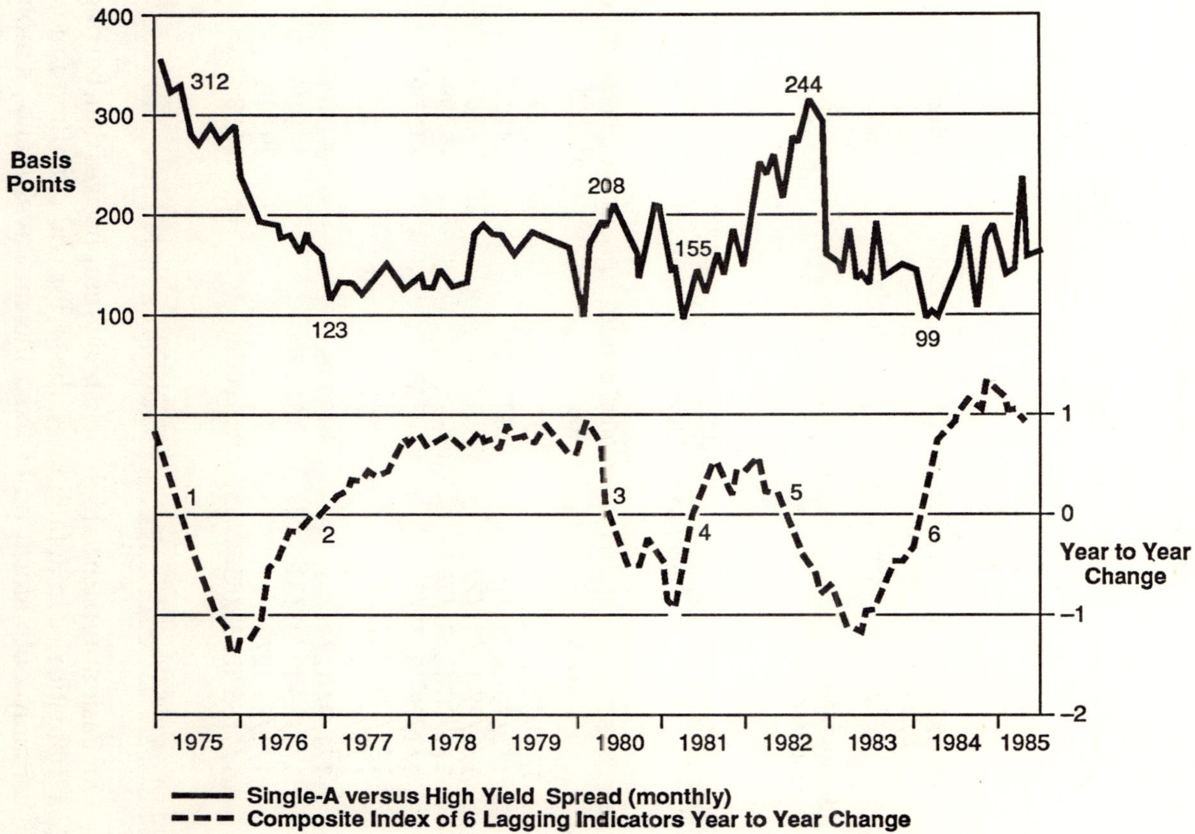

Exhibit 16–5
Results of Swapping by Lagging Indicators
April 30, 1975-August 30, 1985

Dates of Swap Signals	Direction of Swap	Buy and Hold Strategies	
		High Yield	Single-A
4/30/75	High Yield	High Yield	Single-A
2/30/77	Single-A	High Yield	Single-A
7/30/80	High Yield	High Yield	Single-A
7/30/81	Single-A	High Yield	Single-A
8/30/82	High Yield	High Yield	Single-A
4/30/84	Single-A	High Yield	Single-A
8/30/85	Unchanged	High Yield	Single-A
Cumulative Total Return:	336.0%	257.3%	144.5%

Exhibit 16–6
Annualized Total Return Comparison

Period	Historical Spread Method	Lagging Indicator Method
4/30/75-12/31/75	10.47%	10.47%
1/1/76-12/31/76	30.26%	29.01%
1/1/77-12/31/77	5.14%	9.36%
1/1/78-12/31/78	-3.19%	-3.19%
1/1/79-12/31/79	-3.83%	-3.83%
1/1/80-12/31/80	5.74%	-7.40%
1/1/81-12/31/81	4.54%	4.58%
1/1/82-12/31/82	35.23%	37.30%
1/1/83-12/31/83	16.31%	19.91%
1/1/84-12/31/84	16.42%	19.91%
1/1/85-12/31/85	16.00%	14.33%

Conclusion

Our basic approach to high yield bonds emphasizes that, barring a dramatic rise in default rates, the sector will over time almost certainly outperform other fixed income investments, simply due to the power of compound interest. (See Chapter 20, "The

Time Factor in High Yield Market Risk.") We consequently believe that investors with long horizons have a comparative advantage over short-term performance seekers in this part of the market. By the same token, the substantial swings observed in the spread between high yield bonds and higher quality issues constitute a tantalizing prospect for sector swappers. Our findings confirm that there is a substantial reward for correctly synchronizing sector shifts with changes in the Single-A/high yield spread. By combining the use of the spreads themselves as timing devices with a business cycle approach to forecasting changes in spreads, a portfolio manager can potentially achieve superior short-term, as well as long-term performance.

Endnotes

[1] The sample consisted of 440 fixed-rate bonds representing 224 issues from the high yield universe as it existed between 1975 and 1984. Prices were derived from the data tapes of the Interactive Data Corp., which essentially provides exchange-listed prices with a small amount of matrix prices. Month-end closing prices or prices closest to the month-end were used. In the majority of cases we had only "ask" prices, which could have introduced some bias.

CHAPTER 17

Is There a Group Effect in High Yield Bonds?

Investment organizations tend to differentiate themselves according to management styles that reflect their personal inclinations and experience. Some capitalize on highly developed skills in company analysis to excel through superior selection of individual securities. Others rely on exceptional conceptual abilities to identify opportunities in undervalued sectors of the market. Given that both types of managers are represented among the most successful equity and fixed income organizations, it is reasonable to suppose that both styles can produce good results in the high yield sector. That proposition will not go unchallenged in all quarters, though. Most will concede that rigorous credit analysis at the individual company level is a proven formula for high relative performance, since it is imperative in the high yield sector to avoid as much as possible the sharp price declines that accompany defaults. In contrast, the merits of a top-down approach may not be as apparent to all onlookers. The indisputable fact that a company can diverge sharply from the trend of its industry (for example, when only one company in an industry defaults) may create an impression that there is little value to be added by anticipating industry-wide trends.

Experiment Design

Unfortunately, debates of this sort often continue for years, with the disputants relying on anecdotal evidence and filtering events through their existing intellectual biases. Too infrequently does it occur to investment professionals to run a simple experiment, as is possible in this instance.

In asking whether a top-down approach can add value in high yield, we are essentially asking whether there is a discernible group effect in the sector. The alternative conclusion, or null hypothesis, is that each security moves in response to changes in its unique fundamental circumstances (earnings outlook, financial leverage, etc.) and possibly in sympathy with a broad market trend, but that the behavior of its industry peers has no bearing.

As described more specifically in the Technical Note at the conclusion of this chapter the mathematical approach to this problem is to propose two alternative models of the prices observed over time for a sample of high yield bonds. The first is (in simplified terms) M + G + W, or Market Effect + Group Effect + Error Term Associated with the Individual Security. The second is M + W, which attributes no effect to the group. If the null hypothesis is correct (i.e., if the Group Effect equals zero), then M + G + W equals M + W. In that event the relevant F-statistic, which in a sense measures departure from the null hypothesis, would be expected to have a value near 1.0. More precisely, the F-statistic would with high probability not exceed a certain "critical value," which depends on the amount of data and on the number of individual parameters in each model. The null hypothesis is rejected, and the presence of a group effect established, if this ratio exceeds 1.0 by a sufficient margin.

Our empirical test of this proposition involved 18 high yield issues, three in each of six different industries (see Exhibit 17–1). To the extent possible, we selected issues of similar coupons and maturities, intending thereby to minimize the performance impact of differences in duration among the sample bonds. Over the period March 1987 through March 1988 we had available continuous dealer quotations on the entire sample. Combining weekly prices with some intra-week

Exhibit 17–1
List of Issues Tested

Basic Industry		
Colt Industries	12 ½%	10/15/01
Stone Container	13 ⅝%	6/1/95
Wickes Companies	11 ⅞%	6/1/01
Consumer Products		
BCI Holdings	12 ½%	4/15/98
First Brands	12 ½%	9/1/98
Fruit of the Loom	10 ¾%	7/15/95
Energy		
Coastal Corp.	11 ¾%	6/15/06
Mitchell Energy	11 ¼%	1/15/97
Phillips Petroleum	13 ⅞%	3/15/97
Media		
Cablevision Industries	11 ¼%	2/15/02
Comcast	11 ¾%	8/1/06
Continental Cablevision	13 ⅛%	12/1/95
Retailing		
Allied Stores	11 ½%	3/15/97
Macy (R.H.) & Co.	14 ½%	11/15/98
Safeway Stores	12%	11/15/98
Utilities		
Gulf States Utilities	11 ⅜%	1/1/16
Long Island Lighting	11 ½%	12/15/14
Philadelphia Electric	10 ⅜%	2/15/96

prices, we collected a total of 68 observations on each issue. To run the test, we first transformed the raw prices via logarithms, to measure relative price changes from the initial date of the experiment. This transformation eliminated potential distortions arising from absolute price differences among the different securities. In essence, all price movements were put on the comparable scale of percentage change versus the base period.

Results

The F-ratio relative to the complete set of data was found to be 1.21. Since at the 99% confidence level a ratio above 1.18 is not consistent with the hypothesis of "no group effect," this result is highly significant. The group effect can also be detected over shorter time intervals. If only half of each time series is considered at a time, and using a conservative variant of the F-test, we can still be confident of a group effect, at separate confidence levels of 90% for the first half, and 95% for the second—this in spite of our reliance on a mere three issues per industry group.

At least as important as the level of certainty regarding the presence of a group effect, is its magnitude—i.e., its practical significance. The size of the sample does not allow us definitive statements on this. However, the graphical representation of the individual Group Effects in this sample strongly suggests that the industries within the high yield sector do not submit wholly to a broad market pattern, but behave somewhat independently. Exhibit 17–2 filters out the Market Effect and smoothes the data to disclose widely dissimilar price patterns among the industries studied. These non-parallel fluctuations do not appear to be merely unaccountable, random effects. They quite plausibly reflect industry-specific fundamental developments that portfolio managers can profit from by adjusting their industry weightings.

Conclusion

Our findings establish that there is a meaningful industry group effect in the price behavior of high yield bonds. Investment management organizations that favor a top-down, conceptual approach should be encouraged by these results to utilize their skills in the high yield sector. Granted, no manager of speculative-grade bonds can afford to be blase about individual credits, since there is a heavy penalty attached to holding a failing issue. Bottom-up techniques are therefore an essential component of any high yield program. As in other sectors of the capital markets, however, it is probable that more than one strategy can succeed, given satisfactory execution. The presence of an industry group effect points to industry analysis as a potentially fruitful area of research for high yield managers.

Readers should also note that the analytical method used in this study to detect and separate global and industry-specific trends is of general interest. The technique can be adapted and generalized to answer a variety of inquiries into the dynamics of the market, in particular when the objective is to identify and isolate various sources of value fluctuation. It should be substantially clearer and more informative than the use of raw indices, and thus prove to be a valuable tool for handling the evidence in both technical and fundamental analyses.

Exhibit 17–2
Contrasting Industry Group Price Change Patterns

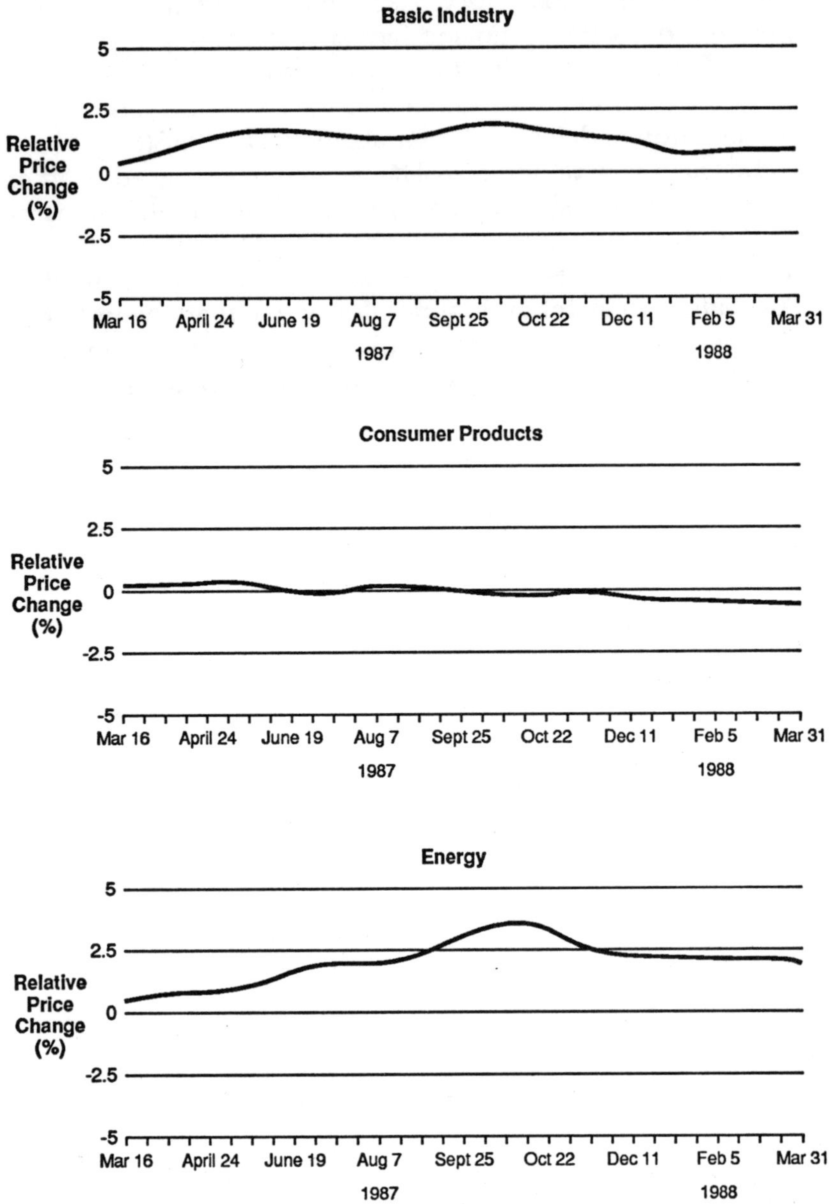

Exhibit 17–2 (Continued)
Contrasting Industry Group Price Change Patterns

Media

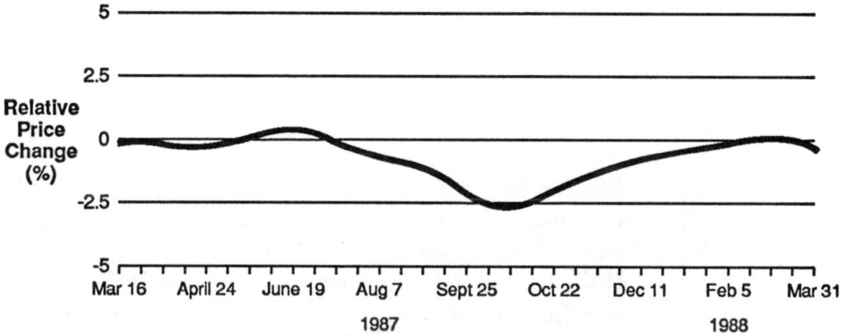

Retailing

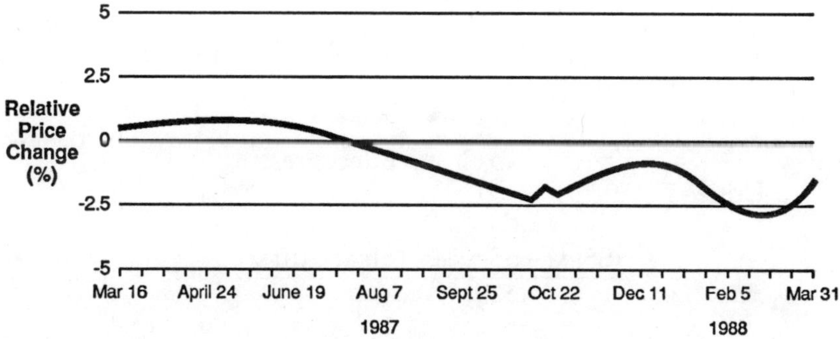

Utilities

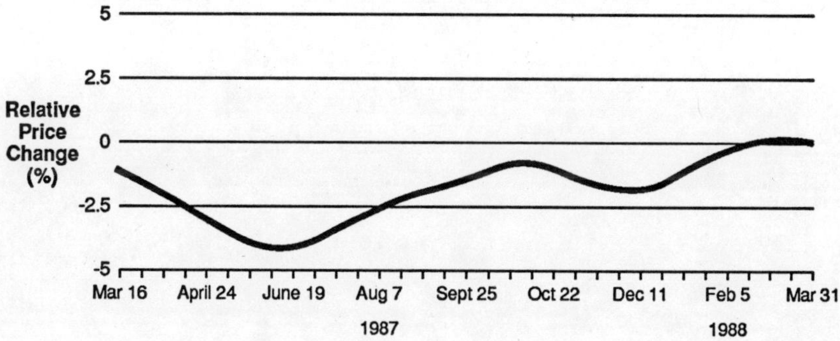

Technical Note

MODEL:

$L_{ij}(t)$ = Log $(P_{ij}(t))$-Log $(Pij(0))$
$L_{ij}(t)$ = $M(t)+G_i(t)+W_{ij}(t)$
$P_{ij}(t)$ = Price of Security j in Group i at Time t
$L_{ij}(t)$ = Transformed Price of Security
M = Market Effect (Securities studied taken as a whole)
G_i = Group Effect
W_{ij} = Error Term Associated with the Individual Security (Independent Wiener processes with 0 drift and common volatility)
i = 1:6 Groups of Related Securities
j = 1:3 Related Securities within each Group
t = 1:68 Times of Quotes

NULL HYPOTHESIS:

$G_i \equiv 0$ No Group Effect present

Utilize F-statistic:

$$F = \frac{(SS_{RM} - SS_{FM}) \div (df_{RM} - df_{FM})}{SS_{FM} \div df_{FM}}$$

F_M : Full Model (Includes Group Effect)
R_M : Reduced Model (Excludes Group Effect)

CHAPTER 18

Market Efficiency: The News Management Anomaly

It is well documented that changes in the issuer's credit quality exert a greater influence on the price behavior of a speculative-grade bond than is the case with an investment-grade bond.[1] One important consequence of this fact is that an individual high yield security's return is more likely to diverge from the return of the high yield sector as a whole, than an investment-grade's return is to vary significantly from its peer group's return.[2]

The potential for divergence cuts both ways. On the one hand, owning a security that substantially underperforms the market is undesirable. Investors generally seek to minimize this effect by diversifying across a number of different issues and across a variety of industries. The impact of an underperformer is thereby reduced (by virtue of its representing only a small percentage of the portfolio's total market value) or—even better—is offset (by a countercyclical name's concurrent better-than-market performance). A portfolio manager who can foresee an issue's underperformance will do still better by selling the security before it begins to diverge. If, on the other hand, a bond is going to outperform the market, the rational decision is to buy.[3] A portfolio manager who correctly anticipates major divergences in individual securities can reap substantial trading profits. To pursue such a strategy, however, one must believe it is possible to beat the market to opportunities of this nature. Many securities analysts, who view the identification of misvalued securities as their *raison d'etre,* believe devoutly in the possibility. Arrayed against them, however, are legions of academics, as well as many practitioners, who subscribe to the Efficient Market Hypothesis, which espouses exactly the opposite view.

Efficient Markets Defined

Briefly, the Efficient Market Hypothesis says that securities prices "fully and instantaneously reflect all available relevant information." [4] By this reasoning, possession of information cannot produce an "excess return," i.e., a return higher than the market's return that does not simply reflect above-average risk. Thomas E. Copeland and J. Fred Weston, adapting the work of Eugene Fama, have defined three forms of the Hypothesis, which we reproduce verbatim below:

1. *Weak-form efficiency.* No investor can earn excess returns by developing trading rules based on historical price or return information. In other words, the information in past prices or returns is not useful or relevant in achieving excess returns.
2. *Semi-strong-form efficiency.* No investor can earn excess returns from trading rules based on any publicly available information. Examples of publicly available information are: annual reports of companies, investment advisory data such as "Heard on the Street" in The *Wall Street Journal*, or ticker tape information.
3. *Strong-form efficiency.* No investor can earn excess returns by using any information, whether publicly available or not.[5]

Of these three definitions, the Semi-strong-form most directly challenges the assumptions of investors who seek to profit from fundamental credit analysis. It indicates that merely gathering information on a firm or its industry cannot help an investor to outperform the market. (Gathering information directly from a company—assuming the information is lawfully and equitably transmitted to anyone who requests it—presumably falls under the definition of "publicly available.") If true, the Semi-strong-form Efficient Market Hypothesis implies that investment organizations are not well served by devoting scarce resources to fundamental analysis aimed at identifying misvalued securities.

A Logical Extension

Of special interest for this article is another proposition that follows logically from the Semi-strong-form, to wit: Once information becomes public, it is immediately incorporated into securities prices. Therefore, merely repeating the same information in a public forum cannot affect prices.

We are interested in this implication offspring of the Efficient Market Hypothesis because evidence presented below appears to contradict it (at least as an absolute statement of how the markets invariably function). The incidents we recount point to market responses to "old news," which—in addition to being an oxymoron—is something that could never influence prices, according to the Efficient Market Hypothesis. A staunch supporter of the Hypothesis would insist that even if "old news" appeared to be the cause of a price change, some other factor must be at work, for example, information of an unrelated nature entering the market at the same time. The most fanatic Efficient Market partisans resemble the proverbial finance professor who spotted a $500 bill on the sidewalk but ignored it and walked on, saying, "If this bill were real, and not just an illusion, somebody else would already have picked it up."

In recent years, Efficient Market theorists have tended to moderate their views, acknowledging that certain information—although technically public—is costly to obtain. As a result, it may not be widely disseminated and fully reflected in prices. Investors should likewise temper theory with observation of real-life conditions and not allow ideological rigidity to cause them to overlook genuine found money (common parlance for "excess returns"). We present below two incidents in which previously available information appears to have had significant market impact when reported in a way that made it seem new. When similar conditions arise in the future, investors who accept our conclusions will feel confident in acting on the assumption that such inefficiencies can and do occur. Those who own the unjustly maligned securities will resist the impulse to sell at distress prices. As prices fall to levels unwarranted by the fundamentals, they may even elect to buy, as will new players who recognize an undervalued situation.

CASE STUDY I: MIDDLE SOUTH UTILITIES

Background

The Middle South Utilities (MSU) case involved litigation related to the Grand Gulf 1 nuclear power plant. Briefly, on February 25, 1987 the Mississippi Supreme Court reversed a September 1985 Mississippi Public Service Commission order that had granted permanent rate relief to Middle South's subsidiary, Mississippi Power & Light (MP&L), for recovery of costs related to Grand Gulf 1. MP&L subsequently filed an appeal of the February 25 decision with the U. S. Supreme Court. On October 5, 1987, the U. S. Supreme Court agreed to hear MP&L's appeal. from that point until June 24, 1988, when the U. S. Supreme Court's decision in favor of MP&L was announced, investors' attention was sharply focused on the case. Had the ruling gone against MP&L, the MPSC rate order could have been modified or canceled. Middle South acknowledged during the period that cancellation or modification of its Grand Gulf rates, without an offsetting reduction in costs, could have quickly rendered MP&L insolvent.

Press Coverage

On April 13, 1988 an article appeared in the *Wall Street Journal* under the headline, "Middle South Utilities Says One or More of Its Units Is Facing Chapter 11 Filing." Quoting a Securities and Exchange Commission filing, the author reported that, "Middle South Utilities Inc. said it 'could be difficult to avoid' bankruptcy-law proceedings for one or more of its units because of a series of adverse rate decisions." The author characterized the disclosure (which was drawn from Middle South's 1987 form 10-K, filed on April 7, 1988) as apparently "the starkest assessment yet of the problems ahead" for Middle South. Elaborating on Middle South's outlook, the article again quoted the SEC filing:

> "Future events either singly or in combination, may result in such adverse changes in business circumstances or such a decrease in liquidity as to make it prudent for one or more of the Middle South companies to file a Chapter 11 petition."

Additional items reported in the article included:

- Retention of special bankruptcy counsel "to study financial relief under a Chapter 11 filing for the parent and two of its units, Mississippi Power & Light Co. and System Energy Resources, Inc."
- Possible insolvency of Middle South subsidiary New Orleans Public Service (NOPSI) as early as 1988's second quarter and a possible need for the subsidiary to redeem up to $115 million of mortgage bonds as early as July 1988.
- A writedown facing the System Energy Resources (SERI) subsidiary due to an earlier Federal Energy Regulatory Commission (FERC) ruling limiting passthrough in rates to 50% of prudently incurred costs of a canceled plant. (Grand Gulf 2's construction had been suspended nearly three years earlier and cancellation was possible.)

The balance of the *Journal* article consisted of background information and a review of events that the author identified as previously reported.

Market Response

There was no unusual price movement in Middle South bonds on the day the *Wall Street Journal* article appeared. Over the following two days, however, a representative MSU subsidiary issue, the System Energy Resources 14% first mortgage bonds due 1994, plummeted from 101 to 93 in over-the-counter trading (Exhibit 18–1). *Bondweek*, a publication of Institutional Investor, Inc., reported in its April 18, 1988 edition that, "Many bonds of Middle South Utilities traded down by seven to 10 points last week" and attributed the selloff to press reports highlighting the potential bankruptcy. Judging by a comparison with the Morgan Stanley High Yield Composite over the same period, the declines observed in Middle South paper did not simply reflect a general slump in lower-rated bonds. On April 8, shortly before the *Wall Street Journal* article appeared, the SERI 14s were priced at a spread of 82 basis points over the Composite. That differential had widened to 286 basis points by April 15, confirming a severe relative decline by the SERI bonds.

Cause and Effect

Summarizing to this point, we have established that a *Wall Street Journal* article reporting a possible bankruptcy at Middle South Utilities was followed, on the day after publication, by a sharp decline, relative to the high yield market, in Middle South subsidiaries' debt. The casual observer would probably regard these two events as more than coincidental, but the evidence presented so far does not demonstrate a causal relationship. Indeed, unequivocal proof is always difficult to obtain in such cases.

Exhibit 18–1
Yield Spread History
System Energy 14% due 11/15/94 versus
Morgan Stanley High Yield Composite

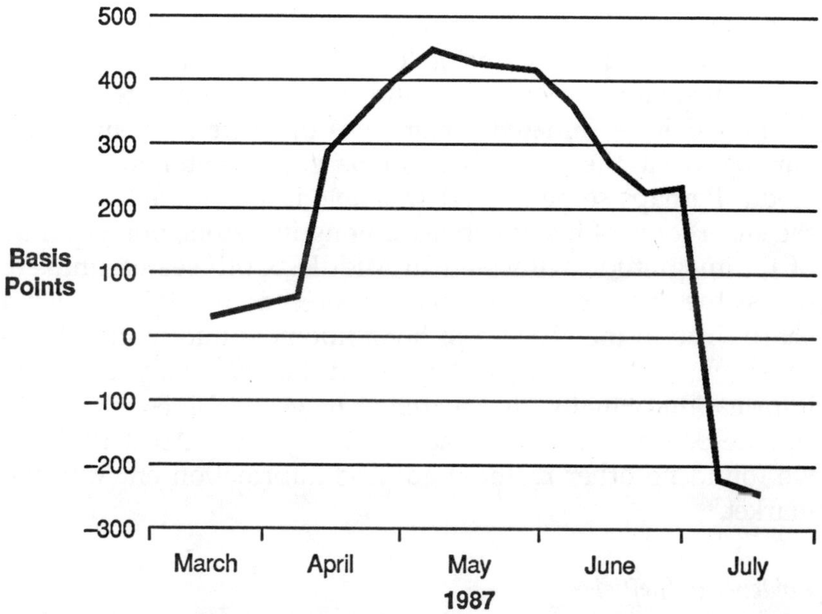

Some market participants have suggested that other factors contributed to the Middle South selloff. For one thing, many of the leading high yield portfolio managers were out of their offices attending an investment bank-sponsored bond conference when the *Wall Street Journal* article appeared. In their absence, less senior officials left in charge of the major portfolios were reportedly reluctant to buy the rapidly cheapening, but still highly controversial Middle South bonds. As a result, some said, there was an absence of the value-oriented support that would ordinarily have curbed the price decline. In addition to this unusual technical situation, some market participants alleged that high yield investors had been motivated to sell Middle South paper by an analyst's presentation that was critical of the credit.

Notwithstanding these possible contributors to the Middle South price decline, we are justified in characterizing the *Wall Street Journal* article as the primary—if not necessarily the sole—cause. If key decisionmakers were away from their offices and consequently unable to buy Middle South paper as it was cheapening, neither would their subordinates in all likelihood have initiated major sales on their own authority, barring what they perceived to be significant news on the credit. Perhaps some analyst was able to move the market by the sheer force of his credibility among investors, but a decline of the magnitude witnessed in Middle South seems unlikely unless the analyst had new facts to present. (Certainly, such a sharp drop in the absence of bona fide new information is inconsistent with the image of a market that efficiently discounts information.) Finally, in a search of news headlines relating to Middle South Utilities for the week beginning April 10, 1988, we found no other material adverse information entering the market.[6]

Evidence of Inefficiency

If it is true that the *Wall Street Journal* article moved the market, then the market moved on old information. We can support this claim by individually examining the facts reported.

Beginning with the article's key point, Middle South's SEC Form 10-Q for 1987's third quarter (filed on November 19, 1987) had already alluded to the possibility of bankruptcy:

> "In the event of any of the foregoing adverse developments, the continuing viability of the Middle South System would be placed in jeopardy, and it could be difficult to avoid a bankruptcy filing by SERI or other affected Middle South System companies. In this connection, MSU, MP&L and SERI have each retained independent special counsel experienced in bankruptcy matters and have been studying the relief and protection that might be available to them under Chapter 11 of

> the United States Bankruptcy Code. While no decisions with regard to bankruptcy filings have yet been made, it must be recognized, in light of the risks discussed herein, that future events, many of which are beyond the control of the Middle South System, either singly or in combination, may result in such adverse changes in liquidity as to make it prudent for SERI or other affected Middle South System companies to file a petition for reorganization under Chapter 11."

It is noteworthy that portions of this excerpt appeared verbatim (as we have in turn quoted above) or were closely paraphrased in the *Wall Street Journal*'s April 13 article. As for the potential bankruptcy of New Orleans Public Service, the November 1987 SEC filing had this to say:

> "Without adequate rates to recover Grand Gulf 1 charges, MP&L and NOPSI could suffer such liquidity constraints that they would, in a short period of time, be unable to meet their contractual obligations to SERI in respect of the Grand Gulf Station and could be rendered insolvent."

The earlier filing also discussed potential mandatory debt redemptions that NOPSI might be unable to meet, although in a slight difference from the *Wall Street Journal*'s reference to $115 million of mortgage bonds, the third quarter 10-Q discussed $75 million of "Rate Recovery Mortgage Bonds."

The last specific point raised in the *Wall Street Journal* article, the potential Grand Gulf 2 writeoff facing SERI, was based on a section of Middle South's 1987 10-K entitled "Uncertainties Relating to Grand Gulf 2." The section mainly summarized previously reported information dating back to September 1985. The most recent event discussed was a January 1988 FERC order regarding recovery of canceled or abandoned plant costs. Since this development had already been reported in the trade press (for example, McGraw Hill's Engineering News-Record covered it in an article entitled "New FERC Rule Changes Cost Recovery of Projects" on January 21), it was certainly not news on April 13. (The *Journal* article included the detail that SERI's investment in Grand Gulf

2 was approximately $890 million as of December 31, 1987, but inasmuch as construction had been suspended since September 1985, the figure was essentially unchanged from what was reported in earlier SEC filings.)

Alternative Explanations

We have now shown that aside from the change in the amount of NOPSI's potential mandatory debt retirement, the *Wall Street Journal*'s April 13, 1988 article presented no new information. This finding draws us closer to the conclusion that SERI 14s fell by eight points on April 14 in response to old information newly (and dramatically) reported. First, however, we must address two alternative explanations, namely, that the Middle South debt declined not because of the *Wall Street Journal* article, but in response to:

a. Other news concurrently reported, or
b. Material new disclosures in Middle South's 1987 10-K that were not reported in the *Wall Street Journal* article yet were material enough to motivate holders to sell Middle South debt.[7]

On the first point, a news search on Middle South Utilities revealed no items on or around April 13, 1988 that could explain the subsequent selloff. Likewise, our reading of the 10-K does not indicate that the *Wall Street Journal* reporter missed anything that would have justified as large a decline as occurred.

Subsequent Market Activity

Unfortunately, from the standpoint of demonstrating market inefficiency, the reaction to the *Wall Street Journal* article did not create a clearcut trading opportunity. Ideally, the initial decline in SERI 14s would have been corrected, after a brief interval, by a sharp "snapback" in price. A pattern of this kind, suggesting that investors eventually recognized their error, would have reinforced the impression that the market initially mistook the old information for new. Instead, the SERI 14s continued to drop in the weeks following the first shock, hitting a low of 85 (a yield of 18.00%) on May 2, with the Composite all the while hovering around 13%. During this period the picture was muddied by additional news, including a year-over-year quarterly earnings decline. By June 24, when the Supreme Court ruled in Middle South's favor (boosting the bonds first to 109 and then to 112 within a few days), the SERI bonds had already begun to recover, reaching 95 by June 14. This move does not really fit the definition of a snapback, however. In short, there was too much going on in Middle South for investors to profit quickly and cleanly from the price decline precipitated by the April 13 *Wall Street Journal* article. Still, the selloff provides strong evidence of market inefficiency in the form of a sharp reaction to information that in theory should already have been incorporated into prices.

CASE STUDY II: BETHLEHEM STEEL

Press Coverage

On March 5, 1987 an article headlined, "Bethlehem Steel Asked Lawyers to Study Chapter 11 Move; No Filing Seen Soon" appeared in the *Wall Street Journal*. The author reported that the nation's third-largest steelmaker had "asked its New York law firm to study the implications of a bankruptcy filing." Furthermore, the article indicated that unnamed sources had said that Weil Gotshal & Manges, "a prominent firm known for bankruptcy work," had briefed Bethlehem's directors about the ramifications of a bankruptcy filing. Walter F. Williams, Bethlehem's chairman, was quoted in the article as acknowledging that management had educated itself about the advantages and disadvantages of Chapter 11, as part of its responsibility to understand all of its options.

Market Response

In the wake of the *Journal* article, Bethlehem Steel's 8.45% debentures due 2005 fell precipitously vis-a-vis the market (Exhibit 18–2). From 56 ¼ on March 4 the bonds fell to as low as 48 on March 10. This represented an increase in yield to maturity from 15.87% to 18.47%, while weekly quotes on the Morgan Stanley High Yield Composite remained in a range of 11.50% to 11.60%.

Cause and Effect

These facts do not by themselves establish a cause-and-effect relationship between the *Wall Street Journal*'s article and the plunge in Bethlehem's bonds. Indeed, the article stressed that neither Williams nor other industry experts expected an imminent Chapter 11 filing. Nonetheless, the specter of default was raised. Considering also that a news search we conducted revealed no other significant disclosures in the first few days of March, there is a strong presumption that the *Journal* story touched off the decline in Bethlehem paper.

Evidence of Inefficiency

If the selloff in Bethlehem bonds in fact resulted from the March 5 article, it was another case of the market responding to old information. About two months earlier, in the *Business Week* dated January 12, 1987, two reporters wrote that one or two more steel bankruptcies could prompt the White House to provide new relief to the steel industry:

> "The financial plight of Bethlehem Steel Corp., the No. 3 producer, could tip the balance. While the company's chief executive, Walter F. Williams, says he has 'made no decision to file Chapter 11 at this time,' he adds that Bethlehem may have to seek it this year."

Not only did Bethlehem's bonds begin to sell off when the *Wall Street Journal* repeated a two-month old story, but they

Exhibit 18–2
Yield Spread History
Bethlehem Steel 8.45% due 3/1/05
Morgan Stanley High Yield Composite

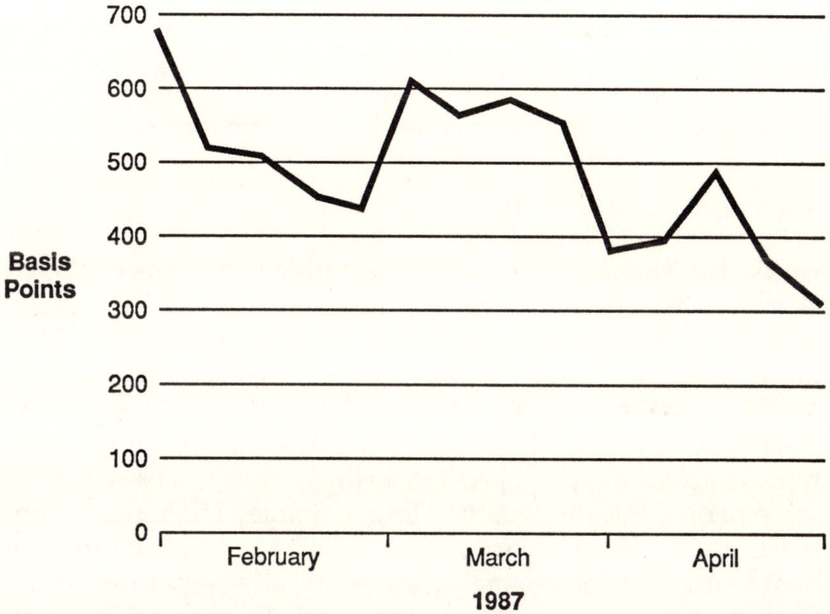

continued to decline even after the Associated Press—on the same day the *Journal* article appeared—quoted Bethlehem spokesman Henry H. Von Spreckelsen as follows:

> "This is not anything new. We said this last year . . . after LTV filed for bankruptcy. It wouldn't be prudent management not to look into this matter after a major competitor did the same thing."

Even the *Journal* article acknowledged that Bethlehem's study of the bankruptcy option had begun "in the months after the July 17 (1986) filing of LTV Corp.," although it did not mention that reports of the same had previously appeared in the press.[8]

One might argue that the *Wall Street Journal*'s March 5 article provided new facts in the form of the specific information that Bethlehem had hired bankruptcy counsel. This information was not directly confirmed by Bethlehem's chairman, however, and Williams had already conceded that bankruptcy was an option in the earlier *Business Week* article. Accordingly, it is a fair inference that the *Wall Street Journal*'s impact derived primarily from the attention it drew to the Chapter 11 option rather than from any specific new information it presented.

Subsequent Market Activity

Unlike the Middle South issues, the Bethlehem bonds exhibited a "snapback," corroborating the thesis that the market initially erred in its response to old news. By the close on March 6, 1987, the Bethlehem 8.45s were down to 50, a yield to maturity of 17.77%. Less than a month later (April 3), without any major new disclosures affecting the credit, the bonds had recovered to 58, representing a 236-basis point drop in yield, to 15.41%. Over the same period, the yield on the Morgan Stanley High Yield Composite *rose* by 11 basis points, from 11.54% to 11.65%. In terms of total return, the Bethlehem 8.45s dramatically outperformed the Composite for the one-month period (17.2% versus 0.7%, both figures non-annualized). Note that to achieve this magnitude of excess return investors did not have to catch the absolute bottom in the Bethlehem 8.45s (48, an 18.47% yield, on March 10).

As a postscript, Bethlehem Steel not only survived but thrived in subsequent quarters, culminating in upgrades by Standard & Poor's in January 1988 and by Moody's in July 1988.

How Could This Happen?

The Middle South and Bethlehem case studies suggest that the Semi-strong-form of the Efficient Market Hypothesis does not apply at all times. Strictly speaking, the evidence we have presented does not establish when it was that the securities in question were misvalued, i.e., before or after the respective *Wall Street Journal* articles appeared. If, however, the bonds fell precipitously on the reporting of information that was demonstrably not new, then they clearly could not have been properly valued both before and after the prices dropped.

Where is the flaw in the Semi-strong argument that permitted these anomalies to occur? In the case studies we have discussed, the problem with the Efficient Market Hypothesis seems to be its inadequate consideration of the way news is reported. "Slanting" and sensationalizing are examples of journalistic techniques that blatantly and consciously seek to elicit reader responses that the facts alone do not justify. Middle South and Bethlehem bonds were affected by a subtler form of news management—an editorial decision about the prominence assigned to a particular item. Unlike the ethically questionable practices of slanting and sensationalizing, a reporter's choice about which facts should go in the article's "lead" may be morally neutral and need not be intentionally manipulative. We in no way desire to impugn the motives of the authors and editors of the articles discussed herein. At the same time, we do wish to underscore how powerfully the presentation of news can shape the public's perception of reality. When the information reported is financial in nature, extraordinarily large economic decisions can proceed from such perceptions.

The Middle South article discussed several matters, but its market impact derived primarily from the prominence it assigned (headline and lead paragraph) to the company's consideration of bankruptcy. In Middle South's 10-K, the same material constituted 1 1/2 pages of a document that ran 137 pages (excluding financial statement schedules). *The Wall Street Journal*'s editorial decision to highlight the bankruptcy angle might have been justified on the grounds that it was the most newsworthy element of the 10-K, except that, as we have already seen, it was not in fact news. Nevertheless, some of the *Journal*'s readers evidently inferred from the two-column headline and the 11 column inches devoted to the item that management's contemplation of a Chapter 11 filing was a significant new development. Editorial decisions played a still clearer role in the Bethlehem Steel episode. The essence of the *Wall Street Journal's* March 5, 1987 article was contained in *Business Week's* article two months earlier. All that differed was the prominence assigned to the bankruptcy angle. the *Wall Street Journal* not only referred to Chapter 11 in its headline, but each of the first 11 paragraphs contained the words "bankruptcy," "Chapter 11" or "filing." In contrast, *Business Week* made no specific reference to a Chapter 11 filing by Bethlehem until paragraph 10 of a story on page 81 entitled "One More Chorus of the Steelyard Blues." Earlier paragraphs dealt with the possibility of "massive bankruptcies" in the steel industry, but Bethlehem's plight was certainly easier to miss in *Business Week*'s account than in the *Wall Street Journal's* later article.[9] Furthermore, even if investors noticed the item in *Business Week,* they may have given it less credence than they subsequently gave to the later *Wall Street Journal* reference, which might have appeared to be better supported by virtue of its greater length.

A Non-Financial Parallel

A student of the media would not regard the huge impact of the editorial choices made by the *Wall Street Journal* and *Business Week* as either remarkable or surprising. Nor, by any means, is such influence confined to the financial arena. Public perceptions of political events, scientific developments and social trends are shaped every day by decisions about which article will rate a front-page banner headline and which response made during a half-hour news conference will provide the lead to the wire service dispatch.

The late Theodore H. White's book, *The Making of the President 1968,*[10] recounted a spectacular example of the power of news management in the political sphere. A comparison with the preceding financial example is instructive.

An Unfortunate Choice of Words

George Romney, then governor of Michigan, was a leading candidate for the 1968 Republican Presidential nomination. A Louis Harris Survey conducted in August 1967 showed Romney running closest to the incumbent, Democrat Lyndon Johnson, among the Republican contenders. His fortunes, however, took a rapid turn for the worse following the "brainwashing" incident, an event that owed a great deal to editorial selectivity.

On August 31, 1967, Romney taped a television interview with Lou Gordon, a Detroit talk show host. At one point in the interview, Gordon asked whether Romney's latest, somewhat "dovish" position on Vietnam was not inconsistent with his earlier views. The candidate replied:

> "Well, you know when I came back from Vietnam, I just had the greatest brainwashing that anybody can get when you go over to Vietnam. Not only by the Generals, but also by the diplomatic corps over there, and they do a very thorough job. And since returning from Vietnam, I've gone into the history of Vietnam, all the way back into World War II and before. And, as a result, I have changed my mind . . . in that particular. I no longer believe that it was necessary for us to get involved in South Vietnam to stop Communist aggression."

Astute News Management

Initially, no one who observed the taping attached particular significance to these few sentences within a lengthy interview. The advance publicity for the Lou Gordon program, which was eventually aired on September 5, mentioned only Romney's disavowal of interest in the Vice Presidential nomination. In reading the interview transcript on September 3, though, Gordon spotted the brainwashing comment and highlighted it in a telephone call to the *New York Times*'s Detroit correspondent, to whom he sent the full transcript. the *Times* correspondent, in turn, gave little prominence to the brainwashing remark in his dispatch, but in New York the editors agreed with Gordon's perception of what the hot story was. On September 5, the day after the Gordon program was aired, the *New York Times* headlined its article, "Romney Asserts He Underwent 'Brainwashing' on Vietnam Trip."

The Campaign Crumbles

Although the *Times* relegated Romney's interview to page 28, the television network news programs picked up the story and that evening broadcast a 30-second clip of Romney's "confession" that he had been brainwashed. Presented out of context and entirely out of proportion to its importance in the interview, the comment not only branded Romney as dangerously suggestible, but also portrayed him as questioning the integrity of General William Westmoreland and Ambassador Henry Cabot Lodge, who had briefed him in Vietnam. Never mind that Romney surely did not intend to suggest that American officials had literally used the insidious mind-control techniques inflicted on U. S. prisoners of war during the Korean conflict. The remark, according to the *New York Times*'s sources, "exposed Romney to ridicule"[11] and his standing in the polls immediately plummeted. A September 1967 Harris poll showed Romney down from first to fourth place among Republican candidates in matchups against Johnson. By late December he trailed rival Richard Nixon by a margin of 64.2% to 12.0% in a private poll. Romney's campaign never recovered from the brainwashing incident. Two weeks before the New Hampshire primary Romney withdrew from the race.

By highlighting one tiny segment of an interview, a snippet that others thought inconsequential, Gordon, the *New York Times* editors and the networks helped change the course of the 1968 Presidential election. By comparison, an eight-point drop in System Energy bonds seems a small thing to achieve through a similar choice of emphasis.

Conclusion

The case studies presented in this article do not suggest to us that the high yield market is rife with inefficiencies, or more prone than other markets to irrational panic selling. In the Bethlehem Steel case, for instance, the equity market also seemed to react to the March 5, 1987 *Wall Street Journal* article, although it snapped back a bit more quickly than the bond market. Between March 4 and March 9, Bethlehem common stock fell from 8 3/8 to 6 7/8, a decline of 17.9% versus a 1.2% rise in the Dow Jones Industrial Average. By March 26, Bethlehem had recovered to its March 4 close of 8 3/8. (At this point the stock was still somewhat lagging the Dow, which was up 5.1% over the period.) Occasional deviations from the idealized conditions imagined by Efficient Market advocates, then, are not unique to high yield. Rather, the lesson to be derived from this study is that theory should not blind one to genuine opportunities. The next time the market appears to be reacting to old news, investors need not assume that some other factor, of which they are unaware, is driving prices.

In particular, portfolio managers should be prepared to recognize a recurrence of the specific conditions that affected Middle South and Bethlehem. A newspaper article suggesting the possibility of a bankruptcy, followed by a sharp decline in the supposedly failing company's bonds, should always be viewed with skepticism. Holders of the issue should not sell at distress prices before verifying that the report reflects new information. If they fail to check their facts, they may later find that they have sold at the bottom, then watch in dismay as the bonds snap back to their previous level. Similarly, value-oriented investors should not automatically reject as too risky a name recently tarnished by intimations of bankruptcy. Upon closer investigation, the newspaper's account may be nothing more than a rehash of information that was already discounted when the bonds were trading several points higher. The Romney brainwashing incident, moreover, shows that the manner in which news is reported can determine how readers will interpret it. Based on the Middle South and Bethlehem Steel precedents, it is quite possible for the market to misinterpret information because of the way it is presented, creating a genuine opportunity to obtain above-market returns on a risk-adjusted basis.

Endnotes

[1] See for example, Richard Bookstaber and David P. Jacob, "The Composite Hedge: Controlling the Credit Risk of High Yield Bonds," Morgan Stanley & Co., Incorporated (March 1985). In essence, a corporate bond can be viewed as a hybrid consisting of a pure interest rate instrument and a short position in a put on the equity of the firm. This put is exercisable against the bondholder only if the firm goes bankrupt, at which point the bondholder becomes the firm's owner. The option is deep out-of-the-money in a highly rated bond, since the probability of bankruptcy in the near term is small. Accordingly, the bond's price movement reflects primarily fluctuations in the general level of interest rates. In contrast, the implicit put in a low-rated bond can significantly affect price movements, since the likelihood of default (and therefore exercise of the option) is much greater than it is for the high-grade bond.

[2] One notable exception is the case of a highly rated company that unexpectedly becomes the target of a hostile takeover or announces that it has agreed to a leveraged buyout. Its bonds may fall sharply, despite a stable or rising market for other fixed income obligations, because of a perception that the issuer's financial risk will increase radically.

[3] Throughout this article, the terms "underperformance" and "outperformance" should be understood to mean, respectively, producing a return less than or greater than the market index, on a risk-adjusted basis. Similarly, an "excess return" by definition does not apply to an above-market return derived simply by taking above-market risk.

[4] Thomas E. Copeland and J. Fred Weston, *Financial Theory and Corporate Policy*, 2nd ed. (Reading, Massachusetts: Addison-Wesley Publishing Company, Inc., 1983) p. 287.

[5] Ibid.

[6] The *Wall Street Journal's* April 13, 1988 article reported, in addition to the disclosures regarding a possible bankruptcy filing, one favorable development for Middle South—a Louisiana Supreme Court affirmation of a Louisiana Power & Light rate increase.

[7] Yet another possible explanation for the severe selloff in Middle South paper is "blind necessity," i.e., a large sale made for no credit-related reason but rather for financial reasons related solely to the seller, such as a need to raise cash to meet obligations. While such a transaction could conceivably have had some price impact, the fact that declines of seven to 10 points were required to clear the market in Middle South debt indicates that as of April 14 potential buyers were extremely averse to the name. It strains credulity to suppose that a chance seller of Middle South paper just happened to come into the market in massive size the day after a negative article appeared in The Wall Street Journal. In such circumstances it is more likely that an investor who needed to raise cash would have selected a less out-of-favor security to liquidate.

[8] Bethlehem's September 30, 1986 10-Q, its first following the LTV bankruptcy, did not specifically refer to an exploration of the same option for Bethlehem. There was an allusion to serious problems, however:

> "The domestic steel industry is in a state of financial crisis. Bethlehem welcomes the recent appointment by the President of a Task Force to further examine the causes and possible solution to the crisis. In addition to Bethlehem's own intensive efforts, prompt and effective action by the government and others is required to ensure the long-term viability of the domestic steel industry."

[9] If the issues selected for our case studies were obscure and illiquid, we could not reject market manipulation as an alternative explanation of the extreme price volatility observed. The SERI 14s and Bethlehem Steel 8.45s, however, are actively traded, regularly quoted high yield securities. If a few dealers or investors artificially drove down the bonds without the aid of significant new information, then the Efficient Market Hypothesis was refuted, as surely as if the cause was, as we contend, a response to "old news." A manipulated price would not accurately reflect all available information, as the Efficient Market Hypothesis demands.

[10] Atheneum Publishers (New York, 1969). The remainder of this chapter, up to the Conclusion, draws heavily on White's account.

[11] Warren Weaver, Jr., "Scope of Romney's Financial and Popular Support Uncertain," *New York Times* (September 18, 1967): p. 4.

CHAPTER 19

The Effect of Dividend Eliminations on Yield Spreads

Problem

Two opposing opinions regarding the impact of dividend eliminations on bond values prevail among market participants. The first view is that elimination of the dividend is most likely to cause the issuer's bonds to appreciate relative to other debt securities. According to this school, the consequent reduction in cash outflow to shareholders makes more cash available to service debt in the future. Following the logic of what we have designated the Cash Flow Hypothesis, the firm's balance sheet strengthens as a result, and higher perceived credit quality causes the yield spread on its bonds to narrow. The alternative interpretation takes into account the firm's bias toward preserving the dividend, in part because controlling directors may depend heavily on it for their personal income. In this view, the firm is unlikely to suspend its dividend until forced to in order to maintain solvency. Therefore, a dividend cut signals investors that its prospects have changed for the worse. The Signaling Hypothesis, as we have named it, logically suggests that perceived credit risk will increase and the spread on the issuer's bonds will widen.

(Note that this chapter focuses on dividend elimination, defined as a decision by a company that paid a dividend in the preceding quarter to cease paying it. Decisions to continue to omit the dividend in future quarters, before it has been resumed, are not considered in this study. Similarly, we have not dealt with dividend reductions that leave dividends at levels greater than zero.)

Methodology

Because these two reasonable hypotheses lead to opposite recommended responses, the fixed income investor who wishes to make a rational decision needs empirical evidence of actual bond behavior following dividend eliminations. To supply this evidence, we collected a sample of all public debt issuers that eliminated their regular quarterly common dividends between 1975 and 1984. We next obtained pricing data for each company's most liquid bond, covering the periods six months prior to and six months following the elimination. Eleven pricing records were unacceptable because of missing or erroneous data, leaving a final sample of 31 companies, shown along with the dates of their dividend eliminations in Exhibit 19–1.

By sorting these data, we first attempted to answer the question: Is a bond's quality spread more likely to widen or to narrow following elimination of the issuer's dividend? Once we answered this question, thereby generating a basic decision rule, we attempted to refine the decision rule further through more detailed analysis of the data.

Findings

Exhibit 19–2 shows that wider spreads followed the majority of dividend eliminations. Measured over the period beginning at the end of the month prior to the elimination and ending six months after the elimination, 61% of the bonds widened versus the Moody's Aaa Corporate Index while 39% narrowed. For those that widened, the spread increased, on average, by 350 basis points, while the remainder narrowed by an average of 223 basis points.

Exhibit 19–1
Dividend Eliminations Among Public Debt Issuers 1975-1984*

Company	Dividend Cut Date
Allied Products	07-12-82
Allis Chalmers Manufacturing (D)	09-21-81
American Airlines	04-17-80
Armco Steel	07-30-84
Braniff Airways (D)	05-08-80
Buttes Gas & Oil Co. (D)	07-14-78
Consumers Power Co.	08-02-84
Crystal Oil Co (D).	11-08-84
Food Fair (Stores) (D)	09-06-78
Inernational Harvester Co.	12-19-80
Itel (D)	07-05-79
Johns Manville (D)	08-05-82
LSB Industries	11-04-82
Mego International (D)	10-16-80
Morton Shoes (D)	05-12-80
Nashua	10-25-82
Oak Industries (D)	05-17-83
Phelps Dodge	07-29-82
Public Service of New Hampshire (D)	04-13-84
Ramada Inns	09-10-81
Savin Business Machines	03-24-81
Sharon Steel (D)	04-22-82
Sunshine Mining Co.	11-30-81
Telecom	04-23-81
Texas International Air (D)	05-04-83
United Merchants & Manufacturers (D)	11-26-76
Universal Resources	12-03-82
Valero Energy	07-25-84
Western Airlines	10-28-80
Western Company of North America (D)	05-03-83
White Motor (D)	05-19-75

* Excludes certain issues for which pricing information was inadequate, as explained in Methodology section of text.

(D) = Companies that have been downgraded to D (signifying default) at Standard & Poor's since eliminating their dividends.

Exhibit 19–2
Analysis of Spread Changes and Dividend Eliminations

	Measurement Period	
Widening*	One Month Prior to Six Months After Dividend Elimination	One Month Prior to One Month After Dividend Elimination
Percent of bonds in sample widening after dividend cut	61%	65%
Average basis point widening	350	111
Smallest basis point widening	68	2
Largest basis point widening	917	270
Narrowing*		
Percent of bonds in sample narrowing after dividend cut	39%	35%
Average basis point narrowing	223	116
Smallest basis point narrowing	34	21
Largest basis point narrowing	407	454

*Versus Moody's Aaa Corporate Index.

The greater frequency, combined with the greater magnitude of widening relative to narrowing, points to a simple decision rule for superior performance: Sell on news of dividend eliminations. (Note that this decision rule applies to selling on the news, as distinguished from actions taken in anticipation of dividend eliminations, which are discussed below.) This finding supports the Signaling Hypothesis, suggesting that firms tend to resist eliminating their dividend until financing distress is imminent. Their belated efforts to conserve cash signal, perhaps unintentionally, that conditions are worse than their previous statements suggested. Further corroboration of this interpretation is the fact that by the end of 1988, 16 of the 31 companies in Exhibit 19–1 had defaulted at some point since they eliminated their dividends. This high (35%) mortality rate strongly supports a strategy of selling in anticipation of still worse news.

To improve on the superior performance promised by following the basic decision rule of selling on dividend eliminations, investors can exploit two other patterns that emerged from further study of the data. These patterns relate to previous dividend actions and industry effects.

Previous Dividend Actions

A company that has repeatedly reduced its dividend before eliminating it altogether has already signaled financial strain to the market. In these cases, the Cash Flow Hypothesis is more relevant. Investors are likely to react primarily to the beneficial effect of funds conservation, causing the quality spread to narrow. The implied decision rule is to buy on the news of a dividend elimination that follows a series of dividend reductions.

Industry Effects

Utility bonds may be more prone to narrow than to widen following a dividend elimination. The small sample size (only two of the 31 bonds in Exhibit 19-1 are electric utilities) prevents us from stating this proposition more emphatically, but the dynamics of utility regulation support it. Public utility commissioners are bound by the legal doctrine that the companies they regulate are entitled to earn a fair return, but they are also political creatures. In order to approve a politically unpopular rate increase, commissioners may have to delay until the eleventh hour, manufacturing a crisis that impresses upon the public the urgency of rate relief to save the utility. This script calls for all parties, including the stockholders, to share the ratepayer's pain. A dividend elimination in these circumstances is a quid pro quo and a sign that the crisis has passed. Frequently, rate relief follows close on the heels of a dividend elimination, Middle South Utilities's 1985 experience being a case in point. Narrowing, rather than widening of quality spreads is the probable consequence as uncertainty is reduced following the elimination.

Therefore, electric utilities apparently constitute a second exception to the general decision rule of selling on news of a dividend elimination.

In addition to decision rules for immediate responses to dividend eliminations, the data compiled for this study suggest strategies for trading bonds in anticipation of and subsequent to dividend eliminations. These additional decision rules, which are most appropriate for aggressive investors, derive from relationships between pre-elimination and post-elimination spread behavior. We observed three characteristic patterns among the spread histories, which we detail here, along with our interpretations of each.

Pattern 1

The largest spread change occurs within the first month following the dividend elimination. Exhibit 19–3, the spread history on Telecom 13 ⅜s of 1999, exemplifies this pattern, with the spread widening by 275 basis points during the month succeeding elimination. Most of the bonds in our sample followed this pattern, which is consistent with the Signaling Hypothesis. It implies that investors were unaware of the gravity of the company's problems until the dividend was terminated.

Pattern 2

The spread widens substantially in the month preceding the dividend elimination, then continues to widen after the announcement. Buttes Gas & Oil (Exhibit 19–4) displayed this pattern, with its 10 ¼s of 1997 widening by 225 points in the month leading up to the dividend elimination and by another 116 basis points in the month following it. This pattern suggests that news of the company's troubles was in the market before the firm suspended its dividend and reinforces the impression that firms tend to defer such actions beyond the point of prudency.

Exhibit 19–3
Telecom
Spread History of 13 3/8% due 10/1/99

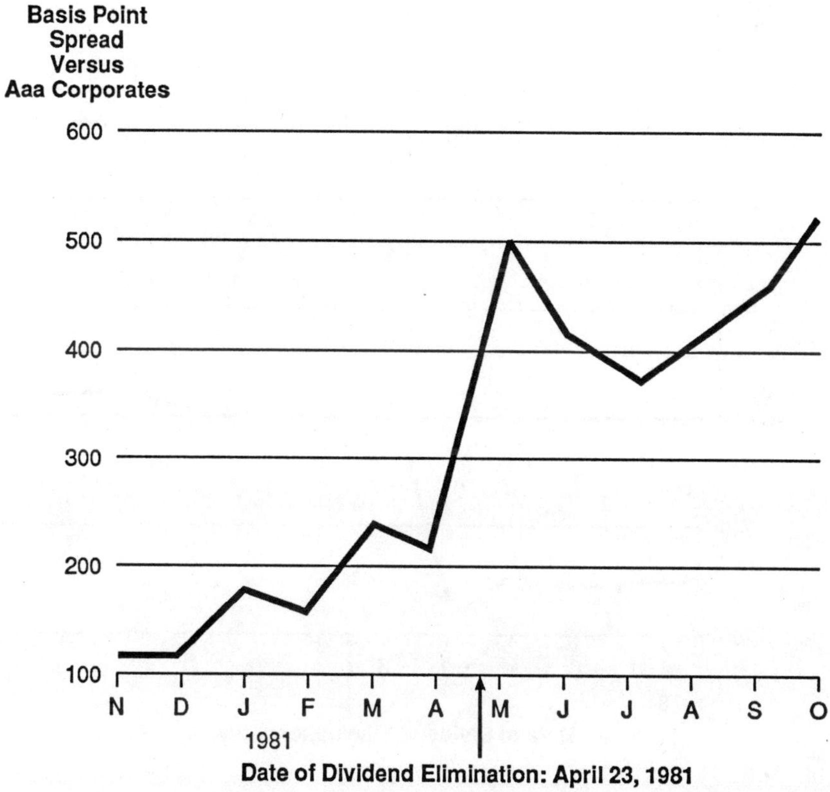

Exhibit 19–4
Buttes Gas & Oil
Spread History of 10 ¼% due 2/1/97

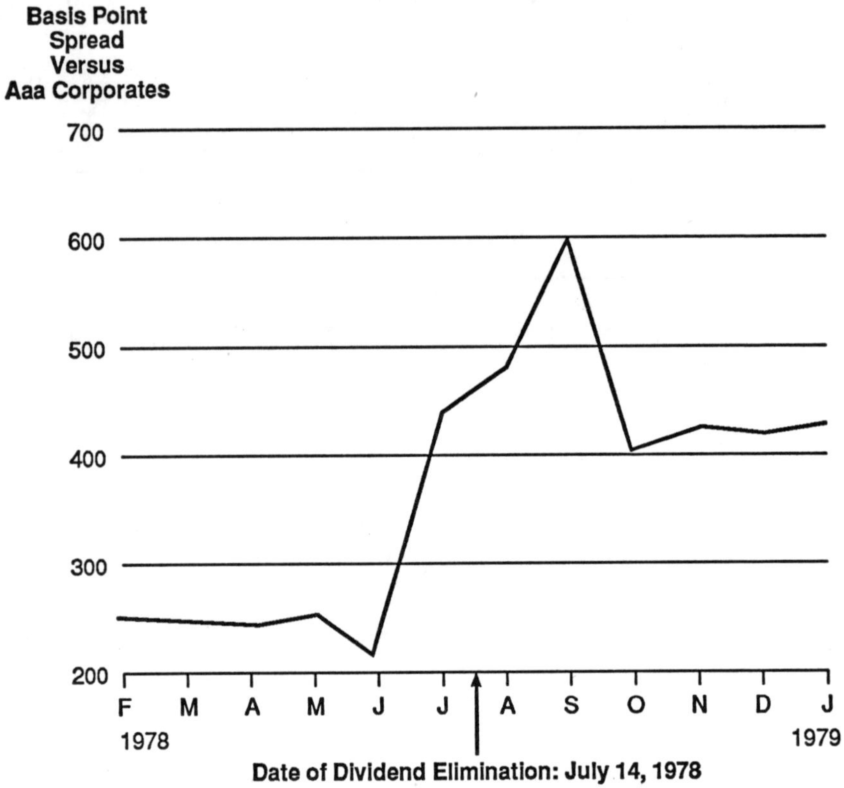

Pattern 3

The spread widens substantially several months before the dividend elimination, then narrows after the announcement. Exhibit 19–5 illustrates this pattern with the spread history of Public Service of New Hampshire's 15s of 2003, which widened by over 500 basis points during the period four to six months before the elimination. The subsequent narrowing conforms to the utility-specific scenario described under "Industry Effects." We believe this pattern reflects an even earlier dissemination of adverse news than shown by Pattern 2 immediately above. In

Exhibit 19–5
Public Service Company of New Hampshire
Spread History of 15% due 5/15/03

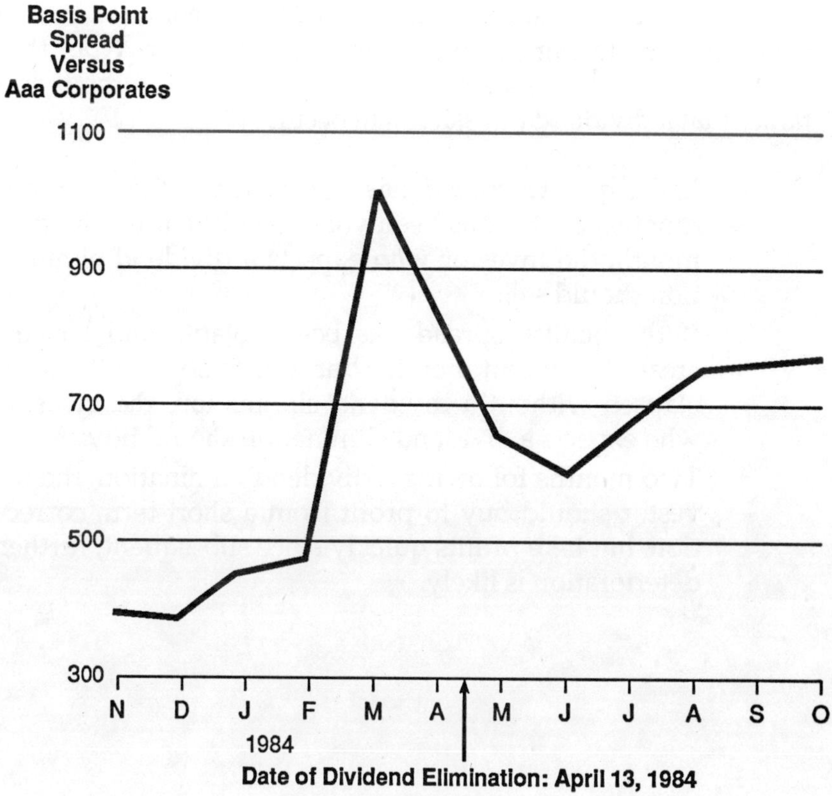

cases like Public Service of New Hampshire, so much time elapses between the market's initial reaction to the problem and the dividend elimination that resolution may already be well underway. It is understandable that narrowing, rather than widening of spreads follows.

A final observation on these trading histories is that in cases where the spread widens following the dividend elimination (Exhibits 19–3 and 19–4), the peak spread typically occurs about two months after the event. Because so many companies that eliminate their dividends subsequently default, long-term investors cannot safely assume that the worst has passed, even though spreads begin to narrow at that point. A short-term trading opportunity may exist, however, as a result of the market initially overshooting the adjustment necessitated by the new information embodied in the dividend elimination.

Based on the observed patterns, we can recommend three decision rules for aggressive, short-term investors. Note that the first two strategies require the investors to act without certainty that a dividend omission will occur.

1. If the quality spread has not been volatile in recent months, or if it has been volatile only within the past month, the investor who expects a dividend elimination should sell.
2. If the quality spread has been volatile and has increased in recent months, but four to six months have elapsed without a dividend elimination, the investor who expects a dividend elimination should buy.
3. Two months following a dividend elimination, the investor should buy to profit from a short-term correction, but take profits quickly since subsequent, further deterioration is likely.

Conclusion

Although by suspending its common dividend a company conserves cash and potentially strengthens its future financial position, the announcement of the dividend elimination usually signals investors that conditions are worse than they had thought. As a result, perceived credit risk in such situations tends to increase, rather than decrease. Moreover, the magnitude of perceived credit risk increases (measured by changes in yield spreads) exceeds the magnitude of the decreases. In general, therefore, investors should sell, rather than buy on news of dividend eliminations. Exceptions to this general rule include eliminations by companies that have repeatedly cut their dividends before eliminating them, and by electric utilities. Short-term trading opportunities exist prior to dividend eliminations, based on evidence that a particular company's problems either have or have not been anticipated by yield spread changes. In the post-elimination period, short-term opportunities result from the market's tendency toward initial overreaction to the revelation of previously unrecognized problems.

PART IV
Value of the High Yield Sector

CHAPTER 20

The Time Factor in High Yield Market Risk

In any analysis of market risk the investment horizon must be a central consideration. An institution with a substantial liquidity requirement may regard the short-term volatility of high yield bonds as a serious disadvantage. On the other hand, a portfolio that offsets 20-year liabilities is relatively unaffected by interim fluctuations in principal and can benefit fully from the power of compounding at a high rate.

Regrettably, this critical differentiation among investment objectives rarely enters the Great Junk Bond Debate. The press understandably emphasizes "the news," which is by definition current events in no particular context. Its sense of history is limited to "big stories" of the past, such as the Fall of the Nifty Fifty and the Collapse of the REITs. Reporters remind us that those catastrophes wiped out massive amounts of net worth, only occasionally noting that the undiversified and the over-leveraged (in other words, the greedy) investors were hardest hit.

Unfortunately, and to some extent unintentionally, the performance measurement industry has exacerbated this weakness of journalism by providing short-term return data that, however newsworthy, may obscure the long-range issues facing serious investment policy-makers. Armed with such data, the critics have characterized interim periods of underperformance by high yield bonds as evidence of their intolerably high risk. In our view, such conclusions overlook the sector's greatest strength—its ability to harness the long-run power of compound interest.

Measuring Market Risk

To reflect this fundamental strength in an analysis of high yield market risk, we have simulated the performance of two hypothetical portfolios (Exhibit 20–1). One portfolio approximates in coupon and maturity the Morgan Stanley High Yield Composite, which includes about 50 issues rated in the Double-B, Single-B and Triple-C categories. The other consists of a likely alternative investment—a portfolio of 21 seasoned issues with approximately the average coupon and maturity of Moody's Single-A Corporate Index. (We have chosen Single-As, rather than Treasuries, for our performance comparison on the premise that most investors who contemplate entry into the speculative-grade field are not so risk-averse as to have previously limited their selections to default-free government obligations.)

Exhibit 20–1
Comparison of Test Portfolios

	Average Coupon	Average Maturity
Single-A	9%	22 years
High Yield	13 ¾%	10 years

Using these portfolios to project future returns, we have assumed a 0% default rate on the Single-A portfolio and held its yield and price constant throughout the projection period. Its total return is therefore equivalent to its beginning yield to maturity over any specified period. As an additional consequence of holding the Single-A portfolio's yield constant, any widening of the Single-A/high yield spread is manifested as a rise in the yield (and a decline in the price) of the high yield portfolio.

For each scenario one chooses to test, a spread widening of a specific number of basis points ("the breakeven amount") will cause a sufficient price decline in the high yield portfolio to offset exactly its yield advantage over the Single-A portfolio. If the spread widens by any amount less than the breakeven amount, the high yield portfolio will outperform the Single-A portfolio. By comparing the size of the breakeven spread "cushion" to the actual historical variability of the Single-A/high yield spread, the investor can determine whether the risk of underperformance in speculative-grade debt is acceptable.

Note that this approach also permits investors to select the expected default loss rate they deem appropriate. In addition, the analysis sheds some light on the question of how large a yield premium over investment-grade paper is required to justify the risk of owning speculative-grade paper.

To understand the results of our simulation (Exhibit 20–2), let us consider a one-year projection with an assumed default loss rate of 200 basis points. (This figure represents the actual principal losses incurred in the portfolio, rather than the percentage of issues defaulting. That is, issues that default do not typically decline to 0% of face amount. Instead, they trade post-default at some price that represents the present value of their eventual worth either in liquidation or following emergence from reorganization proceedings. If on average the issues in the portfolio trade at 40% of face amount after default—approximately the actual historical experience—then an expected 200-basis-point default loss rate represents an expected default rate of .200/(1-.40) or 3.3%. Note that this is an average annual expectation; default rates have historically varied widely from year to year.)Looking at Section A of the exhibit, we observe that if the beginning Single-A/high yield spread is 250 basis points (i.e., a 10.00% yield on the Single-A portfolio and a 12.50% yield on the high yield portfolio), then, net of 200 basis points of expected default losses, the high yield portfolio will perform as well the Single-A portfolio as long as the spread

Exhibit 20–2
Breakeven Spread Widening

(A) One-Year Projection

Expected Annual Default Loss Rate	Beginning Single-A/High Yield Spread				
	150	200	250	300	350
100	10	20	30	40	51
150	0	10	20	30	41
200	-10	0	10	20	31
250	-19	-10	0	10	20
300	-29	-19	-10	0	10

(B) Five-Year Projection

Expected Annual Default Loss Rate	Beginning Single-A/High Yield Spread				
	150	200	250	300	350
100	117	243	378	523	681
150	0	119	247	385	533
200	-113	0	121	251	392
250	-223	-115	0	123	256
300	-330	-227	-117	0	126

Notes:
All amounts are in basis points.
The beginning yield to maturity of the Single-A portfolio is 10.00%.
Coupon income is reinvested at portfolio's beginning yield to maturity.
The default loss rate takes into account post-default residual values. That is, if on average bonds trade at 40% of face value subsequent to default, a default rate of 2% translates into a default loss rate of (1-.40) x 2% = 1.20%, or 120 basis points.

widens by no more than 10 basis points (i.e., from 250 to 260). The high yield portfolio will provide an inferior return if the spread widens by more than this breakeven amount.

Section B of Exhibit 20–2 shows that the cushion increases dramatically (thanks to the impact of compounding) as the investment horizon lengthens. Using the same assumptions as in the preceding example—an expected default loss rate of 200 basis points and a beginning Single-A/high yield spread of 250 basis points—the high yield portfolio will outperform provided the spread does not widen by as much as 121 basis points.

Historical experience suggests that under the assumptions we have made, high yield debt is a rather good bet. A widening of the breakeven amount of 121 basis points from the beginning spread of 250 would imply a future spread of 371 basis points. Exhibit 20–3 shows that the Single-A/high yield spread never reached that great a level during 1985-1988; the maximum differential was 333 basis points in November 1988. In fact, there were only six months out of 48 in which the actual spread came within 50 basis points of the 371 that would have eliminated the high yield portfolio's advantage. A four-year observation period may strike some readers as too short for drawing conclusions. We agree that some caution is warranted, but at the same time point out that during the period the yield on the Morgan Stanley High Yield Composite ranged from as low as 11.54% (March 1987) to as high as 15.32% (January and August 1985). Since future periods of economic stress will affect the perceived risk of Single-A bonds as well as high yield bonds, there is no strong presumption that the quality spread between the two will expand to more than its historical maximum during a recession. Indeed, a longer-term history of the Single-A/high yield spread calculated on a different basis (refer to Chapter 16, Exhibit 16–4) confirms that the differential remained within approximately a 200-basis-point band between 1975 and 1985. Default losses, on the other hand, probably will increase during future economic downturns, yet over a five-year horizon the 200-basis-point assumption looks reasonably conservative. During the period 1985-1988 the actual experience was 160 basis points. In short, an investor with a five-year horizon can be fairly confident of outperforming Single-A corporates when buying at a spread of 250 basis points over Single-As, a bit less than the 1985-1988 average of 268.

Exhibit 20–3
Yield Spread History
Moody's Single-A Corporates versus Morgan Stanley High Yield Composite*

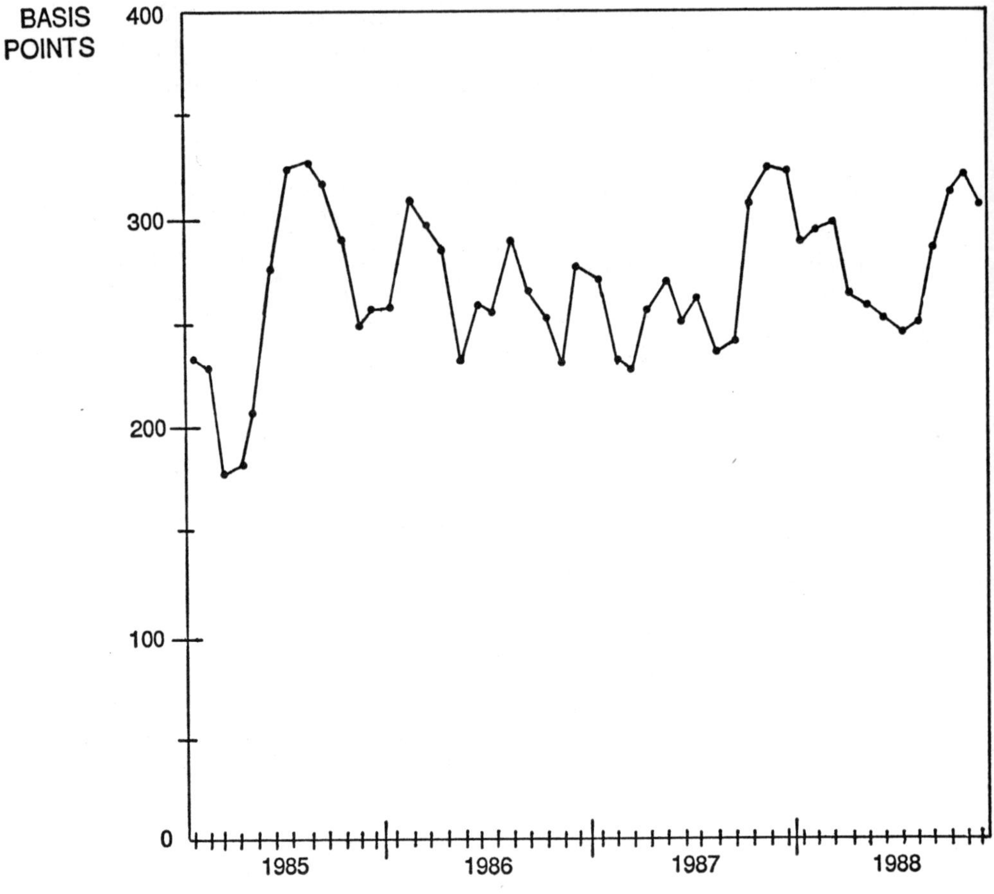

* Spread calculated at mid-month for January 1985 through 1986. From July 1986 onward, spread is the average for the month.

Sources: Morgan Stanley & Co. Incorporated, Moody's *Bond Record*, Moody's *Bond Survey*.

That confidence, it must be acknowledged, is highly dependent on managing credit risk so as to replicate or improve upon historical experience. At the same beginning yield spread of 250 basis points, a portfolio manager who suffers average annual default losses of 300 basis points will underperform Single-A bonds unless the Single-A/high yield spread narrows by 117 basis points to produce a capital gain. A narrowing of that magnitude implies a spread at the end of the five-year period of 133 basis points—a tighter spread than the minimum recorded in Exhibit 20–3 (173 basis points in March 1985).

The fact that the Single-A/high yield spread has rarely dipped below 225 basis points (three months out of 48—all in the first half of 1985) suggests that the investors have either intuitively or analytically grasped the implications of Exhibit 20–2. As explained above, the risk-reward ratio on high yield purchases looks quite reasonable at a beginning Single-A high yield spread of 250 basis points. At a 200-basis-point spread, however, the bet becomes far less compelling. Again assuming default losses of only 200 basis points, any widening at all will cause high yield bonds to fail to outperform Single-As over a five-year horizon. Since the spread has almost always (46 out of 48 months) been wider than 200 basis points, it is an outright gamble to adopt a strategy that will succeed only if the spread narrows. Given the odds depicted in Exhibit 20–2, it is hardly surprising that investors have generally resisted compression of the Single-A/high yield spread to less than 225 basis points. They have behaved rationally in light of their longer-term interest, notwithstanding allegations that "junk bond fever" has periodically bid up the prices of high yield securities to fundamentally unsustainable levels.

Conclusion

Our analysis suggests that annual performance is a questionable test of high yield bonds' investment value. Short-run underperformance does not disprove the validity of investing in the sector, contrary to periodic crowing by the anti-high yield forces.

Quality spreads are volatile enough over short periods to make it risky to try to pick precisely the right times to be in or out of the high yield sector. In this regard, high yield bonds are no different from U.S. Treasuries, which can also produce large losses for investors who guess wrong on short-term fluctuations.

Some high yield investors are willing to take the risk because the rewards of correct short-term decisions can be substantial. (See Chapter 16, "Employing High Yield Bonds in a Sector-Swapping Strategy.") Many other high yield investors, though, take a longer view. They seek to build wealth over a prolonged period by reinvesting high coupons at high rates and letting the brute force of compound interest take over. For these investors, the risks represented by short-term swings in yield spreads are not particularly relevant. As long as they are able to contain default losses, they can feel assured of superior returns in any scenario other than an unprecedented widening of quality spreads.

This does not mean that a long horizon completely eliminates the risks inherent in speculative-grade bonds. It does, however, suggest strongly that there is a place for lower-rated debt even in the portfolios of conservative investors.

Index

J

K

L

M

N

O

P

Z